# Research Handbook and Innovation

*Edited by*

## Gry Agnete Alsos

*Professor, Nord University Business School, Norway*

## Ulla Hytti

*Research Director, University of Turku, Finland*

## Elisabet Ljunggren

*Professor, Faculty of Social Sciences, Nord University, Norway*

Edward Elgar
PUBLISHING

Cheltenham, UK • Northampton, MA, USA

Published by
Edward Elgar Publishing Limited
The Lypiatts
15 Lansdown Road
Cheltenham
Glos GL50 2JA
UK

Edward Elgar Publishing, Inc.
William Pratt House
9 Dewey Court
Northampton
Massachusetts 01060
USA

Paperback edition 2018

A catalogue record for this book
is available from the British Library

Library of Congress Control Number: 2016938580

This book is available electronically in the **Elgar**online
Business subject collection
DOI 10.4337/9781783478132

ISBN 978 1 78347 811 8 (cased)
ISBN 978 1 78347 813 2 (eBook)
ISBN 978 1 78347 812 5 (paperback)

Typeset by Columns Design XML Ltd, Reading
Printed and bound by CPI Group (UK) Ltd, Croydon, CR0 4YY

# Contents

*v*

# Contributors

**Ruta Aidis** is Senior Fellow at the School of Policy, Government and International Affairs, George Mason University, USA. She has more than 20 years' experience teaching, researching, consulting and publishing in the area of comparative entrepreneurship development, gender, institutions and public policy. For the past three years, she has spearheaded an innovative data-driven research initiative, which has resulted in the development of the Global Women Entrepreneur Leaders Scorecard sponsored by Dell Inc. She is also CEO and Founder of ACG Inc., a global research and consultancy firm.

**Gry Agnete Alsos** is Professor in entrepreneurship and innovation at the Nord University Business School, Norway. She conducts research within areas such as business start-up processes, portfolio entrepreneurship, rural entrepreneurship, gender perspectives to entrepreneurship and innovation, and entrepreneurship and innovation policies. She is particularly interested in how different types of entrepreneurs develop their ventures and how they acquire and utilize knowledge and other resources in these processes. She is Editorial Board Member of *Entrepreneurship Theory and Practice*.

**Nina Amble** is Associate Professor in work psychology the Department of Vocational Teacher Education at Oslo and Akershus University College, Norway. She has a Dr. Philos. from the Department of Industrial Economics and Technology Management, Norwegian University of Science and Technology. She is a former employee of the Work Research Institute of Oslo. She is now project manager of an innovation project in public healthcare, funded by the Norwegian Research Council's FINNUT programme. Her research interest is organization of work and gender equality.

**Eira Andersson** is Associate Senior Lecturer at Luleå University of Technology, Sweden, and she studies constructions of masculinity and prerequisites for organizational change in men-dominated organizations in the mining industry. She specializes in participatory research, where new knowledge is developed jointly between researchers and societal actors.

**Lisa Andersson** is a Ph.D. student at Luleå University of Technology, Sweden and studies men-dominated organizations in mining, focusing on issues concerning formal and informal organizational processes and the implications for organizational change, and how gendered power relations are experienced and contested within an organizational context.

**Paula Axelsen** is a Nurse at Sørlandet Hospital at Arendal (SSA), Norway. She was the Sub-project Leader of one of the sub-projects from South-eastern Norway Regional Health Authority (SSHF).

**Knut-Erland Berglund** is a Ph.D. student at Luleå University of Technology, Sweden where he studies gender and empowerment within the context of sustainable development. In order to increase the acceptance, understanding and dispersion of innovative methods, products, organizational forms and societal structures that stems from cooperation between civil society, commercial companies, public authorities and researchers, he uses a participatory research method to explore the concept of 'gendered social innovation'.

**Teita Bijedić** is Researcher at the Institut für Mittelstandsforschung Bonn, Germany. She studied psychology (University of Düsseldorf) and holds a doctoral degree in economics (University of Flensburg). Her doctoral thesis in the field of entrepreneurship education has been awarded by the German Association for Economic Education, Chamber of Industry and Commerce Schleswig Holstein and Flensburg Press Foundation. Her field of research includes gender, diversity, behavioural and learning aspects of entrepreneurship, innovation, and economic education.

**Emma Börjesson** is Project Manager at Health Technology Centre at Halmstad University, Sweden. She has extensive experience in identifying, initiating and managing product development projects in health technology and in coordinating projects with different actors as researchers, and involving healthcare staff and business. She has a background in political science and is currently involved in a research project that combines gender theory and norm-critical design within the framework of gender equality work and innovation.

**Siegrun Brink** is Researcher at the Institut für Mittelstandsforschung Bonn, Germany. She received her university degree in business administration from the University of Göttingen, and her Ph.D. from the Schumpeter School of Business and Economics, Wuppertal. She wrote her Ph.D. thesis on organizational legitimacy and the relevance of venture capital. Her research interests include enterprise management of SMEs, start-up research and innovation, often with a focus on the gender perspective.

**Karin Ehrnberger** is currently doing her Ph.D. in product design at the Royal Institute of Technology (KTH) in Stockholm, Sweden. She has a master's degree in industrial design from the University College of Arts, Crafts and Design in Stockholm, and her thesis explored the correlation of design and gender in technological artefacts. Her research at KTH is focused on norm-critical perspectives in the design process, where she is developing methods to make these visible.

**Kerstin Ettl** is Postdoctoral Researcher at the University of Siegen, Germany and involved in research projects at the Institut für Mittel-standsforschung Bonn, Germany. She takes an individual and contextual perspective on entrepreneurship and SME management, with a particular interest in gender and diversity aspects. She wrote her Ph.D. thesis on women entrepreneurs and success and has worked several years on research exploring the learning and opportunity recognition of women entrepreneurs. Currently she is among other things engaged in research-ing the public image of women entrepreneurs.

**Emília Fernandes** is Assistant Professor at the University of Minho, School of Economics and Management in Braga, Portugal. Her research is focused on feminist theory, entrepreneurship, identity and gender discourses. She has published articles and chapters in international and national publications and, at the moment, she is a member of the executive board of the Master of Human Resource Management in the School of Economics and Management.

**Lene Foss** is Professor in innovation and entrepreneurship at the School of Business and Economics, UiT – The Arctic University of Norway. Her research concentrates on gender in innovation and entrepreneurship, university entrepreneurship/academic entrepreneurship and entre-preneurial education. She is Associate Editor of *Journal of Small Business Management* and Editorial Consultant and Board Member of *International Journal of Gender and Entrepreneurship*. She has been Visiting Fellow at the Department of Sociology, University of North Carolina at Chapel Hill, USA and Cambridge Judge Business School, University of Cambridge, UK.

**Colette Henry** is Professor and Head of Department of Business Studies at Dundalk Institute of Technology, Ireland and Adjunct Professor of Entrepreneurship at UiT – The Arctic University of Norway. Her previous roles include Norbrook Professor of Business and Enterprise at the Royal Veterinary College, London, and President of the Institute for

Small Business and Entrepreneurship (ISBE), UK. She is Editor of the *International Journal of Gender and Entrepreneurship* (*IJGE*), and has published widely on topics relating to women's entrepreneurship, entrepreneurship education and training, the creative industries, social enterprise and the veterinary business.

**Ulla Hytti** is Research Director at the Turku School of Economics within the University of Turku, Finland. She is Associate Editor at the *Journal of Small Business Management* and Editorial Board Member of the *International Journal of Entrepreneurial Behaviour and Research* and the *International Journal of Entrepreneurship and Innovation*. Her research interests are focused on research on entrepreneurs and gender in the contexts of innovation, entrepreneurship, careers and family firms. She has also published research in entrepreneurship education. She is a Board Member of the European Council for Small Business Research (ECSB).

**Sara Ilstedt** is Professor in product and service design at the Royal Institute of Technology in Stockholm, Sweden. She has an MA in industrial design and a Ph.D. in human–computer interaction. Her research focuses on gender issues, sustainability and behavioural changes. She was Editor of the anthology *Under Ytan* about Swedish design research, and Director of Study for Designfakulteten. In 2012, she started Green Leap, an arena for sustainable design that aims to act as a catalyst for change by engaging design in sustainable development. Green Leap initiates projects joining the academy and the design business in multidisciplinary and transformative design research.

**Anna Isaksson** is Senior Lecturer in sociology and Researcher at Halmstad University, Sweden. Her current research focuses on the potential of combining gender theory and norm-critical design within the framework of gender equality work and work for change. Recent research projects have also dealt with equality projects funded by the EU and social and technical innovations in elderly care from a norm-critical perspective.

**Maria Johansson** is a Ph.D. student at Luleå University of Technology, Sweden, and she studies gender in men-dominated contexts and more specifically explores constructions of gender and gender equality in forestry workplaces and how these constructions are intertwined with notions on competence and conceptualizations of (forestry) work. She also takes an interest in how constructions of gender intersect with the constructions of place and class, and how organizational changes are facilitated and/or restricted by the various notions of gender and gender equality.

**Anne Kovalainen** is Professor of entrepreneurship at the University of Turku, Finland. She has been Visiting Faculty Fellow at Stanford University, USA, London School of Economics (LSE), UK, Massachusetts University, USA and Roskilde University, Denmark and worked as Visiting Professor at LSE, at University of Technology Sydney, Australia and at Kingston University, UK. She is Editorial Board Member of *Research in the Sociology of Work*, *Academy of Management Perspectives* and *International Small Business Journal*. She has led large research projects and currently leads a research consortium in Finland, SWiPE, financed by the Academy of Finland Strategic Research. She regularly serves science policy institutions (NORFACE, ESF, NWO, FCT, ACA). Her research focuses on: the relations between entrepreneurship, self-employment and paid work; social research methodology and methods; modes of knowledge production and STS research; and research on gender.

**Silke Kriwoluzky** holds a master's degree in economics from LSE, UK. In her research, she aims at complementing the economic perspective with concepts from other social sciences like sociology and political science. One core area of her work has been the labour market, especially the question of how to organize and shape support for the long-term unemployed in finding a job. In her most recent work, she has been analysing the status quo of SMEs in Germany and the EU with a focus on women and innovation. Her last position held was as Researcher at the Institut für Mittelstandsforschung Bonn, Germany.

**Trine Kvidal-Røvik** is Associate Professor at UiT – The Arctic University of Norway. Her research interests are linked to critical and cultural perspectives on issues of gender, identity, place and communication. She has worked on several research projects focusing on gender and innovation. Her chapter is written as part of her current involvement in the GENINNO project, financed by the Norwegian Research Council.

**Regina Leite** is Assistant Professor in organizational behaviour and human resource management (HRM) in the School of Economics and Management at the University of Minho, Portugal, and Coordinator of the master's course in HRM. Her work has been published in national and international journals and books. Her current research interests include work and non-work spheres, privacy issues, innovation, entrepreneurship, organizational commitment and sexual harassment.

**Malin Lindberg** is Associate Professor at Luleå University of Technology, Sweden. She studies inclusive innovation, with specific focus on social innovation, gendered innovation, women's innovation and place innovation. She specializes in participatory research, where new knowledge is developed jointly between researchers and societal actors.

**Birgitte Ljunggren** is Associate Professor at Queen Maud's University College in Trondheim, Norway. She is also affiliated to Trøndelag R&D Institute as Senior Researcher. Currently she is working on the GENINNO project financed by the Norwegian Research Council, exploring the governance and governmentality of gender and innovation in Norway. Her fields of interest are policy analysis, gender studies and organization studies. She has mostly worked qualitatively using interviews and texts as data but has also developed national surveys.

**Elisabet Ljunggren** is Professor at Nord University, Faculty of Social Sciences, Bodø, Norway. Her research interests include gender aspects of entrepreneurship, innovation and business policies. She is currently leading an innovation research project in Norway, GENINNO, which investigates regional innovation with a gender perspective. She has conducted studies on policy initiatives to enhance entrepreneurship and innovation (e.g. business incubators), and innovation in experience-based industries. She has published in international journals, been a guest editor of the *International Journal of Gender and Entrepreneurship*, and edited several research books. She has an extensive research portfolio and has experience from EU, international and national research projects.

**Selma Martins** is a Generalist Nurse in the emergency room of the Hospital of Setúbal, Portugal. She has a degree in nursing from the Nursing School in Coimbra and, in March 2014, finished her master's degree in management of health units from the University of Minho, which led her to research entrepreneurship in nursing. She participated in the 9th European Conference on Innovation and Entrepreneurship with the presentation of a paper entitled 'Entrepreneurship in Nursing Care: Perspectives, Incentives and Barriers in the Portuguese Context'.

**Seppo Poutanen** is Senior Researcher and Docent of sociology at the School of Economics of the University of Turku, Finland. His areas of expertise include social epistemology, social theory, sociology of science, methodology of social sciences and economic sociology. He has acted as Visiting Fellow in several universities (Stanford University, USA, LSE, UK and UTS Business School, Australia). He is in charge of the Entrepreneurial University research in the SWiPE research consortium, financed by the Academy of Finland and he collaborates in the international GEUM project on the same topic. He has published his research in *Social Epistemology, Critical Public Health, Journal of Critical Realism, Sociological Research Online, International Journal of Gender and Entrepreneurship* and several edited volumes.

**Shruti R. Sardeshmukh** is Senior Lecturer at the University of South Australia. She came to academia after working in IT start-ups. Influenced by her work experience, her research interests lie at the intersection of human resources and entrepreneurship. Focused on start-ups and family-owned businesses, she is passionate about the 'people' dynamics driving the innovation and entrepreneurship processes in individuals and SMEs. She completed her doctoral work at Rensselaer Polytechnic Institute (RPI), USA.

**Ronda M. Smith** is Assistant Professor of management at Ball State University, USA. She earned her Ph.D. in entrepreneurship from the University of Nebraska–Lincoln. She holds degrees in business administration (BS) and industrial-organizational psychology (MS). She has over 20 years of experience in both small business start-ups and established corporations in the areas of human resources, marketing, organizational change and business process re-engineering. Her research includes the nexus of human resources and entrepreneurship, creativity and innovation.

**Liv Karen Snerthammer** is a Nurse in Flekkefjord Municipality, Norway. She was the Sub-project Leader of the four sub-projects from Flekkefjord and Kvinesdal Municipalities.

**Malin Tillmar** is Professor in business administration, Department of Management and Engineering at Linköping University, Sweden and Co-director of the HELIX Competence Centre. Her research centres on the organizing of entrepreneurship and innovation in different contexts, both sectoral and national. Her studies in entrepreneurship and innovation have often had a gender perspective. Her interest in East African society dates back to the 1990s, and she keeps returning to this context for research purposes. Her research has been published in a diversity of journals, including *Entrepreneurship and Regional Development* and *Scandinavian Journal of Management*. She has edited research books and been Guest Editor for *Nordiske Organisasjonsstudier* and *International Journal of Gender and Entrepreneurship*.

**Friederike Welter** leads the Institut für Mittelstandsforschung Bonn and has held a professorship at the University of Siegen, Germany since February 2013. In 2008–2013, she worked at Jönköping International

Business School, Sweden. She has broad experience in applied and policy-related research on entrepreneurship and small business, much of it in an international context. Her main research interests are the nature of entrepreneurship and entrepreneurial behaviour in different contexts, and entrepreneurship/SME policies. She is also Senior Editor of *Entrepreneurship Theory and Practice*.

# PART I

# INTRODUCTION

# 1. Gender and innovation – an introduction

*Gry Agnete Alsos, Ulla Hytti and Elisabet Ljunggren*

## INTRODUCTION

Innovation has become a buzzword in policy and industry as well as scientific discourses, seen as an important element in economic development, and for solving global challenges such as financial crisis, environmental strain, diseases and poverty. Innovation is put forward as a main factor to enhance economic growth in industries, regions and nations (Lundvall, 1992; Malecki, 2002; Malerba, 2002; Verspagen, 2005), and is also suggested to be important at the firm level to recreate and maintain competitive advantage over time. The early scholarly work on innovation includes the influential analysis of Schumpeter (1934), who looked at major innovations as driving economic development. Building on his work, innovation is still often defined as new combinations of production factors in the form of production of new goods or services, introduction of new production processes, the opening of new markets to new sources of raw materials and intermediates, and re-organization of an industry. Contemporary research on innovation is broad in scope and perspectives, including innovation processes within firms, as well as in local, regional or national innovation systems of firms, institutions and governmental bodies (Fagerberg, 2005). Recently, there has been a growing interest in social innovations and innovations taking place in the public sector.

The gender issues of innovation are seldom discussed. One main reason for this deficit is that innovation research seems to lack analyses of where innovation takes place and, particularly, of who participates in innovation (Fagerberg et al., 2005). There seems to be an under-communication of the role of the innovator in innovation literature (Brännback et al., 2012). The lack of focus on individuals as actors tends to make gender invisible (Alsos et al., 2013). However, there are of course individuals within the processes, the organizations and the systems frequently discussed in innovation literature – the question is rather to illuminate the impact of gender by including it in the analyses (Thorslund and Göransson, 2006).

While the literature is still scarce, the issue of gender and innovation has been put on the agenda in the last decade (e.g. Abrahamsson, 2002; Alsos et al., 2013; Blake and Hanson, 2005; Doss and Morris, 2001), and gender and innovation is emerging as an issue for scientific research. Published research suggests on one hand that gender diversity is positive for innovation (e.g. Østergaard et al., 2011) and on the other hand that gendered understandings of innovation lead policy makers – and scholars – to overlook women's involvement in innovation (e.g. Blake and Hanson, 2005; Kvidal and Ljunggren, 2013). This paradox, among others, exemplifies the need for more scholarly work to better understand the role of gender in innovation.

This book addresses these knowledge gaps in several ways. It takes a broad perspective to gender and innovation. The chapters include discussions on innovation in women-owned businesses, larger corporations, public organizations, policy and design. There is a large variety in empirical contexts, with respect both to country contexts and to industry and organizational contexts. The chapters, most of them containing empirical analyses, use a wide range of methodological approaches including action research, discourse analyses, case studies and quantitative analyses of register data. At the general level, the chapters in various ways show that women are indeed involved in innovation, in numerous ways and in many different contexts. However, the dominant idea about innovation seems to be extremely gendered, and women often do not fit the ideas about innovation in one way or another. They may carry out their innovation activity in industries not considered to be the main areas for innovation, or in geographical or social contexts where innovation is seldom looked for. Nevertheless, even when women involve themselves in 'mainstream' innovation related to technology and manufacturing, they still seem to be defined as different and 'the other'. This image is also found in innovation policy, according to analyses reported in this volume. Women's innovation is portrayed as something different, challenging the ideas about what innovation is. Thus this volume documents the masculine connotations associated with innovation in many layers.

We have chosen to start with acknowledging and analysing the scarce, but evolving, literature on gender and innovation. In Chapter 2 of this volume, Lene Foss and Colette Henry review this emerging literature. They develop a framework to analyse how gender is conceptualized in the literature, how innovation is defined and, hence, the connections made between gender and innovation. They find that few articles actually discuss the relationship between gender and innovation. Nor do publications generally discuss the perspective taken to gender. Foss and Henry compare the status of the literature on gender and innovation to the development of the gender and entrepreneurship literature, which so far is more advanced. They conclude that innovation research is lagging behind in its inclusion of a gender perspective, and suggest that the innovation literature would benefit from increasing the number of studies of gender and, specifically, adopting a more feminist epistemology.

Following this literature analysis, which completes Part I, the book is divided into four further parts. Part II deals with gender and innovation in the context of new and small businesses. This is followed by Part III on gender and innovation in large and established firms. From there, the gender aspects of innovation policy are discussed in Part IV, before Part V analyses gender in materiality and design related to innovation.

In the next section of this chapter, each of these parts is presented. The chapter then ends with a reflection on the way forward, focusing on the role of men and masculinities in innovation.

## GENDER AND INNOVATION IN NEW AND SMALL BUSINESSES

Part II of the book comprises four chapters each dealing with gender and innovation in new and small businesses, and growth businesses. The chapters provide a link between innovation and entrepreneurship following the Schumpeterian understanding, i.e. understanding entrepreneurs as innovative actors. The chapters in this part also show how innovation takes place in different geographical and cultural contexts: three countries in East Africa – Kenya, Tanzania and Uganda; three countries in Latin America – Brazil, Bolivia and Colombia; and two European countries – Germany and Portugal. In spite of the different geographical and cultural contexts, the barriers facing innovative women are surprisingly similar throughout the different countries. It seems to be common for the innovation and entrepreneurial activities carried out by women not to be perceived as 'real' innovations or business activities. The chapters draw our attention to everyday innovations, innovation within nursing entrepreneurship, and the particular hurdles and invisibility women innovators face in the different contexts.

In Chapter 3, Teita Bijedić, Siegrun Brink, Kerstin Ettl, Silke Kriwoluzky and Friederike Welter make use of existing data in Germany regarding gender and innovation. They show how women's entrepreneurship does not fit the dominant ideas on innovation as technological and product based. Women are less likely to carry out technologically based product and process innovations compared to men. The authors propose several conceptual explanations for these findings:

that aspects of the institutional frameworks such as taxes and family policies impact individual preferences on educational and professional choices; that context factors foster and perpetuate traditional norms, and that women and men face different role expectations. The authors conclude that women are not less innovative but that a combination of institutional constraints and traditional role models contributes to self-selection into female-typed professions and working structures such as part-time work.

In Chapter 4, Ruta Aidis introduces three successful Latin American women entrepreneurs, from Brazil, Bolivia and Colombia. They have succeeded by being innovative in three quite different industries: industrial services and recycling; personal services; and manufacturing. The data consist of interviews and secondary data, and the author has applied an institutional framework for the analysis. Setting out the facts about women and entrepreneurship in Latin America, based on GEM data, she shows that Latin American women entrepreneurs score at a medium level in innovativeness compared to US and Asian women entrepreneurs. Based on the three cases, Aidis explores the institutional impediments innovative women face: gendered attitudes, access to finance, access to support and networks, access to global markets, and bureaucratic barriers. She claims that successful women entrepreneurs can serve as catalysts for institutional reforms. International recognition gives these women visibility, credibility and access to resources in their domestic countries.

Malin Tillmar argues in Chapter 5 that mainstream perspectives on innovation are not only gender biased, in several dimensions, but also context biased and ethnocentric. Her chapter reports from qualitative studies on innovations occurring in the mundane everyday life of urban female SME owners in the three large countries in East Africa: Kenya, Tanzania and Uganda. The cases illustrate the innovativeness that is exercised, even required, by these women simply to sustain the livelihood of themselves and their families. The phenomenon of innovation is gaining more ground in the literature, and research is expanding the mainstream definition of innovation to include, for example, the everyday innovativeness of women in emerging economies, such as in East Africa. Yet this broader perspective of innovation has not received adequate attention.

In Chapter 6, Selma Martins, Emília Fernandes and Regina Leite analyse how gendered discourses are applied to define innovation in a 'feminine' context: nursing. Following the economic crisis, Portugal has faced an increased number of entrepreneurial endeavours in the nursing care sector. Using personal interviews with 18 nursing entrepreneurs, the authors aim to explore how innovation is constructed in this 'new' sector, which is hallmarked by a gender paradox. The two professional practices are constituted by different gender meanings: nursing is considered to have a feminine nature and is almost exclusively a female-dominated occupation; entrepreneurship is considered a masculine practice and is traditionally associated with men. In their analyses, the authors extend the understanding of innovation within entrepreneurship to inscribe feminine concepts such as 'caring' and 'nurturing'. Further, they discuss whether this construction of innovation implies a hindrance or an opportunity to gender equality and the emancipation of women.

## GENDER AND INNOVATION IN AN ORGANIZATIONAL CONTEXT

Part III consists of three chapters, all addressing innovation in different organizational settings conceptually or empirically, ranging from public sector health care to mining and forestry. Organizational innovation is a well-studied innovation type. Crossan and Apaydin (2010, pp. 1155–1156) suggest that it consists of three components: 'innovation leadership, innovation as process and innovation as an outcome'. However, as found by Alsos et al. (2013), organizational innovation is a research field with a limited understanding of gender and, if studied, it is often with sex as a variable or control variable. The diversity management literature is sometimes applied as a theoretical point of departure when studying organizational innovation, and we have one example of this among the chapters in Part III. Interestingly the chapters in this part cover both public sector and private firms. The chapters also address innovation as a process and as an outcome, but none focuses on innovation leadership. It is particularly interesting that the two chapters studying processes and outcomes find that persisting norms in the organizations need to be changed and that such changes could be understood as innovations per se.

Shruti R. Sardeshmukh and Ronda M. Smith in their conceptual chapter, Chapter 7, discuss that, even if women form almost half of the workforce, women do not seem to be innovative. By applying diversity management literature from the organizational studies and innovation literature they identify structural and social hurdles in two phases of the innovation process: idea generation and idea implementation. When discussing the idea generation phase of innovation, they suggest applying social role theory in order to identify different gender role expectations, to focus on capabilities to highlight developmental opportunities at workplaces and finally to use motivation theories to investigate factors reducing women's motivation for innovation. In the idea implementation phase they suggest applying the theoretical approaches of the role of the social network, social capital and champions. The authors argue that, while idea generation is dependent on individuals and their characteristics, idea implementation relies more on group and organizational characteristics. They claim that female employees are an untapped resource in organizations' innovation work and suggest that organizations should relate to identity-conscious practices to discover innovative ideas. They suggest that the diversity management practices developed within the human resource policies could be useful for organizations' innovation processes, and a diversity management perspective could contribute to the innovation literature.

Nina Amble and the two nurses Paula Axelsen and Liv Karen Snerthammer look at innovation in the care sector in Norway, and in Chapter 8 present new ways of organizing work hours. The innovation consists of both a new rota system and changing the perceived norm of care work as part-time employment to one of full-time employment. They have carried out action research, and the action research process in two health care institutions is described. The process was employee driven and was introduced as a possibility to better organize work, i.e. to get more done with less energy and struggle. They apply Kanter's (2000) definition of innovation as 'the development and exploitation of new ideas' and an understanding of welfare innovation as 'new and familiar knowledge brought into use in new context' (Kristensen, 2008). The new rota system is described as an organizational innovation in the public sector: introducing longer shifts and a new resource team for the nurses. The new system improved care quality and the working arrangements at the workplace. In addition, the authors show how the innovation concept in itself enabled changes and also filled the work shift schedules with new content. The authors apply a gender perspective in their analyses.

Malin Lindberg, Eira Andersson, Lisa Andersson and Maria Johansson in Chapter 9 study organizational innovation and investigate whether gender equality measures in two Swedish firms in highly masculine industries, mining and forestry, can be perceived as organizational innovations. Their theoretical point of departure is the concept of newness, which is central to the innovation literature. They also apply Lam's (2005) classification of organizational innovation into three streams. These are applied in the data analyses, along with a gender perspective. The authors have conducted case studies in one large mining and one large forestry company in Sweden that both have worked with gender equality measures. The authors analyse whether the gender equality measures carried out in the two companies can be understood as organizational innovations, applying two different classifications based on newness: traditional and innovative. They find that three of the measures can be perceived as innovative and contributing to structural changes in the gendered patterns in the firms. These are: 1) creative workshops; 2) cooperation with gender researchers; and 3) engaging in work to challenge masculinities.

## GENDER IN INNOVATION POLICY

Part IV comprises two chapters dealing with gender in innovation policy. Innovation policies are important vehicles at the societal level in determining how we understand innovation, what activities are deemed desirable and what kinds of actors are seen to contribute favourably towards innovations. Thus the innovation policies can be interpreted from the perspectives of inclusion and exclusion: what kind of individuals, activities, organizations and sectors are included in innovations and what is then left out and excluded from them. Both chapters in this part discuss inclusiveness of innovation policies from different angles. First, they examine existing innovation policies to understand the extent to which they are inclusive and allow questioning of the dominant understanding of innovation. Second, they suggest that a refocus of innovation on gendered social innovations opens up the path to new policy making and generating new innovation policies that are more inclusive.

In Chapter 10, Trine Kvidal-Røvik and Birgitte Ljunggren examine gender and innovation articulations in a policy programme in Norway using discourse analysis. They suggest that through this policy women are constituted as different, and it is by this difference that they are legitimized as participants in innovation. Gender is seen as relevant in so far as it represents a resource for innovation. Since innovation is understood to benefit from variety in terms of knowledge, gender balance is framed as something that will contribute to this broad range of knowledge and people. Gender is governed in the policy programme towards a rather narrow and limited space of innovative action for women. Both innovation and gender, and the ways they are articulated in the policy programme, are marked by an advanced liberal governmentality making social subjects relevant only as resources to strengthen some kind of totality.

In Chapter 11, Malin Lindberg and Knut-Erland Berglund first discuss the concepts of social innovation and gendered innovation in order to identify if those debates could enrich each other and contribute towards gender-inclusive innovation policy, research and practice. The chapter suggests that both social innovation and gendered innovation aim at challenging the existing ideas of what innovation is. Both discourses suggest broadening innovation as a theoretical concept and thereby democratizing innovation. From the policy perspective, this focus on gendered social innovations invites a new, more inclusive range of actors, industries, sectors and consequently innovations at the heart of innovation policy.

## GENDER IN DESIGN AND MATERIALITY

Part V, the final part, discusses innovation understood in the classical sense: as new physical products developed by engineers based on research and technical knowledge. Anchored in post-structural feminist theories on 'doing gender' (West and Zimmerman, 1987), both chapters in this part present original and novel analyses of how inventions, innovations and innovation processes are gendered.

In Chapter 12, Seppo Poutanen and Anne Kovalainen take Kanter's (1977) theory of tokenism as their starting point for analysing the evolution process of a female innovator in a chemistry processing plant, where she was the only female engineer. The tokenism perspective allows them to analyse the situation where she represents the numerical minority of one and stands out as different from the others within the organization, as a 'token'. Using a narrative analysis, they effectively illuminate the gendered processes of invention and innovation, and relate this to questions of the visibility, legitimacy and acceptance of an innovator within a large industrial corporation. As a research manager in the R&D department of the corporation, the female chemistry engineer experienced being treated as invisible and looked down upon based on her gender. She made herself visible through taking action and delivering successful innovation, gaining legitimacy through defending her achievements and her management position against the efforts of her male colleagues to hold her back.

In Chapter 13, Emma Börjesson, Anna Isaksson, Sara Ilstedt and Karin Ehrnberger show how norm-critical design can be used to put the gendering of innovation on the agenda and to disclose the built-in but hidden gendered aspects. Following an action-oriented approach, they analyse the invention and testing of a male version of the gynaecological chair, the so-called Androchair, introduced as equipment for better prostate examination, to highlight how innovation is gendered. This is a very efficient way to disclose how the gynaecological examination chair has been normalized and become unchallenged as something that necessarily has to be a certain way despite its making women undertaking gynaecological examination more vulnerable and uncomfortable than necessary. In their study, Börjesson et al. problematize needs based on a gender perspective and, in a novel way, illuminate the importance of a gender perspective to innovation.

Leaning on action network theory, which holds that not only human beings but also physical objects can be studied as active social actors, and as physical manifestations of social relations (Latour, 2003), Poutanen and Kovalainen and Börjesson et al. address the role of materiality for the understanding of how innovation is gendered. They show how innovations, as physical artefacts, can be permeated with gender themselves, distinct from (but also related to) the gendered processes through which they are created. In Chapter 12, the authors describe how titanium dioxide is changed from a masculine artefact used in the production of painting and coating to a feminine artefact used for cosmetic production, not only by the refinement of the product itself but also by changing its packaging. In Chapter 13, the authors consider how the design of the gynaecological chair as a feminine artefact is used to design an examination chair for men, effectively disclosing how the equipment itself has functions that are gendered. Hence, in these two chapters we get an insight into how the design and materiality of innovation are embedded with gender.

## REFLECTION: MEN AND MASCULINITIES' PERSPECTIVE TO INNOVATION

Gender and innovation is an emerging field of research (Alsos et al., 2013), but as can be seen through the chapters in this Research Handbook it has quickly gained a strong and significant foothold. Importantly, the chapters highlight that gender is not about women but about gendered processes and structures (Alsos et al., 2013) that contribute to our understandings of innovation and innovation agents. This gendering view has been advocated also in this volume, and many important insights are put forward. However, most analyses focus on the experiences of women or in the ways gendering processes affect women. For example, the authors discuss how the invisibility of innovations in the public sector affects women, who – at least in the Nordic countries – form the main part of the workforce in the public sector (Amble et al., this volume, Chapter 8), or the ways innovation policies craft a role for women as providers of different resources (Kvidal-Røvik and Ljunggren, this volume, Chapter 10).

The risk with theorizing solely about women and their experiences is that it reinforces the dominant image of men as the unmarked sex, where men and masculinities need not be questioned (Oudshoorn, 2004). Men and masculinities are central to organizational analysis but too often not centred in the investigations. Future research should make men and masculinities explicit objects of theorizing and problematize masculinities (Collinson and Hearn, 1994; Hearn, 2004) in the field of innovation. This problematization also includes being careful when notions of femininity and masculinity are attached to women and men in order to avoid gender essentialism (Poutanen and Kovalainen, 2013; Remneland-Wikhamn and Knights, 2013). Thus our call to focus on men and masculinities in future research on gender and innovation does not aim to suggest an amalgamation of the two but rather invites nuanced analyses of how men experience innovation activities and what kind of masculinities innovation work invokes, for example. Next, we will discuss some perspectives that in our view merit further attention with this particular suggested focus.

Research on gender and innovation suggests that the male-dominated industries are understood as sites for innovation with the automatic association of technology and innovation (Wajcman, 2010). However, to our knowledge there are relatively few studies conducted that investigate what the implications are for men working in these industries. It is possible to develop three trajectories: 1) positive; 2) negative; and 3) mixed effects (Holter, 2014). First, in the positive view, one may advocate that the focus on innovations and being involved in innovations offers intrinsic rewards and improved job satisfaction for the male innovators. For example, Mellström (2004) demonstrates how Swedish male engineers and Malaysian male motorbike repair shop workers, i.e. men who work closely with machines, feel passionately about them: 'machines are culturally defined as an object of men's passion because men have an embodied relationship with the machine and because the machine is often a symbiotic extension of the person, of the man' (Mellström, 2004, p. 379). Thus, it would be interesting to further study how both men and women experience their innovative work and what kind of gendered relationships they develop towards the innovations they are involved in developing. In addition, studies in management and entrepreneurship have highlighted the embeddedness of masculine values in organizations, for example in terms of measures of success (Ahl, 2006; Collinson and Hearn, 1994). Therefore, it might be interesting to develop more insight into how the men working with innovations deal with failures, and the ways these failures are constructed in the context of masculinities. Homosociality – i.e. the preference of men for working with other men – has been highlighted in previous research (Holgersson, 2013). Within organizations, innovation work is often done in teams, and hence the ways homosociality is performed and the practices involved within these innovation teams would be an interesting research avenue.

Second, the negative effects view may suggest that with the pressure to be innovative and produce innovations comes also stress or other health problems, or those not succumbing to the innovation pressures will have to leave the organization or the industry. Since paid work continues to represent the heart of men's life project, and determine the identity of men (Català et al., 2012; Collinson and Hearn, 1994), the ramifications of the marginalization or exclusion of non-innovative men or men who fail in their innovative activities in the innovative industries or companies may also be important. Therefore, studies of the innovation cultures within organizations and in other contexts and studies of how they affect individuals – men or women – and including those who feel excluded from those cultures are needed (Sinclair, 2000). For example, it might be interesting to address what kind of masculinities are available for the men who are not involved in innovation work or fail in their innovative work. Collinson and Hearn (1994) suggest masculine identities are precarious and fragile, and have to be constantly constructed and renegotiated, and that various events, changes and processes may threaten these identities, including the attempts to secure and hold on to the certain clearly defined and coherent identities. For example, Remneland-Wikhamn and Knights (2013) investigate to what extent the open innovation framework challenges masculine discourses of innovation within the automotive industry. They conclude that the industry has not been able to open up to the radical insights offered by open innovation initiatives. Consequently, the masculine discourses are reproduced rather than challenged by open innovation.

When investigating the potential implications of innovations and innovative work on men, it is necessary to ask the further question of 'Which men?', since the effects are likely to vary depending on social class, hierarchy and other divisions. Comeau and Kemp (2007) demonstrate discursively how work in the IT sector is constructed as an arena for sports or war, and these ties normalize the affiliation of youthfulness and technical ability, and consequently at the intersection of age and masculinity older workers were marginalized in small IT firms. Hence, the third mixed effects view suggests that the effects will be different for different groups of men (Holter, 2014) and also that men construct different masculinities in different contexts. For example, a study by

Filteau (2014) demonstrates how men working in the oilfield are able to construct a new dominant masculinity reflecting safety at work (also Lindberg et al., this volume, Chapter 9), while they remain complicit with the hegemonic masculinity in the domestic sphere. The study by O'Connor et al. (2015) suggests that new ways of doing masculinity are being practised within the university sector but still preserving male privileges. Thus, future research could more extensively investigate intersectionality and pay attention to the competing discourses that renew and reproduce masculinities in the context of innovation.

The visibility of men in innovations may also be exaggerated if not scrutinized. For example, Oudshoorn (2004) discusses the ways 'the weak alignment of contraceptive technologies and masculinities constitutes a major barrier for technological innovation in contraceptives for men' (p. 353). Therefore, the story is not so much about developing the technology but of renegotiating masculine identities. This suggests a need for creating the cultural feasibility of technology by articulating the gender identities of users. Börjesson et al. (this volume, Chapter 13) and Oudshoorn (2004) suggest that, while men are generally seen as important and highly visible agents when it comes to innovation, as users of particular health care innovations they remain invisible.

Future research could pay more attention to men and women as (potential) users of innovations and how their gender identities are constructed in the context of different innovations. For example, even if women have traditionally held the main responsibility for domestic chores such as cleaning and taking care of the laundry, what kind of new gendered identities are different family members constructing as the users of the newest high-tech and intellectual models of washing machines capable of diagnosing the laundry and auto-selecting the washing process accordingly? When high technology is pervading our social lives, are we able to witness new demarcations of women's and men's work, be it in organizations or in homes?

## REFERENCES

Abrahamsson, L. (2002), 'Restoring the order: Gender segregation as an obstacle to organisational development', *Applied Ergonomics*, **33** (6), 549–557.

Ahl, H. (2006), 'Why research on women entrepreneurs needs new directions', *Entrepreneurship Theory and Practice*, **30** (5), 595–621.

Alsos, G.A., E. Ljunggren and U. Hytti (2013), 'Gender and innovation: State of the art and a research agenda', *International Journal of Gender and Entrepreneurship*, **5** (3), 236–256.

Blake, M.K. and S. Hanson (2005), 'Rethinking innovation: Context and gender', *Environment and Planning A*, **37** (4), 681–701.

Brännback, M., K. Berglund and A.L. Carsrud (2012), 'Understanding the entrepreneur and innovator nexus as basis for the coming of the science of the artificial', RENT – Research on Entrepreneurship and Small Business Conference, Lyon, France.

Català, V.B., S.M. Colom, L.C. Santamaria and A.G. Casajust (2012), 'Male hegemony in decline? Reflections on the Spanish case', *Men and Masculinities*, **15** (4), 406–423.

Collinson, D. and J. Hearn (1994), 'Naming men as men: Implications for work, organization and management', *Gender, Work and Organization*, **1** (1), 2–22.

Comeau, T. and C. Kemp (2007), 'Intersections of age and masculinities in the information technology industry', *Ageing and Society*, **27** (2), 215–232.

Crossan, M.M. and M. Apaydin (2010), 'A multi-dimensional framework of organizational innovation: A systematic review of the literature', *Journal of Management Studies*, **47** (6), 1154–1191.

Doss, C.R. and M.L. Morris (2001), 'How does gender affect the adoption of agricultural innovations? The case of improved maize technology in Ghana', *Agricultural Economics*, **25** (1), 27–39.

Fagerberg, J. (2005), 'Innovation. A guide to the literature', in J. Fagerberg, D.C. Mowery and R.R. Nelson (eds), *The Oxford Handbook of Innovation*, Oxford, UK: Oxford University Press, pp. 1–26.

Fagerberg, J., D.C. Mowery and R.R. Nelson (eds) (2005), *The Oxford Handbook of Innovation*, Oxford, UK: Oxford University Press.

Filteau, M.R. (2014), 'Who are those guys? Constructing the oilfield's new dominant masculinity', *Men and Masculinities*, **17** (4), 396–416.

Hearn, J. (2004), 'From hegemonic masculinity to the hegemony of men', *Feminist Theory*, **5** (1), 49–72.

Holgersson, C. (2013), 'Recruiting managing directors: Doing homosociality', *Gender, Work and Organization*, **20** (4), 454–466.

Holter, Ø.G. (2014), '"What's in it for men?" Old question, new data', *Men and Masculinities*, **17** (5), 515–548.

Kanter, R.M. (1977), *Men and Women of the Corporation*, New York: Basic Books.

Kanter, R.M. (2000), 'When a thousand flowers bloom: Structural, collective and social conditions for innovation in organizations', in B.M. Staw and L.L. Cummings (eds), *Research in Organizational Behavior*, Greenwich, CT: JAI Press, pp. 169–211.

Kristensen, C.J. (2008), 'Organisatorisk forankring af velfærdsinnovation en analyse med inddragelse af to cases fra aktiveringsområdet', *Tidsskrift for Arbejdsliv*, **10** (3), 73–87.

Kvidal, T. and E. Ljunggren (2013), 'Introducing gender in a policy programme: A multilevel analysis of an innovation policy programme', *Environment and Planning C*, **32** (1), 39–53.

Lam, A. (2005), 'Organizational innovation', in J. Fagerberg, D.C. Mowery and R.R. Nelson (eds), *The Oxford Handbook of Innovation*, Oxford, UK: Oxford University Press, pp. 115–147.

Latour, B. (2003), *Science in Action: How to Follow Scientists and Engineers through Society*, Cambridge, MA: Harvard University Press.

Lundvall, B.Å. (1992), *National Systems of Innovation: Toward a Theory of Innovation and Interactive Learning*, London: Anthem Press.

Malecki, E.J. (2002), 'Knowledge, innovation and economic growth: The theory and practice of learning regions', *Urban Geography*, **23** (2), 198–199.

Malerba, F. (2002), 'Sectoral systems of innovation and production', *Research Policy*, **31** (2), 247–264.

Mellström, U. (2004), 'Machines and masculine subjectivity: Technology as an integral part of men's life experiences', *Men and Masculinities*, **6** (4), 368–382.

O'Connor, P., C. O'Hagan and J. Brannen (2015), 'Exploration of masculinities in academic organisations: A tentative typology using career and relationship commitment', *Current Sociology*, **63** (4), 528–546.

Østergaard, C.R., B. Timmermans and K. Kristinsson (2011), 'Does a different view create something new? The effect of employee diversity on innovation', *Research Policy*, **40** (3), 500–509.

Oudshoorn, N. (2004), '"Astronauts in the sperm world": The renegotiation of masculine identities in discourses on male contraceptives', *Men and Masculinities*, **6** (4), 349–367.

Poutanen, S. and A. Kovalainen (2013), 'Gendering innovation process in an industrial plant – revisiting tokenism, gender and innovation', *International Journal of Gender and Entrepreneurship*, **5** (3), 257–274.

Remneland-Wikhamn, B. and D. Knights (2013), 'Open innovation, gender and the infiltration of masculine discourses', *International Journal of Gender and Entrepreneurship*, **5** (3), 275–297.

Schumpeter, J.A. (1934), *The Theory of Economic Development: An Inquiry into Profits, Capital, Credit, Interest, and the Business Cycle*, Cambridge, MA: Harvard University Press.

Sinclair, A. (2000), 'Teaching managers about masculinities: Are you kidding?', *Management Learning*, **31** (1), 83–101.

Thorslund, J.G. and U. Göransson (2006), *Könsblinda innovationssystem – genusanalys av några centrala begrepp i VINNOVAs verksamhet. Arbetsrapport i FoU-projektet Jämställdhet och Genusvetenskap*, Stockholm: Vinnova.

Verspagen, B. (2005), 'Innovation and economic growth', in J. Fagerberg, D.C. Mowery and R.R. Nelson (eds), *The Oxford Handbook of Innovation*, Oxford, UK: Oxford University Press, pp. 487–513.

Wajcman, J. (2010), 'Feminist theories of technology', *Cambridge Journal of Economics*, **34** (1), 143–152.

West, C. and D. Zimmerman (1987), 'Doing gender', *Gender and Society*, **1**, 125–151.

# 2. Doing gender in innovation: a thematic review and critique of the literature
## Lene Foss and Colette Henry

## INTRODUCTION

Research on innovation has grown rapidly since the 1990s. In current literature and reports, innovation is central to both economic and political debates (European Commission, 2008; Science and Learning Expert Group, 2010), with research on product innovation (i.e. goods) seen as a vehicle for enhancing firm profit and long-term growth (Reynolds et al., 2000; Yuan et al., 2010). Innovation is inextricably linked to entrepreneurship, as the latter involves actively looking for and taking advantage of the former to create new ventures or grow existing ones (Hofstrand, 2010).

Whereas gender has received increased attention in the management (Calas and Smircich, 1991; Courpasson, 2000), organizational (Acker, 1990; Kvande, 2007) and entrepreneurship research literatures (Ahl, 2006; Berg, 1997), little by way of concerted academic attention has been paid to exploring gender within innovation research literatures.[1] Just as the exploration of gender within entrepreneurship has been critical to unveiling the subordination of the feminine and helping to identify alternative forms of entrepreneurship previously considered as 'lacking' (Ahl, 2004; Carter and Shaw, 2006; Marlow, 2002), exploring gender within the innovation literatures will allow us to view innovation from a new perspective and to place it in the context of a gendered society (Pettersson, 2007). Given the inextricable link between entrepreneurship and innovation, as articulated above, this is clearly important. Thus, in this chapter, we focus our research question on how gender is conceptualized in the innovation literatures. In order to answer this question we categorize the thematic focus adopted by those researching innovation in the context of gender, and we discuss their specific gender perspectives. We then explore how researchers actually define innovation, identifying how they illustrate the relationship between gender and innovation. Inspired by the use of discourse analysis in gender research (Ahl, 2004,

2007; Foss, 2010), we also aim to identify areas that, to date, have been omitted from research texts.

The chapter is structured as follows. We begin by presenting the theoretical context for our study, discussing the development of gender theory in entrepreneurship. Next, our methodological approach is presented. This is followed by our analysis of selected articles, which are further critiqued in the discussion section. Finally, we present our conclusions and suggest some avenues for future research.

## THEORETICAL CONTEXT – GENDER THEORY

In this chapter, and by way of laying the foundation for critically analysing the innovation literatures, we base our understanding of gender in accordance with developments in gender theory in the context of entrepreneurship. Over the last 40 years, research on gender and entrepreneurship has developed from 'feminist empiricism' (gender-as-variable), to 'feminist standpoint theory' (gender-as-relationship) through to 'post-structural feminism' (gender-as-process) (Ahl, 2006; Berg, 1997). The two first approaches have been criticized for being essentialist[2] in nature, as they assume that certain traits are unique to men and women. Further, these approaches reinforce the sameness (empiricist feminism) or difference (feminist standpoint) between men and women, thus taking little account of within-sex variation. Indeed, the majority of the earlier studies on entrepreneurship were highly male gendered; they were based mainly, or in some cases solely, on the experiences of men, thus establishing a seemingly acceptable benchmark against which to judge women in their entrepreneurial endeavours. As a consequence, such research failed to recognize the socially constructed aspects of gender (Ahl, 2004, as cited in Hill et al., 2006, p. 160). The focus was placed firmly on the differences rather than the similarities between men and women. This type of research emphasized the specific challenges or barriers faced by women aspiring to or engaging in entrepreneurship, and was problematic, as it manifested an androcentric approach, exaggerated perceived 'male' successes, excluded women and collectively served to reproduce the gendered subordination of women within the entrepreneurial domain.

According to Neergaard et al. (2011), in contrast to the 'gender-as-variable' approach, feminist scholars recognize and analyse the scope and variations of women's structural subordination to men in different societal and geographical contexts. Socialization is exposed as a process that constructs different opportunities, possibilities and choices for men and women. In relation to entrepreneurship, for example, research adopting a feminist standpoint seeks to make women entrepreneurs more visible and, where comparisons are appropriate, compares them to other women rather than to their male counterparts (Bowden and Mummery, 2009).

The third approach – post-structural feminism – analyses how gender is constructed through history, geography and culture (Bordo, 1990; Di Stefano, 1990; Haraway, 1991). What appears as masculine and feminine may vary over time and place and across discourses (cf. Pettersson, 2004). Thus, gender is analysed by how it is formed as a result of the relationships in which it is situated and the context in which it is expressed (Bruni et al., 2005). As McDowell (2000) posits, gendered relations are not simply binary, but rather unruly and complicated. In this regard, gender becomes a cultural code to be negotiated. Research adopting a post-structural feminism approach analyses gender as some-thing separate from biological sex; rather than being studied as a specific characteristic of men or women, it is studied through discursive practices (Kelan, 2009). As explained by Ahl (2004), this means that femininity and masculinity can be distinguished in performance by males as well as females, thus suggesting that a female entrepreneur (or innovator) can exhibit the sort of behaviour that would normally be expected of her male counterpart, and vice versa (Neergaard et al., 2011). Researchers using a post-structuralist standpoint approach in their work are not, according to Ahl (2006, p. 597), concerned with what men or women *are* but with how masculinity and femininity are *constructed*. In this regard, gender is something that is 'done', 'accomplished' or 'performed' (Acker, 1999; Butler, 1990; Fenstermaker et al., 2002; West and Zimmerman, 1987). For example, post-structural research on female entrepreneurship distin-guishes that entrepreneurship per se is embedded within a masculine discourse, one that positions men as the entrepreneurial normative actor and women as 'other' (Neergaard et al., 2011). The problem here – for women entrepreneurs, scholars, practitioners and policy makers – is that 'other' typically means 'lacking', 'in deficit' or 'less'.

## DATA AND METHODOLOGY

For the purposes of this study, we focused on published scholarly research that purported to analyse innovation in the context of gender. We chose to review literatures in the form of empirically based journal articles, omitting books and book chapters. We further excluded book reviews, editorials, calls for papers, and articles with only a passing reference to our key search terms. The ISI website of science was searched for entries in peer-reviewed journals containing at least one of the following phrases in the title, abstract, key words or full text: 'innovation and gender', 'innovation and women' or 'innovation and sex'. We deliberately sought these combinations to avoid exploring purely mainstream innovation literatures or only those literatures that analysed innovation in isolation from gender. We further needed to choose subcategories in the ISI web of science. Recognizing that innovation is a cross-disciplinary theme, we sought to broaden the potential scope of contributions through the following subcategories: Management, Business, Geography, Economics, Women's Studies, Planning and Development, Social Science and Interdisciplinary research. Also, in order to cover the earliest possible contributions, we chose the time period 1956–2010. After this search, we realized that many of the current publications with a focus on gender and innovation were not covered by ISI. We thus expanded our search through Google Scholar to include articles published after 2010. This exercise generated a total of 168 articles from ISI and 50 further articles from Google Scholar.

The ISI database combined with the Google Scholar database covers most, but admittedly not all, of the published journals in the field of social science (i.e. Sociology, Management, Business). Thus, the reference lists in the total of 218 selected articles were examined to identify additional articles published in journals that are not included in the chosen databases. We also examined the within-article citations. Surprisingly, upon further examination, several published articles with 'innovation' in both their title and their key words did not contain any discussion of innovation in the main body of the text. Thus, from the 218 articles initially selected, only 46 were deemed sufficiently relevant to our study. After a more thorough reading of these articles, we eliminated further on the basis of both relevance and level of exploration of the concept of innovation in the context of gender. This process resulted in a final total of 22 core articles selected for exploratory analysis (see Table 2.1).

We do not suggest that ours is an exhaustive list of articles, sufficient for a thorough critical discourse analysis of the field. However, given our aim to identify some of the key trends in the gender and innovation discourse, such a list can provide valuable insights into how gender is contextualized in innovation research, and help lay the foundation for further debate in this area. The next section presents our approach to analysing the selected articles.

*Table 2.1 Selected articles*

| Theme and author(s) | Year | Journal | Web of Science citations | Google Scholar citations | Scopus citations | Five-year impact factor | Article influence score |
|---|---|---|---|---|---|---|---|
| *Thematic category: Traditional innovation and associated definitional issues:* | | | | | | | |
| Carrasco, I. | 2014 | Management Decision | 0 | 5 | 1 | 0.622 | |
| Hunt, J., J. Garant, H. Herman and D.J. Munroe | 2013 | Research Policy | 8 | 18 | 9 | 3.989 | 1.42 |
| Østgaard, C.R., B. Timmermans and K. Kristinsson | 2011 | Research Policy | 45 (7.5) | 180 | 67 | 3.989 | 1.42 |
| Blake, M.K. and S. Hanson | 2005 | Environment and Planning A | 36 (3.0) | 140 | 61 | 2.177 | 0.877 |
| Wilson, M. | 2004 | Journal of Information Technology | 25 (1.92) | 62 | 40 | 3.097 | 0.773 |
| Sonfield, M., R. Lussier, J. Corman and M. McKinney | 2001 | Journal of Small Business Management | 31 (1.94) | 149 | 55 | 1.554 | 0.363 |
| *Thematic category: Management styles, performance and teams:* | | | | | | | |
| Baer, M., A.K. Vadera, R.T. Leenders and G.R. Oldham | 2014 | Organization Science | 0 | | 1 | 5.61 | 2.88 |
| Idris, A. | 2009 | African Journal of Business Management | 4 (0.5) | 12 | | 0.107 | 0.000 |
| Ruiz-Arroyo, M., M. del Mar Fuentes-Fuentes, A.M. Bojica and L. Rodríguez-Ariza | 2012 | Journal of Small Business and Entrepreneurship | | 7 | | | |

*Table 2.1 (continued)*

| Theme and author(s) | Year | Journal | Web of Science citations | Google Scholar citations | Scopus citations | Five-year impact factor | Article influence score |
|---|---|---|---|---|---|---|---|
| Welbourne, T.M., C.S. Cycyota and C.J. Ferrante | 2007 | *Group and Organization Management* | 18 (1.8) | 69 | 24 | 1.914 | 0.777 |
| Miller, T. and M.C. Triana | 2009 | *Journal of Management Studies* | 87 (10.88) | 272 | 105 | 3.485 | 1.386 |
| Cady, S.H. and J. Valentine | 1999 | *Small Group Research* | 39 (2.17) | 126 | 51 | 1.288 | 0.523 |
| *Thematic category: Organizational structures and networks:* | | | | | | | |
| Foss, L., K. Woll and M. Moilanen | 2013 | *International Journal of Gender and Entrepreneurship* | | 11 | 4 | | |
| Lindberg, M., M. Lindgren and J. Packendorff | 2014 | *Journal of Knowledge Economy* | | 11 | 0 | | |
| Smith-Doerr, L. | 2010 | *Industry and Innovation* | 3 (0.43) | 7 | 3 | | |
| Gray, M. and A. James | 2007 | *Environment and Planning A* | 13 (1.30) | 29 | 19 | 2.177 | 0.877 |
| *Thematic category: Gendered stereotypes, feminist resistance, and gendered processes of innovation:* | | | | | | | |
| Eriksson, A.F. | 2014 | *International Journal of Gender and Entrepreneurship* | | 3 | 1 | | |
| Pettersson, K. and M. Lindberg | 2013 | *International Journal of Gender and Entrepreneurship* | | 6 | 6 | | |

| Poutanen, S. and A. Kovalainen | 2013 | International Journal of Gender and Entrepreneurship | 4 | 3 |
| Rönnblom, M. and B.I. Keisu | 2013 | International Journal of Gender and Entrepreneurship | 3 | 1 |
| Wikhamn, B.R. and D. Knights | 2013 | International Journal of Gender and Entrepreneurship | 4 | 2 |
| Johansson, A.W. and M. Lindberg | 2011 | Annals of Innovation and Entrepreneurship | 4 | |

*Notes:*
ISI has changed name to Web of Science citations – by Thomson Reuters.
Scopus citations – by Elsevier.
Five-year impact factor and article influence score – from Web of Science.
Numbers in parenthesis are average citations per year.
Updated 25 May 2016.

## ANALYSIS OF THE SELECTED ARTICLES

In this chapter, our analysis of the gender and innovation literatures is inspired by Ahl's (2002) discourse analysis of women's entrepreneurship, Foss's (2010) discourse analysis of research on entrepreneur networks, and Henry et al.'s (2015) analysis of the gender and entrepreneurship literatures. According to Butler (1990) 'gender' as a word is a linguistic marker; it is not neutral, as it reveals the social and political dialect of academia. Given that academics are the agents of scholarly discourse, they have the power to control how gender is conceptualized in research. The extent of this control can be detected by exposing the underlying assumptions in the texts that relate gender and innovation to one another in a particular way (Ahl, 2007). These underlying assumptions may demonstrate hegemonic voices (Foss, 2010) as well as damaging discourses (Sunderland, 2004). Discourse analysis is different to ordinary content analysis in terms of how the material is interrogated: the analysis focuses not only on what the content *is* but also on what it *does*, what is included and what is not, and what is implied and what is asserted (Ahl and Nelson, 2015, p. 277). We argue that this is a legitimate exercise for contributing to extant research on gender in innovation.

Our analytical approach was three-fold. First, we categorized our selected articles according to their thematic focus. In so doing, we noted that, with a few exceptions, the majority of our articles, while not always explicit in their chosen gender perspective, adopted either a gender-as-relationship or a gender-as-process perspective, where they identified the masculine biases inherent in innovation and highlighted women's consistent exclusion from the process. Second, we discussed how researchers actually defined innovation and, third, we identified how they illustrated the relationship between gender and innovation.

In thematically analysing our selected articles, we identified four broad categories: 1) articles dealing with innovation in its traditional form that also recognize the inherent gender biases associated with accepted definitions in current literatures; 2) articles exploring management styles in the context of innovation, with a particular emphasis on performance, teams and team diversity; 3) articles with organizational structures and networking in technologically developed industries as their key focus; and 4) articles on gendered stereotypes, feminist resistance, and gendered processes in innovation.

## 1) Traditional Innovation and Associated Definitional Issues

This category covers articles that deal with innovation in its traditional form as well as those articles focusing mainly on how innovation is defined. We included six articles in this category, published between 2001 and 2014, and these are listed in Table 2.1. With the exception of one article that adopted a conventional gender-as-variable approach (Sonfield et al., 2001), all of the articles in this category adopted either a gender-as-relationship or gender-as-process perspective. Current understanding of innovation, as argued by Blake and Hanson (2005), is predominantly technology- and product-driven, devoid of context and overly masculine. Thus, by considering the various definitions of innovation used in mainstream literatures to date, Blake and Hanson (2005) help lay the foundation for our analysis. The authors suggest that the very concept of innovation has been constructed to focus solely on particular types of economic activity, which by their very nature tend to exclude women (i.e. high-growth businesses in traditionally male-dominated industries that are scientifically or technologically based, export oriented, etc.). Interestingly, not everyone, but more so the women, interviewed in their study viewed their particular product or service as innovative in the traditional sense; rather, they felt they were innovative because they brought a new idea to a particular place and, as a consequence, created a positive change in that place (p. 682). In this regard, Blake and Hanson (2005) highlight the potential value of geographic context for revealing the true nature of both the innovation and the innovative opportunity. This in turn, they suggest, would lead to a more inclusive definition and enhanced understanding of innovation.

Using comparative case examples, Blake and Hanson (2005) platform the role of gender in shaping the start-up process and location decisions of entrepreneurs. It is through these examples that the inherently masculinized perspective, which has traditionally underpinned our understanding and acceptance of the concept of innovation, is demonstrated. For example, businesses based on a care home facility or a Mexican restaurant, as discussed in Blake and Hanson's (2005) study, would not, in the context of traditional, mainstream literatures, be viewed as innovative; they are not new in the 'novel' sense and may potentially cause displacement. However, using cases such as these, the authors highlight their innovative element when contextual and motivational factors are considered, that is, the entrepreneur's choice of geographical location and the business objective. In both of the examples referred to above, the women entrepreneurs realized that there was a particular need to be filled in *that* place; they were familiar with *that* place and thus capitalized on the locality aspect. They could have easily chosen to locate to a more central geographic city or region, or export their product or service, but preferred to focus on a 'specific local need where local may refer to the scale of a city, a neighbourhood or a church catchment area' (p. 690).

Commercial science, a traditionally accepted source of innovation, is the focus of Murray and Graham's (2007) article. Here, the authors argue that the exclusion of women early on in their scientific careers leaves them with fewer opportunities in the marketplace and directly contributes towards the weakening of their commercial science and socialization skills. Interviews with life science academics at a high-calibre university are used to highlight the significant gender gap in commercial science. The findings reveal a series of embedded gender biases ranging from women's initial exclusion from commercial opportunities through to the underlying construct of the commercial scientist as being predominately male coded. This has resulted, in practice, in women being less prepared for the commercial selling of their science and less confident than their male counterparts in their own commercial science abilities. This was particularly evident when metrics such as publications, industry collaborations and patents were applied. The women in the study had a significantly lower percentage of the above when compared to their male colleagues. Furthermore, while there was a general consensus that men were supportive of their female colleagues' scientific endeavours, they tended to disregard them as potential commercial collaborators. Essentially, the women felt excluded from much of the commercial opportunity process, while men did not. The typical issues that have dominated the gender literatures over the years constituted the dominant narratives among many of the women in Murray and Graham's study, including a sense of exclusion, limited opportunities, the perception that male scientists were more highly regarded by industry, and the presence of a 'boys' club'. Consistent with findings from other gendered domains, such underlying biases impact negatively on women's competency levels and serve to further masculinize the field.

With parallels to the above debate, Hunt et al. (2013) explore the under-representation of women amongst patentees. Using a sample of academic science and engineering Ph.D.s, the authors investigate commercial patent holders and find that only 5.5 per cent are women. The authors suggest that growth in innovation and technological progress would be much higher if the whole workforce (i.e. both males and females) was exploited. They further highlight that, while not all innovations are patented, patents tend to be used as the traditional measure of innovation, thus allowing assumptions to be drawn about women's participation in innovation. While challenging the traditional view of innovation with respect to gender equality in terms of participation, their study does not offer a counter-definition or alternative perspective. Rather, the authors conclude that increasing women's participation in patent-intensive fields of study would increase female patenting. They suggest that early intervention is required.

At a more conceptual level, the paper by Wilson (2004) discusses the lack of theorization of gender within the information systems (IS) literature. The author adopts a critical feminist approach to the organizational context of IS development. Clearly, Wilson rejects the masculine way of defining technology and technological ability, and suggests broadening the scope to include the use of technology as a change process in order to view the important role women play as users. By drawing on insights from four areas – 1) gender and computing (the differences and inequalities of development and use of IS), 2) gender and society concerning the existence of gendered spheres, 3) gender and organizations concerning the social division of labour, and 4) gender and technology – the author argues for a social constructivist account of gender phenomena, claiming that both technology and gender are socially and mutually defining. Although it is not explicit, Wilson employs a 'gender-as-process' perspective, using a post-structuralist analysis of gender.

Gender differences in venture innovation and risk among business owners are the focus of Sonfield et al.'s (2001) paper. Here, the authors use the entrepreneurial strategy mix as their analytical framework. This situational model, developed by Sonfield and Lussier (1997), suggests appropriate strategies for new and on-going ventures based on identifying different levels of innovation and risk. 'Innovation' is defined as creating a new, unique and different product or service, whereas 'risk' is defined as the probability of major financial loss. In a cross-sectional study of a national sample of 184 firms, the results showed no differences in innovation or risk among male and female firm owners, nor in the strategies they choose to employ. Thus, the study contradicts previous studies where women have been found to have a higher aversion to risk than men do. However, in terms of satisfaction with business performance, men scored higher. While this article employs a conventional 'gender-as-variable' approach, owing to mixed results the authors suggest that future studies investigate possible differences among women entrepreneurs, which reflects a more modern gender approach.

How environments affect the process of innovation as conceptualized by women is the focus adopted by Carrasco (2014). This article is especially interesting because it contrasts the 'doing gender' perspective in that the author only acknowledges a gender gap in innovation in terms of the number of women represented in technological innovation, leaving the technological masculine norms inherent in traditional definitions intact. Carrasco (2014) has developed an empirical model seeking to explain how the institutional environment affects innovation development as conceptualized by women. A latent model containing data from 40 countries was developed, and it was proposed that three different constructs affect women's innovations in male-dominated, technological industries: 1) indicators of an informal environment; 2) the general economic, social and family environment; and 3) educational character-istics and general education at an institutional level. Carrasco found that innovation by women is determined by various aspects of the social, political and economic environment surrounding them; thus, the insti-tutional environment is important when encouraging innovation by women.

Using data from an innovation survey merged with data on employees, Østgaard et al. (2011) investigate the relationship between employee diversity and innovation in terms of gender, age, ethnicity and education. Their findings reveal a positive correlation between employee diversity and the innovative performance of firms. This is most significant for employee diversity in gender and education, while age diversity seems to have a negative impact. Their analysis showed that gender was one of the variables that had the strongest positive relationship to a firm's likelihood to innovate.

## 2)   Management Styles, Performance and Teams

This category covered articles dealing predominately with innovation in management styles as related to organizational performance and teams. As with the previous category, as illustrated in Table 2.1, we included six articles under this heading, all published between 1999 and 2014. In this category, while the gender-as-relationship and gender-as-process perspec-tives predominated, we noted at least one study that adopted a traditional gender-as-variable approach (Cady and Valentine, 1999). The study by Baer et al. (2014) could also be perceived as adopting a traditional gender approach, while the study by Miller and Triana (2009) did not appear to adopt any specific gender perspective. While it is generally accepted in the literature that management style directly affects organ-izational innovation and, as a consequence, overall performance, rela-tively little is known about the way in which women manage innovation. Consistent with Blake and Hanson's (2005) view that the very concept of innovation is predominately male coded, Idris (2009) highlights the underlying gendered assumptions relating to management style. Studies on management styles have been traditionally based on male norms, mainly because most studies on innovation management have been based on men rather than women. Thus existing typologies fail to consider the particular challenges faced by women entrepreneurs, their specific characteristics, their response to environmental stimuli, and the manner in which they operationalize their innovations (i.e. whether product, service or process). An understanding of women's interpersonal relationships and the impact of culture is also lacking in current innovation management theory, thus biasing the concept of management towards traditional male models. Through the study of Malaysian women entrepreneurs and their management of innovation, the author constructs a typology of female entrepreneurial managers in which she identifies four distinct leadership styles: mother, teacher, boss and chameleon (p. 421). The styles are essentially shaped by the individual women's experiences and, to some degree, reflect gendered norms to the extent that they are, with the exception of the 'boss' category, highly feminine in nature. This is further reflected in the author's hypothesis that some women entrepreneurs may adopt such styles, that is, those that reflect their traditional roles in society, in order to fit in 'so that society will be more tolerant and accepting towards their leadership' (p. 423). Paradoxically, such predominantly male constructs do little to create an improved and more gender-balanced understanding of innovation management styles.

Taking the view that innovativeness is a key factor explaining a firm's competitive advantage and superior performance, Ruiz-Arroyo et al. (2012) explore the capabilities needed to obtain and sustain competitive advantage. The authors analyse the innovativeness of women-owned businesses, its relationship to performance, and the role of knowledge acquisition from relationships with customers. In their study of 111 women-owned firms, they show innovativeness to be positively related to different types of operational and financial performance, with knowledge acquired from customers shown to improve innovativeness. The authors acknowledge that studies of innovation among women-owned firms are scarce, and refer to the 'adaptor' rather than 'innovator' label traditionally associated with women's entrepreneurial endeavours. In demonstrating that women's level of innovativeness is quite significant and is positively related to all measures of performance, Ruiz-Arroyo et al. (2012) directly challenge traditional gender-biased views of innovation. They suggest that innovation does not belong to a specific sector or activity; rather, it can relate to an organizational culture or strategic orientation. Thus researchers should focus on the capabilities that need to be developed to acquire knowledge, and should examine networks and social capital.

Welbourne et al.'s (2007) examination of gender diversity in top management teams shows how Wall Street is beginning to recognize the contribution women can make to managing innovative new firms, as illustrated in both initial public offering (IPO) and long-term firm performance. While the authors acknowledge that current literatures include conflicting views on the issue of women managers and their impact on firm performance, they provide valuable evidence that Wall Street is possibly becoming gender neutral when it comes to share value and other purely commercial business metrics. Their hypotheses relating to the positive relationship between the percentage of women on top management teams and initial IPO pricing of innovative firms, and similarly between this and stock price and earnings per share, were supported by their study. Their findings suggest that investors perceive having women in a firm's top management team as a benefit. In contrast, Welbourne et al. (2007) uncover evidence of a strengthening male-oriented culture within larger innovative firms and public limited companies (PLCs); here there are significantly fewer women managers and, it is suggested, highly skilled and experienced female managers are continuing to exit the larger corporates to take up senior roles in smaller innovative IPO firms. This suggests that the traditional glass ceiling has not yet been fully cracked.

Gender diversity in the boardroom is the focus of Miller and Triana's (2009) article. They suggest firm reputation and innovation as mediators in the relationship between racial and gender diversity and firm performance. The authors define innovation as strategies that provide new opportunities for the firm to create products or services. Based on signalling theory and behavioural theory of the firm, five hypotheses are developed predicting positive relationships between board gender diversity or board racial diversity and innovation and reputation. They posit that innovation mediates the relationship between board gender diversity and firm performance, and between board racial diversity and firm performance. Demographic data on Fortune 500 firms were analysed with OLS regression; these showed that both reputation and innovation mediated the relationship between board racial diversity and firm performance. Thus, consistent with behavioural theory, firms may benefit from the diverse human and social capital on diverse boards that support an innovation strategy. The results supported the diversity hypothesis that both board gender and racial diversity are positively related to innovation, as measured by R&D expenditures. Further, innovation was a mediator between racial diversity and firm performance. However, the hypothesis that gender diversity was positively related to reputation received mixed support. The authors do not use an explicit gender perspective in their theoretical framework.

In a similar vein, Cady and Valentine (1999) explore the impact of diversity (age, race, sex and function) on team innovation. The authors present a field study where they measure the team diversity of 50 teams using an entropy-based formula. The results revealed that none of the diversity dimensions affected the quality of innovation. Sex had a negative impact on the quantity of innovation, whereas race had a positive impact. Further, both sex and gender influenced perceptions of team consideration.

Building upon social role theory, Baer et al. (2014) present both a field and a laboratory experiment measuring how the extent of intergroup competition is affected by the sex composition of those groups, resulting in either a surge or a constriction of creativity. Both studies supported their hypothesis. As anticipated by the authors, competition boosted the creativity of groups composed mostly or entirely of men. Little or no evidence was found to support the expected decline in creativity among groups composed largely or exclusively of women. However, when considering the non-linear effects on intergroup competition, a negative relationship between competition and creativity among the all-female groups emerged. Thus, this study is consistent with and further extends the contingency perspective by suggesting that the composition of groups in terms of sex also plays a vital role in moderating the effects of intergroup competition on outcomes such as group creativity (p. 904). In line with social theory, the Baer et al. study found groups composed of women to be more creative than groups composed of men.

### 3)  Organizational Structures and Networks

From our review, just four articles were identified in this category dealing with innovation in the context of organizational structures and networks. All of these were published over a period of seven years, between 2007 and 2014. While not overly explicit in their chosen gender perspective, the papers in this category appeared to adopt a gender-as-relationship and/or gender-as-process approach. Innovation is inherently gendered through structures and networks, as illustrated by Smith-Doerr (2010), who considers women's participation in the early US film industry, and explores the reasons for women's sudden demise, which coincided with the introduction of 'talking' rather than 'silent' movies. In the early 1900s, women dominated the US film industry not just as successful screenwriters but also as editors, continuity writers and scenarists. Smith-Doerr attributes their success in no small part to the informal organizational network form that prevailed at that time. This particular non-bureaucratic organizational structure gave women both visibility and power, allowing them to draw on their vast networks to deliver entire film productions. Analysing women's participation with a gender lens, Smith-Doerr cites Tuchman's (1989) argument that women first succeeded in this field because it was 'open' and 'lacked the cultural legitimacy and economic incentives for attracting men' (Smith-Doerr, 2010, p. 17). Interestingly, the technological innovation that led to the talking movies changed the basic organizational structure upon which the industry had previously operated, resulting in a type of 'credentialist' system that inherently discriminated against women and encouraged men to the field.

Gray and James (2007) critique the tendency in regional and innovation literature to divorce learning and innovation processes from people with real gendered identities and commitments that shape their daily work activities. A case study of the ICT sector in Cambridge demonstrates significant inequalities in the dominant patterns of work and social interaction among female and male employees. These inequalities potentially constrain female workers' abilities to contribute fully to the key processes that, theoretically, are purported to drive the economic competitiveness of firms in a region. This article is important because it provides empirical evidence for the further integration of feminist and regional economic geographies.

Lindberg et al. (2014) adopt an exploratory case study approach to analyse the inherent gendered norms within traditional Triple Helix innovation models. Their study identifies four roles that non-governmental organizations (NGOs) could potentially fulfil in order to bridge the gender gap: the creation of collaborative platforms for women-led SMEs; linking women-led firms to government and academia; developing competence- and process-based innovation outside of traditional Triple Helix constellations; and highlighting the individual and societal aspects of entrepreneuring. The authors challenge the Triple Helix model by drawing attention to the 'cultural gap' in how innovation is viewed, suggesting that policy makers' expectations of innovation are based on high-tech, high-growth and individual ventures, that is, traditional masculine ways of entrepreneuring. Lindberg et al. (2014) suggest that the Triple Helix model sustains gendered views of innovation because it is mainly situated within male-dominated settings, and suggest, as an alternative, a Quadruple Helix model that incorporates civil society as a fourth partner. Such a model could highlight the role of non-profit actors within innovation networks, and allow marginalized groups (including women) to play central roles (p. 109). Studies of this nature help broaden extant conceptualizations of innovation.

The study conducted by Foss et al. (2013) supports the view that the effects of a work environment and the organizational structure of a workplace on innovation are both mediated and non-mediated by gender. The mediated effects support a 'doing gender' approach. Idea generation and implementation is gendered in the sense that female employees tend to work in fields such as customer service, human resources, accounting, and research and analysis, whereas male employees work in management, technical and practical operative work, and technical research and planning. Thus, the innovative potential of female employees is not often exploited, because innovation becomes masculine coded in keeping with the work activities of male employees. Both the technology-related industrial context and the male-dominated environment of a corporation prove challenging for encouraging employee-driven innovation in women.

### 4) Gendered Stereotypes, Feminist Resistance, and Gendered Processes of Innovation

Our final category included those articles that dealt specifically with the gendered stereotypes and processes of innovation. Here we found six papers published between 2011 and 2014, five of which were published in the niche and relatively new *International Journal of Gender and Entrepreneurship*. As with the previous category, the papers in this group appeared to adopt a gender-as-relationship and/or gender-as-process approach, with evidence of slightly more emphasis on the latter. This category of papers contains more recent literature that broadens the understanding of how innovation is inherently gendered. For example, Pettersson and Lindberg (2013) use Rose's concept of paradoxical space to analyse the feminist approaches used to articulate and perform resistance to hegemonic masculinist discourses on innovation. The paper focuses on Swedish gender and innovation research and development projects. Using Rose's framework as a theoretical lens, the authors focused on research and evaluations in which they had been involved as 'outsiders within' (p. 323). The empirical material used was collected through literature and internet research as well as interviews. Following Rose (1993), the analyses utilized the following four aspects of feminist resistance: 1) movements between centre and margin; 2) reaching beyond representation and definition; 3) separatism and free spaces for women; and 4) recognizing differences among women. The authors conclude that all of these approaches are used in the discursive landscape of Swedish gender and innovation R&D. The latter approach (recognizing differences among women), however, was generally lacking in the material analysed, except in a few cases.

Johansson and Lindberg (2011) argue for a more inclusive view on innovation related to gender. By interpreting the story of a particular innovating businesswoman as an example of innovation as an everyday phenomenon, the paper analyses innovation as something that emanates from creativity and from the routines of everyday practice. This view of innovation clearly deviates from the standard.

Eriksson (2014) utilizes a more conceptualized starting point, exploring whether a gender perspective contributes to or functions as a driving force for innovation within organizations. Through a qualitative case study, the article describes innovation in the local organizational context of an upper secondary school in Sweden. The school stood out as a good example of gender awareness and gender mainstreaming within the municipality. When compared to six other local workplaces, the school distinguished itself in terms of the adoption and generation of innovation. Findings revealed that, by adopting a gender perspective, the school's staff members were able to identify the necessary areas of improvement, all of which had gender implications for both male and female pupils. This allowed the school to identify several problems and areas of need, which led to the development of a number of gender-sensitive innovations.

In a narrative case study of a large chemical corporation, Poutanen and Kovalainen (2013) illustrate how gender is related to the process of innovation. By using interview data from a single case, they illustrate how women are left out of the innovation process. They are not included in the workplace groups that define and participate in the negotiation of technologies – even if they hold a position in the R&D department and are responsible for R&D work. The article also demonstrates that, as a product becomes feminized in the innovation process, male colleagues tend to lose interest in the process, which makes it possible for the female inventor to reclaim her position.

Rönnblom and Keisu (2013) investigate the construction of innovation in Swedish universities and relate it to how gender and gender equality are produced. By combining aspects from gender theory and feminist theory, they introduce a framework for studying gender and policy. They use this framework to analyse the gendered meaning of marketization in the Swedish academy. The findings show that the ambition to broaden the understanding of innovation in the university context results in a conventional representation of innovation.

Wikhamn and Knights (2013) study the open innovation process by following the transformation of AB Volvo from a company providing engineer-oriented products (such as vehicles and construction equipment) to a transport solution provider of 'soft products' (such as software, telematics and services). These enhance customer satisfaction as well as safety and environmental care, but do not improve the actual vehicle. To achieve this goal, an open innovation process was seen as a necessary approach, with the potential to introduce softer and possibly less masculine ways of organizing innovation. By conducting more than 50 interviews with key managers and project leaders at Volvo, the researchers could analyse the gendering of open innovation in practice as the development of soft products continued. The results show that, despite open innovation activities aiming to support creativity and changes in organizational culture, they were nevertheless infiltrated by masculine discourse on innovation when put into practice.

## Definitions of Innovation

In our review, we identified 14 research texts that offered a more precise definition of innovation. For example, Miller and Triana (2009) define innovation as 'strategies that provide new opportunities for the firm to create products and services' (p. 756). M. Wilson's (2004) article delves deeper by developing a framework that she argues contributes to information systems research (IS) by 'providing access to additional explanations for organisational phenomena (such as user rejection); by deepening our understanding of the innovation process; by improving IS through increased awareness of social issues (especially gender) and by promoting further potential topics for IS researchers' (p. 81). However, the concept of innovation processes is not used as a conceptual tool in the article; rather, technology becomes the dominant concept. In contrast, Cady and Valentine's (1999) article is more concerned with the quantity rather than the quality of innovation, which they define as the number of new ideas generated (p. 731). They refer to the concept of sustaining innovation (cf. Dougherty and Hardy, 1996), defining it as an organization's capability to generate product and service ideas. According to the extant literature, however, this is usually denoted as innovation where technology helps companies sustain their growth in the existing market in order to ensure market domination and growth (Walsh and Kirchhoff, 2003). Notwithstanding the above, Cady and Valentine (1999) also include some consideration of the quality of innovation by referring to the concept of adoption (cf. Damanpour, 1991), that is, the degree to which an idea that fills a need or solves a problem can be successfully adopted by an organization. As Cady and Valentine are dealing with team innovation, an averaging approach is used, where each idea developed by a team is evaluated to compute an overall score for the quality of innovation. Sonfield et al. (2001) build on Sonfield and Lussier's (1997) entrepreneurial strategy mix, where innovation is defined as creating a new, unique and different product or service.

Blake and Hanson (2005) argue for a revised definition of innovation to better facilitate those types of innovations typically led by women but not viewed as innovations in the traditional male sense. In this regard, contextual and motivational factors become additional yet valuable components of the innovation mix. In a similar vein, Idris (2009) helps to redefine how innovation is managed, by identifying particular styles associated with women managers but which would not typically be seen as legitimate or mainstream. Interpersonal relationships and culture are highlighted as additional aspects that need to be considered when defining innovation management style.

While Smith-Doerr's (2010) article does not overtly define innovation in the traditional sense, it does highlight the potential negative impact of technological *innovation* on women's participation within an industry; in this regard, the introduction of 'talkies' rather than 'silent' movies played a significant yet negative role, creating a new type of organizational structure that was inherently gender biased. In many ways, Smith-Doerr is calling for a return to informal, networked organizational types where, clearly, women have been proven to flourish; this is an innovation in itself.

Eriksson (2014) uses an explicit and broad definition of innovation, defining innovation as the implementation of a new or significantly improved product (good or service) or process, a new marketing method, or a new organizational method in business practices, workplace organization or external relations. This definition is justified by acknowledging both innovation-generating and innovation-adopting aspects in organizations (Eriksson, 2014, p. 165). The article analyses innovation in the public sector, and focuses on product innovation, process innovation and organizational innovation.

Carrasco (2014) highlights the connection between innovation and environment, emphasizing the role of different players and the links among them in innovation processes (p. 412). Pettersson and Lindberg (2013) discuss the masculine aspects of innovation, emphasizing that innovation is an area characterized 'either by blindness or male dominance' (p. 327). They problematize that innovation is usually described in reference to mechanical machines and technical products, and not so often in relation to subjects considered feminine, such as social, organizational and service innovation. Wikhamn and Knights (2013) similarly argue that, when analysing an open innovation process, one must consider the open innovation in relation to masculine and/or feminine discourse. Johansson and Lindberg (2011) highlight that innovation policy tends to associate innovation with large-scale industrial product development, and neglects the kinds of innovation taking place within the service and creative industries, which employ mostly women. They argue that this marginalization is related to how innovation is conceptualized. Poutanen and Kovalainen (2013) discuss the gendered aspect of the innovation process, where the product itself could be gendered and considered undervalued if labelled as 'feminine' in a workplace with a predominance of men. In Østgaard et al. (2011), innovation is used as the dependent variable in their logistic regression. In order to have a manageable measure of innovation, they explicitly define innovation in its traditional way 'as the introduction of new products or services, excluding minor improvements on already existing products and services' (p. 504). They also include important organizational changes as a measure of innovation.

In Rönnblom and Keisu (2013), the very concept of innovation, and how it is represented in universities, is the subject of analysis. The article presents three interrelated representations of innovation, ranging from viewing innovation as a catalyst for growth to a broader representation that includes aspects of teaching. The results show that a definition of innovation that is too narrow excludes many academic activities, thus favouring a broader representation on a general level. On the other hand, when the concept of gender equality was introduced into discussions with researchers, the understanding of innovation narrowed to activities that generate a product capable of being commercialized.

## Relationship between Gender and Innovation

In this section, we review how the texts link gender to innovation.[3] Miller and Triana's (2009) main argument is that boardroom diversity (including gender) provides strategic human and social capital to firms, thereby increasing innovation (p. 759). The authors build on the behavioural theory of the firm by focusing on how the extensiveness of the search and the decision-making process can influence innovation in the firms. Thus, homogeneous groups may hamper innovation because the high level of cohesion causes pressure to conform.

Heterogeneous groups should produce a broader range of ideas and information because they contain a diverse body of knowledge. The authors further refer to the connection between demographic diversity and differences in social capital and network resources. The more diverse the ties, the more resources can be acquired. Miller and Triana (2009) refer to a study where heterogeneous managerial knowledge from network structures positively impacts innovation. They subsequently refer to studies showing that the social networks of females and minorities tend to be more diverse than those of white males; since women and minorities must maintain multiple networks in order to secure their career and social resources, they maintain a broad range of contacts and are more likely to maintain so-called weak ties. Such ties have been proven to be successful because they provide non-redundant information. Thus, information from females and minorities can be a pivotal source of information supporting innovative activity. Their hypothesis is, therefore, that both gender and racial diversity on boards are positively related to firm innovation. Our immediate interpretation of this text is that the underlying rationale relies on a feminist argument that women and men are essentially different; thus, they acquire diverse knowledge, information, networks and resources. We concur that heterogeneity in human resources is positively linked to the diversity of resources and networks. However, Miller and Triana's (2009) argument seems to be based on the perception that women and men come to the boardroom with completely different mindsets.

In Smith-Doerr's (2010) paper, the relationship between gender and innovation is very much seen as a negative one. Here innovation in its traditional form impacted negatively on women's participation in film writing, and led to a rapid gender shift towards a predominantly male-led industry. Technological innovation led to an organizational change through which structures and roles were more hierarchical and more formal, rather than the previously more networked and less formal environment, which had allowed women to flourish. It seemed that the network form of organization afforded women more visibility and authority, which they subsequently lost in the more bureaucratic formal structure.

The relationship between gender and innovation in its truest sense is possibly best illustrated in Murray and Graham's (2007) paper. Here, the authors platform the gender inequalities between women and men operating in the commercial science arena. Once again, as a result of long-standing gender inequalities in the academic system, male scientists and male-led innovations were perceived as being of higher value within both the academic and the commercial arenas. In contrast, Welbourne et al. (2007) highlight how Wall Street is finally starting to take a more commercial view of women's participation in top management teams (TMTs). These IPO firms, led by more gender-balanced management teams, appear to be attracting investment based on evidence of women's innovative contribution at the strategic management level.

In Eriksson (2014), the relationship between gender and innovation is at the very core of the article, highlighting a gender perspective as a driving force for innovation. Innovation and gender perspective are positively linked, as a focus on gender perspective allowed problems to be defined and specific areas of improvement to be identified within the school. When these problems were identified, it was possible to measure them and suggest alternative actions (p. 174). In Carrasco (2014), gender segregation in innovation is explained by job market segmentation and gender differences in education and training, which create some barriers for women seeking to engage in high-technology entrepreneurial activity. In Pettersson and Lindberg (2013), the relationship between gender and innovation lies in their emphasis on a gendered perspective in innovation.

In a conceptualization of their Quadruple Helix model, Johansson and Lindberg's (2011) fourth pillar may serve as a bridge over the gender gap of innovation. Their model – with a fourth group of actors – consists of NGOs running their activities in a non-profit manner. They must fulfil their role of linking and legitimizing small women-led businesses to the other helixes. This is a novel way of exploring the relationship between innovation and gender.

The study by Poutanen and Kovalainen (2013) links gender theories to innovation by analysing how the gendering of a product innovation takes place. Østgaard et al. (2011) link employee diversity to innovation, where gender is one of several variables seeking to explain this relationship. Their main argument is that aspects of diversity in terms of human capital cannot be ignored in relation to a firm's innovative capabilities (p. 508). They also highlight how the impact of gender diversity is overlooked in the innovation literature.

In Wikhamn and Knights (2013), the relationship between gender and innovation is illustrated by how the masculine discourse enters the open innovation process and hinders the alternative feminine discourse, which could otherwise enrich the radical and creative features of the open innovation paradigm (p. 275). Finally, through their analysis of how the concept of innovation is produced in academia, Rönnblom and Keisu (2013) highlight the different understandings of gender equality.

## DISCUSSION

The most prominent feature of the research articles we analysed was the lack of a clear definition of innovation. Of the 22 papers included in our review, only 14 specifically defined innovation, as discussed above. Interestingly, innovation is defined in numerous ways in these articles, ranging from very traditional definitions that focus on strategies for creating products and services (Miller and Triana, 2009; Sonfield et al., 2001) or technology (Wilson, 2004) to the quantity and quality of new ideas in teams (Cady and Valentine, 1999) and more contextual and non-gender-biased definitions (Blake and Hanson, 2005; Smith-Doerr, 2010). While others did not specifically define innovation per se, they did offer specific operationalizations, such as patenting (Hunt et al., 2013) or competitive advantage and superior performance (Ruiz-Arroyo et al., 2012). We take this as signal of the multidisciplinary characteristic of innovation research.

A second feature prevalent in the articles we reviewed was that, in analysing the relationship between gender and innovation, several of them did not use an explicit gender perspective. This finding supports prior studies of gender and entrepreneurship (Ahl, 2004, 2006) and gender and networks in entrepreneurship research (Foss, 2010). Further, some of the articles did not use the term 'gender'; rather, they used the term 'women entrepreneurs' (Idris, 2009), 'women in management' (Welbourne et al., 2007) or 'women-owned firms' (Ruiz-Arroyo et al., 2012). Thus, in many cases, these papers neither refer to the most basic elements of gender theory nor develop arguments for the gendered aspects of innovation. Other papers use an implicit feminist standpoint perspective by hypothesizing that women differ on certain variables (Hunt et al., 2013; Miller and Triana, 2009; Sonfield et al., 2001). The most explicit gender theory-driven articles with regard to post-structuralist feminism include those by Blake and Hanson (2005), Gray and James (2007), Murray and Graham (2007) and Smith-Doerr (2010). Although not explicitly citing feminist theory, these articles provide more elaborate arguments for the intersectional nature of gender and innovation. Interestingly, the article by Lindberg et al. (2014) was the only one to admit that traditional innovation models, such as the now well-established Triple Helix model, are inherently gender biased, and offer their more inclusive Quadruple Helix framework as a potential solution.

Based on our analysis, we suggest that the definition of innovation itself is inherently gendered, as it refers to objective 'things' (products, markets, technologies) and does not include the (often individual) actors implementing these innovations. Indeed, within innovation research, gender has become almost hidden. According to Ahl (2007, p. 238), it is the epistemological position in research, treating gender as something we *are*, rather than something we *do*, which hinders us in viewing how gender is accomplished in different contexts. This calls for revitalizing innovation research by drawing upon knowledge of how gender stratifies organizations, as developed in other research fields (Acker, 1990; Calas and Smircich, 1991; Kvande, 2007). Future innovation research could be expanded by drawing upon structural, cultural and institutional factors, as well as by being more comparative and international in nature (cf. Ahl, 2004, 2006, 2007). Our analysis of a sample of research papers here, while admittedly small, illustrates clear potential for an increased scholarly awareness of the gendered aspects of innovation. Interestingly, this observation is congruent with our experience of innovation conferences and symposia: gender is included as a (control) variable in quantitative analysis of the antecedents of innovation, but not as a part of an explanatory scheme. When gender has a significant effect, authors and discussants struggle to explain why.

The analysis of the reviewed papers in some cases[4] also reveals an underlying assumption that women are essentially different from men and bring different assets to the innovation process, an observation congruent with standpoint feminism. A contribution within organizational gender research calls for understandings of gender that encompass more paradoxes, variation and complexity (Kvande, 2007). In this regard, the potential of innovation research is yet to be fully realized. Below, we discuss some ideas for future research in this field.

**Towards a Feminist Epistemology**

Developing future research on innovation and gender immediately raises the question: what kind of knowledge are we seeking? According to feminist epistemology, knowledge is situated. Engelstad and Gerrard (2005) argue that situated knowledge recognizes science as a culture and the idea of science as culturally constructed. Haraway (1988) posits that partiality (i.e. individual perspectives influenced by societal norms, one's own experiences and the opinions of others) and not universality is the condition for making rational knowledge claims. Since partial perspectives are embodied and situated, they are responsible and accountable; thus, they are objective. There is potential here to link Haraway's concept of situatedness with geographers' concept of 'space' (Massey, 1995). While people's lives are lived through time, they are also lived in place and through space (Pratt and Hanson, 1993). In our study, the research paper by Gray and James (2007) illustrates how the literature disconnects learning and innovation processes from people with real gendered identities and commitments that motivate and shape their work activities. It is this intersection with time, place and space that makes innovation culturally, contextually and even historically embedded. In order to accomplish this, we follow Ahl (2007) and Foss (2010) in the need to move from an objectivist to a constructionist epistemological position in research. Innovation research would benefit from viewing gender as something that is done and embedded in various contexts (cf. Acker, 1990; Butler, 1990; Fenstermaker et al., 2002; West and Zimmerman, 1987). Future scholars of innovation may want to move beyond normal discourse practices because they are essentialistic in their forms. Ahl (2007, p. 239) suggests: 'The way to give women a voice in the field in which they are marginalized is to speak through the normal discourse – which oppresses women. It's a "Catch 22" situation.'

## Towards Methodological Diversity

Following the above, we claim that innovation research needs to develop more methodological diversity by exploring methods that can reveal the situated knowledge of innovation. In a recent special issue of the *International Journal of Gender and Entrepreneurship*, for example, Wilson and Tagg (2010) studied business owners' views on the role of sex by using personal construct theory and repertory grids. Without providing the informants with any predefined alternatives, the authors were able to show remarkable variation in their data; there are hardly any gender stereotypes, and the business owners do not consider themselves either as entrepreneurs or as heroes. Thus, this study illustrates the importance of moving beyond predefined alternatives in data gathering, and demonstrates how researchers actually reproduce stereotypes by hanging on to binary constructs.

Following Haraway (1991), Engelstad and Gerrard (2005) argue for recognizing 'the researched' as subjects, 'as an objectification creates essentialist and monolithic categories that in no way represent the diversity of the subject researched' (p. 4). Following this, narrative methods (Boje, 1991; Czarniawska, 1998) may provide stories of innovation from organizational members themselves. Hosking and Hjorth (2004) argue that narratives are situated in contextualized relationships to multiple local – cultural – historical acts. Other avenues of creativity such as creative dialogue, art, poetry and theatre (Broussine, 2008) may also help to articulate the voice of the 'innovateur' within innovation research. How would men and women in small enterprises and larger corporations label innovations if they were allowed to describe what innovation meant to them and how they handled innovation? Or what would men and women conceive as their main challenge regardless of the researcher's predefined alternatives in questioning? Another method is the repertory grid (Tan and Hunter, 2002), which helps researchers to understand people's cognitive developments. This is an underused method in innovation research that can elicit information on how people imagine the concept of innovation.

**Towards a Change in Journal Practices**

We believe the reason that much of the research on gender and innovation tends to be so mainstream and essentialist in nature is due to the practices of academic journals. Innovation journals, along with academic journals in general, typically have more interest in empirical articles that are mainstream and generalizable and use traditional quantitative methods. This point has also been raised concerning qualitative methodology (see Smith and Anderson, 2007). If we had not included any journals in our study apart from those listed in the ISI database, we would have missed five important articles published in the special issue of the *International Journal of Gender and Entrepreneurship* in 2013 that were focused on 'Gender and Innovation', four of which were inherently non-essentialist in their approach. Owing to the difficulties of getting qualitative and non-mainstream research published, we further believe that many of the innovation-intensive streams of research will continue to appear outside of mainstream journals, that is, in books and in book chapters. Without the leadership of strong, mainstream journals, it will be impossible to change this trajectory.

## CONCLUSIONS

This chapter explored how gender is conceptualized in the gender and innovation literatures. A review of relevant literatures yielded only a small number (n=22) of gender and innovation articles for analysis. These articles were categorized according to their thematic focus as follows: traditional innovation and definitional issues; management styles, performance and teams; organizational structures and networks; and gendered stereotypes, feminist resistance, and gendered processes of innovation. We subsequently analysed the content of the papers and identified the particular gender perspective adopted by the authors, how they defined innovation, and how they perceived the relationship between innovation and gender. Following this, a case was made for both a feminist epistemology and methodological diversity, with some ideas proposed for future research.

The most prominent finding in our review is that very few scholarly articles actually contain a robust discussion of the relationship between gender and innovation. There were hardly any articles explicitly referring to gender theory and positioning themselves within specific gender perspectives. This was surprising, given that the relationship between, for example, gender and entrepreneurship, as articulated at the outset of this chapter, is well documented in the business and entrepreneurship literatures. Several reasons may be offered to explain this phenomenon. Firstly, while the concepts of entrepreneurship and innovation are inextricably linked, they do differ in the sense that the former more clearly relates to an 'actor', that is, the entrepreneur. The concept of innovation, however, as defined in the literature, seems less attributed to a clear individual 'actor' and more to the results of various actions, that is, new products, new markets or new ways of organizing. Secondly, the innovation field is more influenced by technology, scientific and marketing scholars, whereas the entrepreneurship field has been more influenced by social science researchers. As a consequence, over the years, entrepreneurship research has adopted feminist theories developed within sociology and anthropology. We posit, therefore, that innovation research is lagging behind in terms of its perspectives on how gender is 'done', compared to other fields such as entrepreneurship where feminist epistemology is more developed.

Notwithstanding the limitations of the methodological approach adopted, which admittedly yielded considerably fewer relevant articles than had been initially anticipated, our exploratory analysis strongly suggests that innovation research is inherently gendered towards a dominant male perspective. In accepting traditional definitions of what constitutes innovation, the field has become restricted and narrow to the extent that only male innovation norms are studied and platformed. This has serious implications for both innovation policy and practice; if the field does not become open to a more gender-balanced reconceptualization of innovation, only those traditional models of innovation will continue to be supported, valued and, subsequently, practised. Such traditional models include innovations which are based on high-level technologies, commercialized scientific discoveries, high performance, and so on, and appear to exclude 'other', equally valuable and mostly female-led types of innovation in which motivation, context and style play a significant role. In this context, it is not surprising that there are significantly fewer female than male innovators and high-tech or scientific entrepreneurs reported in most developed economies.

# NOTES

1. One exception here is the special issue 'Gender and Innovation' in *International Journal of Gender and Entrepreneurship*, with guest editors Alsos, Ljunggren and Hytti (2013).
2. The term 'essentialism' in this chapter refers to differences due to biology and not to differences due to the varying life experiences of women and men (e.g. from a gender-segregated labour market or uneven distribution of household work).
3. It should be noted that several of the contributions in our final selection were not explicit about this relationship.
4. See Hunt et al. (2013); Miller and Triana (2009); Sonfield et al. (2001).

# REFERENCES

Acker, J. (1990), 'Hierarchies, jobs, bodies: A theory of gendered organizations', *Gender and Society*, **4** (2), 139–158.

Acker, J. (1999), 'Gender and organisation', in J. Saltzman Chafetz (ed.), *Handbook of the Sociology of Gender*, New York: Kluwer Academic/Plenum, pp. 177–194.

Ahl, H. (2002), 'The construction of the female entrepreneur as the other', in B. Czarniawska and H. Höpfl (eds), *Casting the Other: The Production and Maintenance of Inequalities in Work Organizations*, London: Routledge, pp. 52–67.

Ahl, H. (2004), *The Scientific Reproduction of Gender Inequality: A Discourse Analysis of Research Texts on Women's Entrepreneurship*, Solna, Sweden: Liber.

Ahl, H. (2006), 'Why research on women entrepreneurs needs new directions', *Entrepreneurship Theory and Practice*, **30** (5), 595–621.

Ahl, H. (2007), 'A Foucauldian framework for discourse analysis', in H. Neergaard and J.P. Ulhøi (eds), *Handbook of Qualitative Research Methods in Entrepreneurship*, Cheltenham, UK and Northampton, MA, USA: Edward Elgar, pp. 216–250.

Ahl, H. and T. Nelson (2015), 'How policy positions women entrepreneurs: A comparative analysis of state discourse in Sweden and the United States', *Journal of Business Venturing*, **30** (2), 273–291.

Alsos, G.A., E. Ljunggren and U. Hytti (2013), 'Gender and innovation: State of the art and a research agenda', *International Journal of Gender and Entrepreneurship*, **5** (3), 236–256.

Baer, M., A.K. Vadera, R.T. Leenders and G.R. Oldham (2014), 'Intergroup competition as a double-edged sword: How sex composition regulates the effects of competition on group creativity', *Organization Science*, **25** (3), 892–908.

Berg, N.G. (1997), 'Gender, place and entrepreneurship', *Entrepreneurship and Regional Development*, **9** (3), 259–268.

Blake, M.K. and S. Hanson (2005), 'Rethinking innovation: Context and gender', *Environment and Planning A*, **37** (4), 681–701.

Boje, D.M. (1991), 'The storytelling organization: A study of story performance in an office-supply firm', *Administrative Science Quarterly*, **36** (3), 106–126.

Bordo, S. (1990), 'Feminism, postmodernism and gender-scepticism', in L.J. Nicholson (ed.), *Feminism/Postmodernism*, London: Routledge, pp. 133–156.

Bowden, P. and J. Mummery (2009), *Understanding Feminism*, New York: Acumen Press.

Broussine, M. (ed.) (2008), *Creative Methods in Organizational Research*, London: Sage.

Bruni, A., S. Gherardi and B. Poggio (2005), *Gender and Entrepreneurship*, New York: Routledge.

Butler, J. (1990), *Gender Trouble: Feminism and the Subversion of Identity*, London: Routledge.

Cady, S.H. and J. Valentine (1999), 'Team innovation and perceptions of consideration – what difference does diversity make?', *Small Group Research*, **30** (6), 730–750.

Calas, M.B. and L. Smircich (1991), 'Voice seduction to silence leadership', *Organization Studies*, **12** (4), 567–601.

Carrasco, I. (2014), 'Gender gap in innovation: An institutionalist explanation', *Management Decision*, **52** (2), 410–424.

Carter, S. and E. Shaw (2006), *Women's Business Ownership: Recent Research and Policy Development*, Research report, London: Small Business Service.

Courpasson, D. (2000), 'Managerial strategies of domination: Power in soft bureaucracies', *Organization Studies*, **21** (1), 141–161.

Czarniawska, B. (1998), *A Narrative Approach in Organization Studies*, London: Sage.

Damanpour, F. (1991), 'Organizational innovation: A meta-analysis of effects of determinants and moderators', *Academy of Management Journal*, **34** (3), 555–590.

Di Stefano, C. (1990), 'Dilemmas of difference: Feminism, modernity and postmodernity', in L.J. Nicholson (ed.), *Feminism/Postmodernism*, London: Routledge, pp. 63–82.

Dougherty, D. and C. Hardy (1996), 'Sustained product innovation in large, mature organizations: Overcoming innovation-to-organization problems', *Academy of Management Journal*, **39** (5), 1120–1153.

Engelstad, E. and S. Gerrard (2005), 'Challenging situatedness', in E. Engelstad and S. Gerrard (eds), *Challenging Situatedness: Gender, Culture and the Production of Knowledge*, Delft: Eburon, pp. 1–26.

Eriksson, A.F. (2014), 'A gender perspective as trigger and facilitator of innovation', *International Journal of Gender and Entrepreneurship*, **6** (2), 163–180.

European Commission (2008), *Evaluation on Policy: Promotion of Women Innovators and Entrepreneurship Final Report*, Brussels: Enterprise and Industry Directorate-General, accessed at http://ec.europa.eu.

Fenstermaker, S., C. West and D. Zimmerman (2002), 'Gender inequality: New conceptual terrain', in S. Fenstermaker and C. West (eds), *Doing Gender, Doing Difference: Inequality, Power, and Institutional Change*, New York: Routledge, pp. 25–39.

Foss, L. (2010), 'Research on entrepreneur networks: The case for a constructionist feminist theory perspective', *International Journal of Gender and Entrepreneurship*, **2** (1), 82–101.

Foss, L., K. Woll and M. Moilanen (2013), 'Creativity and implementations of new ideas: Do organisational structure, work environment and gender matter?', *International Journal of Gender and Entrepreneurship*, **5** (3), 298–322.

Gray, M. and A. James (2007), 'Connecting gender and economic competitiveness: Lessons from Cambridge's high-tech regional economy', *Environment and Planning A*, **39** (2), 417–436.

Haraway, D.J. (1988), 'Situated knowledge – the science question in feminism and the privilege of partial perspective', *Feminist Studies*, **14** (3), 575–599.

Haraway, D.J. (1991), *Simians, Cyborgs, and Women: The Reinvention of Nature*, London: Free Association Books.

Henry, C., L. Foss and H. Ahl (2015), 'Gender and entrepreneurship research: A review of methodological approaches', *International Small Business Journal*, online 27 January, 1–25.

Hill, F.M., C.M. Leitch and R.T. Harrison (2006), 'Desperately seeking finance? The demand for finance by women-owned and -led businesses', *Venture Capital*, **8** (2), 159–182.

Hofstrand, D. (2010), *Peter Drucker and Innovation*, Ag Decision Maker website, accessed 15 October 2011 at http://www.extension.iastate.edu/agdm/wholefarm/pdf/c5-10.pdf.

Hosking, D.M. and D. Hjorth (2004), 'Relational constructionism and entrepreneurship: Some key notes', *Narrative and Discursive Approaches in Entrepreneurship*, Cheltenham, UK and Northampton, MA, USA: Edward Elgar, pp. 255–268.

Hunt, J., J. Garant, H. Herman and D.J. Munroe (2013), 'Why are women underrepresented amongst patentees?', *Research Policy*, **42**, 831–843.

Idris, A. (2009), 'Management styles and innovation in women-owned enterprises', *African Journal of Business Management*, **3** (9), 416–425.

Johansson, A.W. and M. Lindberg (2011), 'Making a case for gender-inclusive innovation through the concept of creative imitation', *Annals of Innovation and Entrepreneurship*, **2**, 8440.

Kelan, E. (2009), *Performing Gender at Work*, London: Sage.

Kvande, E. (2007), *Doing Gender in Flexible Organizations*, Bergen: Fagbokforlaget.

Lindberg, M., M. Lindgren and J. Packendorff (2014), 'Quadruple Helix as a way to bridge the gender gap in entrepreneurship: The case of an innovation system project in the Baltic Sea region', *Journal of Knowledge Economy*, **5**, 94–113.

Marlow, S. (2002), 'Self-employed women: A part of or apart from feminist theory?', *Entrepreneurship and Innovation*, **2** (2), 83–91.

Massey, D. (1995), *Spatial Divisions of Labor: Social Structures and the Geography of Production*, Basingstoke, UK: Macmillan.

McDowell, L.M. (2000), 'Feminists rethink the economic: The economics of gender/the gender of economics', in G. Clark, M.P. Feldman and M. Gertler (eds), *The Oxford Handbook of Economic Geography*, Oxford, UK: Oxford University Press, pp. 497–517.

Miller, T. and M.C. Triana (2009), 'Demographic diversity in the boardroom: Mediators of the board diversity–firm performance relationship', *Journal of Management Studies*, **46** (5), 755–786.

Murray, F. and L. Graham (2007), 'Buying science and selling science: Gender differences in the market for commercial science', *Industrial and Corporate Change*, **16** (4), 657–689.

Neergaard, H., S. Frederiksen and S. Marlow (2011), 'The emperor's new clothes: Rendering a feminist theory of entrepreneurship visible', Paper presented at the 56th ICSB Conference, June, Stockholm.

Østgaard, C.R., B. Timmermans and K. Kristinsson (2011), 'Does a different view create something new? The effect of employee diversity on innovation', *Research Policy*, **40**, 500–509.

Pettersson, K. (2004), 'Masculine entrepreneurship – the Gnosjö discourse in a feminist perspective', in D. Hjort and C. Steyaert (eds), *Narrative and Discursive Approaches in Entrepreneurship: A Second Movements in Entrepreneurship Book*, Cheltenham, UK and Northampton, MA, USA: Edward Elgar, pp. 177–193.

Pettersson, K. (2007), *Men and Male as the Norm? A Gender Perspective on Innovation Policies in Denmark, Finland and Sweden*, Nordic Research Programme, 2005–2008, Report 4, Stockholm: Nordregio.

Pettersson, K. and M. Lindberg (2013), 'Paradoxical spaces of feminist resistance', *International Journal of Gender and Entrepreneurship*, **5** (3), 323–341.

Poutanen, S. and A. Kovalainen (2013), 'Gendering innovation process in an industrial plant – revisiting tokenism, gender and innovation', *International Journal of Gender and Entrepreneurship*, **5** (3), 257–274.

Pratt, G. and S. Hanson (1993), 'Women and work across the life course: Moving beyond essentialism', in C. Katz and J. Monk (eds), *Full Circles: Geographies of Women over the Life Course*, Abingdon, UK: Routledge, pp. 27–54.

Reynolds, P., M. Hay, W.D. Bygrave, M.S. Camp and E. Autio (2000), *Global Entrepreneurship Monitor*, Executive Report, Kansas City, MO: Kauffman Center for Entrepreneurial Leadership.

Rönnblom, M. and B.I. Keisu (2013), 'Constructions of innovation and gender (equality) in Swedish universities', *International Journal of Gender and Entrepreneurship*, **5** (3), 342–356.

Rose, G. (1993), *Feminism and Geography: The Limits of Geographical Knowledge*, Minneapolis: University of Minnesota Press.

Ruiz-Arroyo, M., M. del Mar Fuentes-Fuentes, A.M. Bojica and L. Rodríguez-Ariza (2012), 'Innovativeness and performance in women-owned small firms: The role of knowledge acquisition', *Journal of Small Business and Entrepreneurship*, **25** (3), 307–326.

Science and Learning Expert Group (2010), *The Science and Learning Expert Group Report*, 25 February, London: Department for Business, Innovation and Skills.

Smith, R. and A.R. Anderson (2007), 'Daring to be different: A dialogue on the problems of getting qualitative research published', in H. Neergaard and J.P. Ulhøi (eds), *Handbook of Qualitative Research Methods in Entrepreneurship*, Cheltenham, UK and Northampton, MA, USA: Edward Elgar, pp. 434–459.

Smith-Doerr, L. (2010), 'Flexible organizations, innovation and gender equality: Writing for the US film industry 1907–27', *Industry and Innovation*, **17** (1), 5–22.

Sonfield, M.C. and R.N. Lussier (1997), 'The entrepreneurial strategy matrix: A model for new and ongoing ventures', *Business Horizons*, **40** (3), 73–77.

Sonfield, M., R. Lussier, J. Corman and M. McKinney (2001), 'Gender comparisons in strategic decision-making: An empirical analysis of the entrepreneurial strategy matrix', *Journal of Small Business Management*, **39** (2), 165–173.

Sunderland, J. (2004), *Gendered Discourses*, Basingstoke, UK: Palgrave Macmillan.

Tan, F.B. and M.G. Hunter (2002), 'The repertory grid technique: A method for the study of cognition in information systems', *MIS Quarterly*, **26** (1), 39–57.

Tuchman, G. (1989), *Edging Women Out: Victorian Novelists, Publishers and Social Change*, New Haven, CT: Yale University Press.

Walsh, S. and B. Kirchhoff (2003), 'Entrepreneurs' opportunities in technology-based markets', in P. Phan (ed.), *Technological Entrepreneurship*, Greenwich, CT: Information Age Publishing, pp. 17–31.

Welbourne, T.M., C.S. Cycyota and C.J. Ferrante (2007), 'Wall Street reaction to women in IPOs: An examination of gender diversity in top management teams', *Group and Organization Management*, **32** (5), 524–547.

West, C. and D.H. Zimmerman (1987), 'Doing gender', *Gender and Society*, **1** (2), 125–151.

Wikhamn, B.R. and D. Knights (2013), 'Open innovation, gender and the infiltration of masculine discourses', *International Journal of Gender and Entrepreneurship*, **5** (3), 275–297.

Wilson, F. and S. Tagg (2010), 'Social constructionism and personal constructivism: Getting the business owner's view on the role of sex and gender', *International Journal of Gender and Entrepreneurship*, **2** (1), 68–82.

Wilson, M. (2004), 'A conceptual framework for studying gender in information systems research', *Journal of Information Technology*, **19** (1), 81–92.

Yuan, L., S. Zhongfeng and L. Yi (2010), 'Can strategic flexibility help firms profit from production innovation?', *Technovation*, **30** (5/6), 300–309.

# PART II

# GENDER AND INNOVATION IN NEW AND SMALL BUSINESSES

# 3. Women's innovation in Germany – empirical facts and conceptual explanations

*Teita Bijedić, Siegrun Brink, Kerstin Ettl, Silke Kriwoluzky and Friederike Welter*

## INTRODUCTION

Innovation is a crucial factor for economic development, growth and sustainability on the national and international level, both in traditional industrial countries like Germany and in emerging countries. Thus, over the past decades, innovation has been a major topic in international research. One strand of literature which has gained importance recently focuses on women and innovation (e.g. Alsos et al., 2013). Previous research and current studies show that women's participation in innovative activities lags behind men's participation in innovative activities in Germany (Brink et al., 2014) as well as in other countries. According to the Innovation Indicator, which measures the willingness and the ability of the entire population of a country to participate in innovation, participation of women in innovation processes is below average in Germany when compared to 16 leading industrialized countries. The conditions for the participation of women in innovation in Germany are also less favourable (DIW, 2006a, 2006b). These facts are in line with the wide-spread notion in previous innovation research that women in general and women-led enterprises in particular are less innovative than their male counterparts. This chapter reassesses the empirical facts that support this notion for Germany, questioning whether and – if so – why women are less innovative.

In the following section, we present the most widely used definition of innovation and explain which caveats emanate from this definition when analysing innovation through a gender lens. We then take a look at existing statistical data concerning the innovation activities of women in Germany and check if we can identify gender-dependent innovation patterns. Next, we propose a number of possible explanations for the statistical findings, particularly with regard to the importance of women entrepreneurs' preferences and role expectations, taking into account different contextual influences on these factors. After a short introduction as to how a contextualized view helps to explore entrepreneurial behaviour, we discuss contextual effects on educational and career preferences, and on professional careers. Finally, we summarize the explanations concerning the nature and extent of women's participation in innovative activities in Germany and give an outlook on future research needs.

## THE DEFINITION OF INNOVATION

In its broadest understanding, innovation in economic life is usually understood as 'doing things differently' (following, for example, Schumpeter, 1939). However, elaborating this broad notion into a definition which is both comprehensive and operational turns out to be challenging. Schumpeter, for example, used to focus on new or better ways to combine production factors (Schumpeter, 1934). This approach makes it less intuitive to apply his definition to the service sector or to organizational aspects of production. In the scientific discourse today, a broad definition of innovation prevails, including various kinds of novelties with economic relevance, such as organizational, marketing and social developments (Damanpour, 1991; Knight, 1967).

The most common and frequently used definition of innovation today is the official OECD definition formulated in the *Oslo Manual*. It states that an innovation is 'the implementation of a new or significantly improved product (good or service), or process, a new marketing method, or a new organisational method in business practices, workplace organisation or external relations' (OECD, 2005, p. 46). A distinction has to be made between innovation and invention, which is the first occurrence of an idea that might be turned into innovation through the process of commercialization. This process of economic exploitation occurs mostly in firms in the commercial sphere (Fagerberg, 2005). The OECD definition poses two major caveats when dealing with women's innovation, especially in empirical research. First, it does not mention the person who innovates. When considering gender issues, however, it is essential to know who the relevant actor is in order to then determine his or her sex. However, a multitude of single innovations involve teamwork and take place within larger organizations. They are the result of a lengthy process involving many interrelated innovations (Fagerberg, 2005). If we take the organizational dimension into account, we automatically place innovation on an elevated management level – one where in many countries women are sharply underrepresented. Kay (2007) shows that in Germany only 18.5 per cent of all board members, company directors and company owners are female. In fact, in most empirical studies, the act of innovation is ascribed to the owner or director of a company, even though the relevant activities might be carried out at a lower level of the hierarchy (e.g. Ruiz-Arroyo et al., 2012; Tonoyan and Strohmeyer, 2006).

Second, operationalizing concepts such as 'a new organisational method in business practices, workplace organisation or external relations' and capturing them empirically is difficult. Therefore, in most empirical studies and public support programmes, innovation is operationalized in a much narrower sense: The concept is usually restricted to the development of new products or processes, often in a technological context. This implies that a large part of innovative activities, such as other types of innovations and innovations in non-technologically based contexts, are ex ante excluded from the analysis. If there exists a gender bias between types of innovation, this will lead to erroneous conclusions with respect to the innovation activities of men and women (Lindberg et al., 2011). The narrow operationalization of innovation also leads to a bias in empirical studies, which tend to focus on certain sectors, that is, on those sectors which are expected to feature a high level of technology-based product and process innovations. Findings on innovative activities in other sectors remain scarce both for Germany and for other countries (Nählinder et al., 2012).

## INNOVATIVE ACTIVITIES OF WOMEN IN GERMANY

Since empirical data regarding innovative activities usually provide information on the institutional level, as recommended by the OECD (2005), the respective data sets do not contain information on the innovator and his or her personal characteristics, including gender. Therefore, most statistics do not provide information with respect to gender-dependent innovative activities. In Germany, there are only two data sets which contain information on the gender of the persons involved in innovative activities.

The statistics of the German Patent and Trademark Office (DPMA) provide a first source of information which includes gender-specific data. Burkhardt and Greif (2001) show that women are strikingly under-represented in patenting: in 1999 only 7.5 per cent of the applicants for a patent were women or teams that included women. According to a data set which combines labour market and patent register data for Germany, only 5.2 per cent of 42 375 patents in 2002 were filed by women (Dorner et al., 2014). While this share is higher than the proportion of women filing a patent at the European Patent Office (1.6 per cent), the numbers are low in comparison to for example Sweden, where the share of women among applicants for a patent increased substantially between 1985 and 2007: in 1985 less than 2.4 per cent of the patent applications were filed by women, but in 2007 this share increased to over 9 per cent (Dorner et al., 2014).

Given that only technological inventions can be protected by patents, patent applications can only provide a first impression of the innovative activities of women. Data on other types of innovation need to be gathered in representative surveys. Although there are several data sets with information on the innovative activities of companies in Germany, only one of them provides information which can be used as a proxy for the sex of the innovator. This is the IAB[1] Establishment Panel, an annual panel survey of German companies which discloses the sex of the company's owner or director. Based on this data set, Tonoyan and Strohmeyer (2006) confirm the underrepresentation of women in developing product and process innovations. Only 33 per cent of female-led firms carried out product innovations and 16 per cent introduced process innovation in 1998/1999, while the share amounts to 42 per cent for either type of innovation in male-led firms (Tonoyan and Strohmeyer, 2006).

Not surprisingly, the findings by Tonoyan and Strohmeyer (2006) indicate a link between product and process innovations and the respective industry. They show that product and process innovations are more likely to be developed or implemented in male-dominated sectors (Tonoyan and Strohmeyer, 2006). A comparison of the rate of innovators by sector in Germany and the rate of German female entrepreneurs illustrates this relationship (see Figure 3.1).

The comparison shows that female entrepreneurs are underrepresented in sectors with a high percentage of innovators such as manufacturing of transport equipment and telecommunications, computer programming and information service activities (see also Jennings and Brush, 2013). Instead, female entrepreneurs are more active in sectors like manufacture of textiles, apparel, leather and related products, media services and business support activities. However, within these sectors the percentage of innovators is near or below average.

The gender-specific sector preferences are also visible in data on business registrations in Germany (see Table 3.1). The majority of female business founders in 2013 started their companies in retail and in private and public service activities, while female start-up companies in construction and other technology-intensive sectors like information and communications are considerably less frequent.

The underrepresentation of women in innovative start-ups is confirmed by Ripsas et al. (2013), who show that only 13 per cent of all founders of

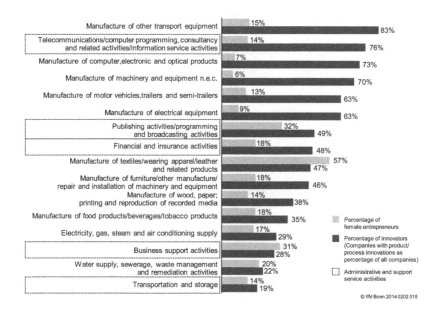

*Source:* BMBF (2014); Brink et al. (2014, p. 19, ZEW Mannheimer Innovationspanel); Statistiches Bundesamt (2012); own calculations.

*Figure 3.1 Rate of innovators and rate of female entrepreneurs by sector in Germany (2010)*

young and growth-oriented companies are female. Moreover, women form a minority among recipients of public support which is targeted at funding start-ups in technology- and knowledge-based fields. Under the scheme EXIST, the largest programme of supporting academic entre-preneurship in Germany, less than 20 per cent of recipients of start-up funding are women (Becker et al., 2011).

When interpreting these facts and data on women's innovation, one has to take into account the underlying conceptualization and operationaliz-ation of innovation as described in the previous section. All statistics quoted above are based on a narrow definition of innovation: the statistics of the German Patent and Trademark Office and of the European Patent Office, in definition of a patent, include only products and processes which present 'a solution to a specific problem in the field of technology' (WIPO, 2008, p. 17); the IAB Establishment Panel considers product and process innovations in general, but implicitly refers to industrial produc-tion and to technology areas (Tonoyan and Strohmeyer, 2006).

*Table 3.1    Start-up companies in 2013 by industry*

| Sector | Total | Female-led | Share of female-led start-ups in sector as percentage of all female-led start-ups (%) | Share of female-led start-ups per sector (%) |
| --- | --- | --- | --- | --- |
| Wholesale and retail trade; repair of motor vehicles and motorcycles | 134 473 | 47 993 | 23.7 | 35.7 |
| Public administration and defence; compulsory social security; other service activities | 61 630 | 43 171 | 21.3 | 70.0 |
| Administrative and support service activities | 80 602 | 26 489 | 13.1 | 32.9 |
| Professional, scientific and technical activities | 61 804 | 23 942 | 11.8 | 38.7 |
| Accommodation and food service activities | 36 213 | 12 564 | 6.2 | 34.7 |
| Manufacturing | 23 566 | 9 475 | 4.7 | 40.2 |
| Human health and social work activities | 8 007 | 5 951 | 2.9 | 74.3 |
| Education | 11 813 | 5 731 | 2.8 | 48.5 |
| Real estate activities | 14 036 | 4 548 | 2.2 | 32.4 |
| Financial and insurance activities | 17 133 | 4 276 | 2.1 | 25.0 |
| Construction | 96 935 | 4 138 | 2.0 | 4.3 |
| Information and communication | 22 704 | 3 982 | 2.0 | 17.5 |
| Transportation and storage | 19 670 | 3 719 | 1.8 | 18.9 |
| Arts, entertainment and recreation | 12 892 | 3 579 | 1.8 | 27.8 |
| Electricity, gas, steam and air conditioning supply | 8 866 | 1 962 | 1.0 | 22.1 |
| Agriculture; forestry and fishing | 4 335 | 1 130 | 0.6 | 26.1 |

| Sector | Total | Female-led | Share of female-led start-ups in sector as percentage of all female-led start-ups (%) | Share of female-led start-ups per sector (%) |
|---|---|---|---|---|
| Water supply; sewerage, waste management and remediation activities | 1 119 | 123 | 0.1 | 11.0 |
| Mining and quarrying | 158 | 28 | 0.0 | 17.7 |
| Total | 615 956 | 202 801 | 100.0 | 32.9 |

*Source:* Statistisches Bundesamt (2014); own calculations.

Therefore, all we can conclude from existing empirical data is that in Germany: 1) female-led firms are underrepresented in sectors with a high level of technology-based product and process innovations; and 2) female-led firms are less likely to carry out technology-based product and process innovations. In the following section, we will provide contextual explanations for these empirical observations.

## CONTEXTUAL PERSPECTIVES ON INNOVATIVE ACTIVITIES OF WOMEN

### The Concept of Context as an Explanation for Entrepreneurial Behaviour

One way to analyse and understand economic behaviour and decisions is to take into account contextual aspects, that is, social, institutional, spatial, temporal and historical circumstances and conditions. The context provides opportunities, but also sets barriers for individual action (Welter, 2011). There are different ways of implementing a context approach as the conceptual basis of explaining individual behaviour. Within this chapter, we focus on social and institutional context dimensions, following Welter (2011) and Welter et al. (2014). Our focus will be on how contextual factors influence women's preferences and how these in turn shape their innovative behaviour. We thus provide explanations for the empirical evidence regarding gender-dependent differences in innovative behaviour in Germany stated above.

Social context includes the relations between individuals, networks, families, households or friends; the institutional context refers to the regulative and normative environment. All context factors interact and overlap (Welter et al., 2014), thus providing a multidimensional explanation of gender-dependent differences in innovative behaviour (Welter, 2011). This allows us to derive a more inclusive understanding of innovative behaviour. Based on the context perspective, the lower inclination of women to carry out technologically based product and process innovations can be traced back to two main determinants: the social context has an impact through individual experiences on the one hand and through role models provided by friends, family and colleagues and the overall individual socialization on the other hand. This social context shapes women's expectations and preferences with respect to educational choices and professional life.

The institutional context includes normative aspects such as conceptions and images that are provided by culture and society, frequently conveyed through media and the educational system, and the regulative context, that is, laws, regulations and (economic) policy. These context factors are mutually interdependent and also continuously interact with the individual. Thus, the context determines the existence of stereotypes and their persistence within the individual environment, but is also modified through the actions of individuals or groups. In other words, individual behaviour can contribute to the perpetuation of gender stereotypes as well as being a result of them.

**Contextual Effects on Educational Preferences**

Creativity is not the only prerequisite for innovation. Besides creative ideas and the ability to recognize and exploit opportunities in the market, the motor of technology-driven innovation is technological know-how. In addition to ingenuity, an educational background in a technological, engineering or science discipline is almost inevitable in order to generate technological innovation. However, data show a persisting underrepresentation of women in these fields, which is especially pronounced within higher education, where women on average prefer arts and humanities, whereas men tend to choose engineering and science subjects, as illustrated in Figure 3.2. Although this phenomenon can be observed in most industrialized countries, it is especially striking within German higher education (European Commission, 2010). Moreover, such educational preferences have been stable over years

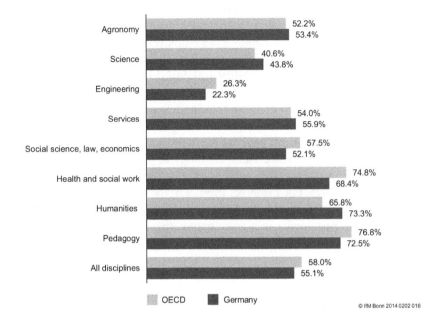

© IfM Bonn 2014 0202 016

*Source:* Brink et al. (2014, p. 35); OECD (2011).

*Figure 3.2   Percentage of female students in different subject groups
(OECD and Germany)*

despite extensive political efforts to change the educational preferences
of girls and young women.

Educational and vocational preferences are shaped during childhood
within the family and household environment. According to socialization
theories, the individual absorbs norms and values that prevail in the
parental household. These values are determined by historically developed and persistent images of roles and responsibilities within the family,
which are transported by parents' behaviour and which also are ingrained
in the institutional framework (Welter, 2011). These internalized role
distributions and role expectations form an influential social context, as
they lead to gender-specific attitudes towards vocational choices and
career expectations (Busch, 2013; Hurrelmann et al., 2008). For example,
the probability of young women choosing a non-traditional profession is
higher if the role distribution between their parents did not follow
traditional patterns and if the mother herself was employed (Busch,
2013). Almost every second employed woman in Germany works part
time. Furthermore, 30 per cent of women between 15 und 65 years are

not in employment at all, whereas this holds for only 18 per cent of men. This difference becomes more pronounced when children are involved: 65 per cent of women with children are employed, with three out of four working part time, whereas the situation of employed men remains unchanged with or without children (BMFSFJ, 2010). These results indicate the pertaining and predominant traditional gender roles within families and the retention of these role models for further generations.

Early attributions of gender-specific roles and responsibilities within the parental household, as well as the behaviour of role models, also affect the affinity for science and technology in general. This in turn can influence academic and career choices long before a career is established (Quesenberry, 2007). For example, even at a young age differences exist between boys and girls regarding the use of modern technology: While boys deal with new media in a more explorative way, girls use the same technology more reactively and in a consumption-oriented way (Hoffman and Vance, 2007; Katz et al., 2006). These initial patterns shape the relationship to technology later in life. As a result, girls and young women seem to have a lower inclination for technology-driven professions and industries than men, dispose of a lower level of technological know-how and thus are less likely to carry out technology-driven innovations.

Another influencing factor for gender differences in educational preferences is the experiences and preferences built at school. Since the affinity for certain subjects develops during primary education, choosing a technical field of study within higher education is more likely if related courses have already been taken at school (EFI, 2012). Germany has put substantial efforts into programmes to attract girls to engineering and science disciplines and to make them pursue their education in these fields. Several initiatives have been set up over the last few decades. For example, the national programme 'Komm mach MINT' aims at improving the image of STEM disciplines among girls and provides different courses and events especially for girls as well as mentoring programmes. Another nationwide programme is the 'Girls' Day', which once a year provides the opportunity for girls to get to know technology- and crafts-related workplaces.[2]

However, despite various initiatives for girls and young women, the gender gap in technical and engineering fields remains relatively stable (see Figure 3.2), in schools as well as within higher education. Even when they perform well in the respective fields, girls are still less inclined to choose STEM subjects (Bahmani et al., 2012; Brush et al., 2009).

## Contextual Influences on Self-perception as an Innovator

Role assignments and cultural stereotypes influence not only women's educational choices, but also their willingness and ability to consider themselves as innovators. Similar to the image of an entrepreneur, the image of an innovator is (still) masculine (Achtenhagen and Welter, 2011; Ahl, 2006; Klyver et al., 2012; Pettersson and Lindberg, 2013). Since technology and masculinity are closely linked, technology-driven innovation is widely perceived and presented as a male activity (Kugele, 2010; Marlow and McAdam, 2012). This promotes cultural values and role stereotypes which make it difficult to align the role as a woman with that of an innovator. As a result, women do not perceive themselves as innovators although, viewed objectively, they might be one (Nyberg, 2009).

Besides the media, one important source of (re-)producing and promoting the public image of an innovator and entrepreneur is curricula and textbooks in schools. On the one hand, textbooks often reflect existing cultural stereotypes. On the other hand, they ensure the stereotypes' perpetuation by inculcating them into the students (Piorkowsky, 2006). In Germany, where entrepreneurship is not anchored within school curricula but is only a part of extra-curricular activities, entrepreneurs and innovators are rarely explicitly mentioned in textbooks. Their presentation is rather implicit in different contexts and subjects. For example, résumés and biographies of prominent and outstanding innovators (e.g. Mark Zuckerberg or Bill Gates) are presented, reflecting a male-dominated image of an innovator as well as a narrow and traditional representation of the innovation context. In history books, entrepreneurs are still represented as the heroes and pioneers of early industrialization, that is, as technology innovators. The representation is mostly dominated by male characters, roles and professions (Grindel and Lässig, 2007, pp. 22ff.). Furthermore, the representation of occupational profiles in German textbooks is still predominantly based on gender stereotypes. The textbook analysis conducted by Wiepcke and Pickard (2011) shows that lessons in occupational orientation contain gender-stereotypical roles and situations.

Thus, girls have little opportunity to identify with entrepreneurial and innovative personalities or – in a more general manner – with male-dominated occupations and to find role models during school life. This lack of role models continues during higher education or vocational training and the course of their early career years, making it difficult for young women to identify with the roles of innovators. These mechanisms in turn consolidate a male image of an entrepreneur and innovator, thus contributing to the persisting gender-related occupational segregation.

**Contextual Effects on Professional Careers**

Besides the social context, a major influencing factor on women's innovativeness is the institutional context, which consists of normative components, such as cultural and societal norms, and regulatory components, such as formal legal regulations and economic regulations (Welter et al., 2014). These institutional aspects consolidate the traditional division of labour and impose barriers for certain career paths, thus affecting women's innovation activities.

The traditional and still predominant model of labour division in (West) Germany is a conservative one with one partner (usually the man) working full time and one partner (usually the woman) being responsible for the household and the children. This male-breadwinner model is strongly supported by legal provisions, for example the tax system, and institutional standards such as an insufficient infrastructure for day care, especially in West Germany (Welter, 2004). This institutional framework sets clear disincentives for female labour market participation. As a result, the share of women working part time in Germany is far above the EU average. In 2010, 69.6 per cent of all 20- to 64-year-old women were in employment in Germany, with 45.6 per cent of them working part time and 54.4 per cent full time. The EU average part-time rate was 30.8 per cent (Statistisches Bundesamt, 2012). Asked for reasons for their part-time employment, every second woman (51.3 per cent) mentioned child care or other family duties, and 18.9 per cent were not able to find full-time employment (Statistisches Bundesamt, 2012). However, part-time work, especially combined with family duties which require strict time management at work, leaves little time for the creative activities that are the basis for innovations (Kugele, 2010). This applies for part-time employed working women as well as for part-time self-employed women. In Germany less than 45 per cent of self-employed women work more than 40 hours per week, compared to 70 per cent of all self-employed men reporting they work full time (Bögenhold and Fachinger, 2010, 2013). The number of women working part time for less than 15 hours per week is much higher than the number of men working less than 15 hours per week (Bögenhold and Fachinger, 2012). A part-time self-employed business usually operates in a smaller market, so that investments, for example in innovations, take longer to pay off. This makes innovations less profitable and improbable.

The conservative breadwinner model in Germany is similar to that in other conservative welfare countries (e.g. Austria or the Netherlands). But, even in countries which are considered more equal in terms of their regulatory framework, work-related gender differences persist. For female entrepreneurs in Denmark, Neergaard and Thrane (2011) show how regulatory institutions on the one hand create equal treatment in public life and the labour market, but on the other hand perpetuate a male pattern of family life at home. The regulatory aspects of the institutional context also influence societal norms; for example, family-related roles are still attributed to women (Holst, 2001). This leads to discrimination against women entrepreneurs, who have to bear the double burden of entrepreneurship and family responsibilities (see also Welter et al., 2014).

The persistence of the societal context which is shaped by regulatory norms becomes visible when comparing West and East Germany. Over 40 years of division, the two parts of Germany developed different institutional contexts, at both the normative and the regulatory level. Re-unification harmonized most regulatory aspects, but not necessarily the normative components. For instance, it remains much more common in East Germany for mothers with small children to work full time. In 2007 only 18 per cent of mothers in West Germany worked full time (over 30 hours a week), compared to 50 per cent full-time working mothers in East Germany. In West Germany 27 per cent of mothers were not working and not searching for a job, but in East Germany this number was only 14 per cent (Geisler, 2010). Day care infrastructure is designed accordingly, so that in East Germany almost 70 per cent of children between three and five were in full-time day care in 2013, whereas in West Germany the share amounted only to 32 per cent (Statistisches Bundesamt, 2013a). This makes it easier for women in East Germany to find time to pursue a career or to set up a company. Therefore, female entrepreneurship in East Germany has shown a higher growth rate and a higher rate of full-time self-employment, and women entrepreneurs exhibit stronger entrepreneurial intentions than their counterparts in West Germany, although the overall rates of female entrepreneurship are still lower in East than in West Germany (Welter, 2006).

Fagenson and Marcus (1991) point out another way that the institutional context influences entrepreneurship and innovative activities: in societies where traditional gender roles persist (as is the case for Germany), entrepreneurship is typically perceived as a masculine behaviour and activity. This societal norm can discourage women, so that rates of women's entrepreneurship tend to be lower than for men (see Welter et al., 2014). In this regard, the West German institutional framework which fosters conservative traditional role stereotypes is constraining women from prospering within male-dominated fields, including entrepreneurship (Welter, 2006). This societal context has led to an image of female leadership as less desirable, which in turn affects the social context (see above), as well as individual self-perception and choices towards career preferences.

The effect of institutional regulations, norms and values on (working) women and their effect on women's innovation is also reflected in the so-called pipeline leak: women who choose a career in science withdraw from the scientific field significantly more often than men, dropping out along the career ladder (Svinth, 2006). The pipeline leak is especially pronounced with regard to knowledge commercialization in universities, which is a significant source of technological innovation (Polkowska, 2013, p. 156). It can also be observed that women who are active in knowledge transfer in universities often choose activities that do not generate but rather support innovation, such as consulting, while men are more likely to be involved in spin-off activities (Polkowska, 2013). Different determinants for the pipeline leak can be identified: owing to career breaks, for example during maternity leave (Kay et al., 2014), women tend to have lower human capital than men. Since 2007, the German government has provided financial support for a maximum of 14 months of parental leave that allows parents to stay at home and take a 'paid' career break beyond the existing 12-week maternity leave for women before and after childbirth. The reason for this support is the German subsidy guideline to foster a family-friendly environment (BMFSFJ, 2013). Thus, since 2007 the number of parents who make use of parental leave has grown substantially. Hand in hand with the traditional gender roles in Germany, more mothers with children under three years take parental leave (26.2 per cent) than men (2.0 per cent) (Statistisches Bundesamt, 2015). What seems to be good for family reasons on the one hand, however, seems to be negative for the professional human capital of these women, and their likelihood of acting innovatively. Especially in the case of an academic career, it is vital to stay up to date with regard to new scientific developments and trends and to be active in research and publishing (Polkowska, 2013).

Furthermore, women form a minority among professorships in science and technology in Germany. In 2012 there were 43 800 professors in Germany, about 20 per cent of them women. The total number of female professors has doubled since 2002, but the number of female professors in engineering is still low (10 per cent), as well as in mathematics and natural sciences (14 per cent) (Statistisches Bundesamt, 2013b). Moreover, women are rarely represented on the relevant decision-making advisory boards (Polkowska, 2013), which impedes networking and lobbying. Finally, barriers like a lack of personal support and networks, men-oriented workplace structures and the gender distribution in teams lead to a higher drop-out rate among women in the course of the academic career (Buré, 2007). All this can have an impact on the extent and type of ventures created by women from academia.

## CONCLUSIONS

Our data show that there are some obvious differences between men and women entrepreneurs in Germany in terms of their innovation behaviour. On interpreting this finding, we first have to take into account the general understanding of an innovation and the innovator. The term 'innovation' is narrowly restricted to technologically based innovations and specific types of innovations. This narrow definition is usually applied by empirical research studies, official statistical data sources, and public programmes supporting innovation across Germany. In line with current research (e.g. Alsos et al., 2013; Welter et al., 2014) we suggest that narrowing down the whole concept of innovation to these forms of innovation does not give sufficient consideration to the diverse manifestations of innovation and ex ante excludes women and women-led companies. Therefore, it is a worthwhile task for researchers when designing empirical studies as well as for politicians when designing support programmes to widen the definition of innovation in order to capture other forms of innovation – like social or marketing innovations – too. Such a wider perspective would also include a view on 'women sectors', which are considered to be less innovative by definition and previously have been neglected in studies. Nevertheless, a wider definition of innovation alone will not change the behaviour and preferences of women towards innovation, and hence gender differences will not automatically vanish.

The innovator is supposed to be the person who implements a novelty. In most research, especially in empirical research, the owner or director of a firm is considered to be this person, even though the actual innovative activities might have been carried out by someone else. Given the underrepresentation of women in top management positions, this might lead to an underestimation of the innovation activities of women. It is therefore necessary for research, policy and practice to dig deeper and to carefully determine to whom an innovation is ascribed.

Applying the narrow definition of innovation, we found only two data sets with information on the gender of the persons involved in innovation activities. It is obvious that we need more studies about innovation in

Germany that cover the sex of the innovator. The existing data show that women in Germany are underrepresented in innovative activities: they file fewer patent applications, tend to set up a company in sectors with a rate of innovators near or below average, and develop product and process innovations to a lesser extent than men. We traced these differences back to contextual influences, especially the social and institutional context in which women act. Internalized role expectations and ensuing individual preferences lead to the lower inclination of women to choose education in a technological, engineering or science discipline, which is a typical path towards technology-based innovations.

Although there are a number of initiatives in Germany attempting to make girls aware of job and career options in male-dominated sectors, the gender gap in those disciplines is relatively stable. Moreover, even within the same professional disciplines, gender-specific differences exist regarding the course of careers. Therefore, sensitization of women is still an ongoing topic, but studies are necessary that analyse previous sensitization activities and their effects.

Previous research demonstrated that the career breaks of women, especially child-rearing periods, often result in the lower human capital of women relative to their male counterparts. A previously neglected but interesting aspect for future research is *how* such career breaks can influence human capital in a *positive* way (e.g. by increasing one's organizing abilities) and what that means for innovation behaviour. Further barriers like a lack of personal support and networks, men-oriented workplace structures, and the gender distribution in teams intensify the pipeline leak in the course of the academic career. Investment in the human capital of women could increase their propensity to start an enterprise and possibly also to become an innovator (Kay et al., 2014). Owing to the regulatory framework in Germany, which supports a male-breadwinner model, many women work part time, which leaves little time and resources for innovative activities. Finally, the image of an innovator, similar to the image of an entrepreneur in Germany, is still masculine, which makes it less likely that women perceive themselves as innovators. Concerning these aspects, we suggest that we need to further enhance gender equality in Germany by attempting to change internalized role expectations. Still low, but increasing, numbers of women entrepreneurs and professors in Germany help to create more and more 'real' role models and may help to change images in the long term. Many of our findings apply not only to women and innovation in Germany but to women and innovation in other countries, too. Therefore, we see a need for further cross-national studies, especially European-wide comparisons. Countries with a lower participation of women in innovation could learn from other, good-practice countries; for example, Germany could learn from the Nordic ones.

We want to end with a positive conclusion from our observations: women in Germany are not less innovative as such, but a combination of existing institutional constraints and traditional role models contributes to them self-selecting into less innovation-prone professions and working structures, such as part-time work. Women contribute to innovation, but often in the background, invisible. Thus, the main task for future research about women and innovation in Germany is to point out the invisible contribution of women to innovation and to further develop ideas about how to change framework conditions. From this point of view we do not have to change the women – they make the best of what's possible within the existing framework – but we have to change the framework itself. It is also important to increase recognition of women and women entrepreneurs and not only to compare them to a masculine-embossed norm. Alsos et al. (2013) accentuated the need for more research on structural factors such as education and social expectations, and the female socialization processes in relation to their career perspectives and roles in innovation. In addition to their call, we suggest that the causalities and interaction between the framework factors that lead to traditional role expectations and a gender-dependent innovation behaviour must also be examined deeper in future research. The present chapter aims to contribute to this with a view on social and institutional aspects. Future studies should in addition focus on important aspects such as spatial, temporal and historical circumstances and conditions for women entrepreneurship and innovation activities.

## NOTES

1. Institute for Employment Research.
2. During a Girls' Day, technical enterprises and vocational training facilities, universities, and research centres hold an open day for girls and present a wide range of professions and activities for girls from 5th grade (see http://www.girls-day.de/). 'Komm mach MINT' is a networking initiative to sensitize girls and young women for STEM professions (see http://www.komm-mach-mint.de).

## REFERENCES

Achtenhagen, L. and F. Welter (2011), '"Surfing on the ironing board" – the representation of women's entrepreneurship in German newspapers', *Entrepreneurship and Regional Development: An International Journal*, **23** (9–10), 763–786.

Ahl, H. (2006), 'Why research on women entrepreneurs needs new directions', *Entrepreneurship Theory and Practice*, **30** (5), 595–621.

Alsos, G.A., E. Ljunggren and U. Hytti (2013), 'Gender and innovation: State of the art and a research agenda', *International Journal of Gender and Entrepreneurship*, **5** (3), 236–256.

Bahmani, S., F. Escribano Sotos and I. Pardo Garcia (2012), 'Women, research, and entrepreneurship', in N. Galindo and D. Ribeiro (eds), *Women's Entrepreneurship and Economics: New Perspective, Practices, and Policies*, New York: Springer, pp. 35–52.

Becker, C., T. Grebe and T. Lübbers (2011), *Evaluation der Fördermaßnahmen 'EXIST-Gründerstipendium' und 'EXIST-Forschungstransfer'. Studie im Auftrag des Bundesministeriums für Wirtschaft und Technologie*, Berlin: Gesellschaft für Innovationsforschung und Beratung.

BMBF (Bundesministerium für Bildung und Forschung) (2014), 'Bundesbericht für Forschung und Innovation 2014', accessed 18 August 2014 at http://www.bmbf.de/pub/bufi_2014.pdf.

BMFSFJ (Bundesministerium für Familie, Senioren, Frauen und Jugend) (2010), *Ausgeübte Erwerbstätigkeit von Müttern*, Berlin: BMFSFJ, accessed 16 January 2015 at http://www.bmfsfj.de/RedaktionBMFSFJ/Broschuerenstelle/Pdf-Anlagen/Ausge_C3_BCbte-Erwerbst_C3_A4tigkeit-von-M_C3_BCttern,property=pdf,bereich=bmfsfj,sprache=de,rwb=true.pdf.

BMFSFJ (Bundesministerium für Familie, Senioren, Frauen und Jugend) (2013), *Förderrichtlinien des Bundes*, Berlin: BMFSFJ, accessed 16 January 2015 at http://www.bmfsfj.de/BMFSFJ/Service/foerderrichtlinien.html.

Bögenhold, D. and U. Fachinger (2010), 'How diverse is entrepreneurship? Observations on the social heterogeneity of self-employment in Germany', accessed 6 March 2015 at http://mpra.ub.uni-muenchen.de/23271/1/MPRA_paper_23271.pdf.

Bögenhold, D. and U. Fachinger (2012), *Unternehmertum: Unterschiedliche Facetten selbstständiger Berufstätigkeit*, IfS Discussion Paper 01/2012, Klagenfurt, Austria: University of Klagenfurt.

Bögenhold, D. and U. Fachinger (2013), *Weibliche Solo-Selbständigkeit zwischen Notwendigkeit und Innovationsherausforderung: Beobachtungen über Geschlecht und Unternehmertum in Deutschland*, IfS Discussion Paper 01/2013, Klagenfurt, Austria: University of Klagenfurt.

Brink, S., S. Kriwoluzky, T. Bijedić, K. Ettl and F. Welter (2014), *Gender, Innovation und Unternehmensentwicklung*, IfM Materialen No. 228, Bonn, Germany: IfM Bonn.

Brush, C.G., A. de Bruin and F. Welter (2009), 'A gender-aware framework for women's entrepreneurship', *International Journal of Gender and Entrepreneurship*, **1** (1), 8–24.

Buré, C. (2007), 'Gender in/and science, technology and innovation policy: An overview of current literature and findings', Strategic commissioned paper for Innovation, Policy and Science Program Area, International Development Research Centre (IDRC), Ottawa.

Burkhardt, D. and S. Greif (2001), *Frauen im Patentgeschehen der Bundesrepublik Deutschland (Ergebnisbericht)*, On behalf of Federal Ministry of Education and Research, Bonn, Germany: Bundesministerium für Bildung und Forschung.

Busch, A. (2013), 'Die Geschlechtersegregation beim Berufseinstieg – Berufswerte und ihr Erklärungsbeitrag für die geschlechtstypische Berufswahl', *Berliner Journal für Soziologie*, **23** (2), 145–179.

Damanpour, F. (1991), 'Organizational innovation: A meta-analysis of effects of determinants and moderators', *Academy of Management Journal*, **34** (3), 555–590.

DIW (2006a), 'Innovationsindikator Deutschland 2006', accessed 20 August 2014 at http://www.innovationsindikator.de/fileadmin/user_upload/Dokumente/innovationsindikator2006.pdf.

DIW (2006b), 'Zu wenig Frauen in Forschung und Innovation', *DIW Wochenbericht*, **73** (45), 643–651, accessed 20 August 2014 at http://www.diw.de/documents/publikationen/ 73/diw_01.c.44824.de/06-45-2.pdf.

Dorner, M., S. Bender, D. Harloff, K. Hoisl and S. Patrycia (2014), 'The MPI-IC-IAB-Inventor Data 2002 (MIID 2002): Record-linkage of patent register data with labor market biography data of the IAB', FDZ-Methodenreport 06/2014, accessed 18 August 2014 at http://doku.iab.de/fdz/reporte/2014/MR_06-14_EN.pdf.

EFI (Expertenkommission Forschung und Innovation) (2012), *Gutachten zu Forschung, Innovation und technologischer Leistungsfähigkeit Deutschlands. Gutachten 2012*, Berlin: EFI.

European Commission (2010), *Report on Equality between Women and Men 2010*, Luxembourg: European Commission.

Fagenson, E.A. and E.C. Marcus (1991), 'Perceptions of the sex-role stereotypic characteristics of entrepreneurs: Women's evaluations', *Entrepreneurship Theory and Practice*, **15** (4), 33–47.

Fagerberg, J. (2005), 'Innovation: A guide to the literature', in J. Fagerberg, D.C. Mowery and R.R. Nelson (eds), *The Oxford Handbook of Innovation*, Oxford, UK: Oxford University Press, pp. 1–26.

Geisler, E. (2010), 'Mütterwerbstätigkeit', in J. Goldstein, M. Kreyenfeld, J. Huinink, D. Konietzka and H. Trappe (eds), *Familie und Partnerschaft in Ost- und Westdeutschland: Ergebnisse im Rahmen des Projektes 'Demographic Differences in Life Course Dynamics in Eastern und Western Germany'*, Rostock: Max-Planck-Institut für demografische Forschung, pp. 11–12.

Grindel, S. and S. Lässig (2007), *Unternehmer und Staat in europäischen Schulbüchern. Deutschland, England und Schweden im Vergleich*, Braunschweig, Germany: Georg-Eckert-Institut.

Hoffman, M.E. and D.R. Vance (2007), 'Gender difference trends in computer literacy of first-year students', *ACM SIGCSE Bulletin*, **39**, 404–409.

Holst, E. (2001), *Institutionelle Determinanten der Erwerbsarbeit. Zur Notwendigkeit einer Gender-Perspektive in den Wirtschaftswissenschaften*, Berlin: DIW.

Hurrelmann, K., M. Grundmann and S. Walper (2008), 'Zum Stand der Sozialisationsforschung', in K. Hurrelmann, M. Grundmann and S. Walper (eds), *Handbuch Sozialisationsforschung*, 7th edn, Weinheim, Germany: Beltz Verlag, pp. 14–31.

Jennings, J.E. and C.G. Brush (2013), 'Research on women entrepreneurs: Challenges to (and from) the broader entrepreneurship literature?', *Academy of Management Annals*, **7** (1), 663–715.

Katz, S., D. Allbritton, J. Aronis, C. Wilson and M.L. Soffa (2006), 'Gender, achievement, and persistence in an undergraduate computer science program', *Data Base for Advances in Information Systems*, **37**, 42–57.

Kay, R. (2007), *Auf dem Weg in die Chefetage: Betriebliche Entscheidungsprozesse bei der Besetzung von Führungspositionen*, IfM-Materialien No. 170, Bonn, Germany: IfM Bonn.

Kay, R., S. Schneck and O. Suprinovič (2014), *Erwerbsbiografische Einflüsse auf das Gründungsverhalten von Frauen*, IfM-Materialien No. 230, Bonn, Germany: IfM Bonn.

Klyver, K., S.L. Nielson and M.R. Evald (2012), 'Women's self-employment: An act of institutional (dis)integration? A multi-level, cross-country study', *Journal of Business Venturing*, **28** (4), 474–488.

Knight, K.E. (1967), 'A descriptive model of the intra-firm innovation process', *Journal of Business*, **40** (4), 478–496.

Kugele, K. (2010), 'Analysis of women's participation in high-technology patenting', in S. Marlow and P. Wynarczyk (eds), *Innovating Women: Contributions to Technological Advancement*, Contemporary Issues in Entrepreneurship Research, Vol. 1, Bingley, UK: Emerald, pp. 123–151.

Lindberg, M., M. Lindgren and J. Packendorff (2011), 'The role of NGO's in supporting women's entrepreneurship: A study of Quadruple Helix innovation systems in the Baltic Sea region', accessed 3 March 2015 at http://media1.lindgren-packendorff.com/2014/02/CMS_2011_final.pdf.

Marlow, S. and M. McAdam (2012), 'Gender and entrepreneurship: Advancing debate and challenging myths; exploring the mystery of the under-performing female entrepreneur', *International Journal of Entrepreneurial Behavior and Research*, **19** (1), 114–124.

Nählinder, J., M. Tillmar and C. Wigren-Kristoferson (2012), 'Are female and male entrepreneurs equally innovative? Reducing the gender bias of operationalisations and industries studied', in S. Andersson, K. Berglund, E. Gunnarsson and E. Sundin (eds), *Promoting Innovation: Policies, Practices and Procedures*, Vinnova Report 2012:08, Stockholm: Vinnova, pp. 351–372.

Neergaard, H. and C. Thrane (2011), 'The Nordic welfare model', *International Journal of Gender and Entrepreneurship*, **3** (2), 88–104.

Nyberg, A.-C. (2009), 'Making ideas matter: Gender, technology and women's invention', Doctoral thesis, Luleå University of Technology, Sweden.

OECD (Organisation for Economic Co-operation and Development) (2005), *Oslo Manual: Guidelines for Collecting and Interpreting Innovation Data*, 3rd edn, Paris: OECD Publishing.

OECD (Organisation for Economic Co-operation and Development) (2011), *Bildung auf einen Blick. OECD-Indikatoren*, Paris: OECD Publishing.

Pettersson, K. and M. Lindberg (2013), 'Paradoxical spaces of feminist resistance: Mapping the margin to the masculinist innovation discourse', *International Journal of Gender and Entrepreneurship*, **5** (3), 323–341.

Piorkowsky, M.-B. (2006), 'Institutionelle Einflüsse auf das Unternehmerbild. Das Unternehmerinnenbild in Deutschland. Ein Beitrag zum Gegenwärtigen Forschungsstand', in A.D. Bührmann, K. Hansen, M. Schmeink and A. Schöttelndreier (eds), *Das Unternehmerinnenbild in Deutschland. Ein Beitrag zum gegenwärtigen Forschungsstand*, Hamburg, Germany: LIT, pp. 122–160.

Polkowska, D. (2013), 'Women scientists in the leaking pipeline: Barriers to the commercialisation of scientific knowledge by women', *Journal of Technology Management and Innovation*, **8** (2), 156–165.

Quesenberry, J.L. (2007), 'Career values and motivations: A study of women in the information technology workforce – a thesis in information sciences and technology', accessed 4 February 2015 at https://etda.libraries.psu.edu/paper/8071/3366.

Ripsas, S., B. Schaper and F. Nöll (2013), *Deutscher Startup Monitor 2013*, Berlin: Bundesverband Deutsche Startups.

Ruiz-Arroyo, M., M. del Mar Fuentes-Fuentes, A.M. Bojica and L. Rodriguez-Ariza (2012), 'Innovativeness and performance in woman-owned small firms: The role of knowledge acquisition', *Journal of Small Business and Entrepreneurship*, **25** (3), 307–326.

Schumpeter, J.A. (1934), *The Theory of Economic Development*, Cambridge, MA: Harvard University Press.

Schumpeter, J.A. (1939), *Business Cycles: A Theoretical, Historical and Statistical Analysis of the Capitalist Process*, New York: McGraw-Hill.

Statistisches Bundesamt (2012), 'Teilzeitquote von Frauen in Deutschland deutlich über EU-Durchschnitt', Press Release No. 078, accessed 20 August 2014 at https://www.destatis.de/DE/PresseService/Presse/Pressemitteilungen/2012/03/PD12_078_132.html.

Statistisches Bundesamt (2013a), *Kindertagesbetreuung regional 2013. Ein Vergleich aller 402 Kreise in Deutschland*, Wiesbaden, Germany: Statistisches Bundesamt.

Statistisches Bundesamt (2013b), 'Frauenanteil in Professorenschaft 2012 auf über 20% gestiegen', Press Release No. 235, 11 July, accessed 15 January 2015 at https://www.destatis.de/DE/PresseService/Presse/Pressemitteilungen/2013/07/PD13_235_213.html.

Statistisches Bundesamt (2014), *Unternehmen und Arbeitsstätte. Gewerbeanzeigen Dezember und Jahr 2013*, Fachserie 2, Reihe 5, Wiesbaden, Germany: Statistisches Bundesamt.

Statistisches Bundesamt (2015), 'Personen in Elternzeit', accessed 15 January 2015 at https://www.destatis.de/DE/ZahlenFakten/Indikatoren/QualitaetArbeit/Dimension3/3_9_Elternzeit.html.

Svinth, L. (2006), '"Leaky pipeline" – to be or not to be a useful metaphor in understanding why women to a disproportional degree exit from scientific careers', Paper presented at the 6th European Gender Research Conference – UPGEM.

Tonoyan, V. and R. Strohmeyer (2006), 'Employment growth and firm innovativeness: An empirical investigation of women- and men-owned small ventures in Germany', in A.-K. Achleitner, H. Klandt, L.T. Koch and K.-I. Vogt (eds), *Jahrbuch Entrepreneurship 2005/2006: Gründungsforschung und Gründungsmanagement*, Berlin: Springer, pp. 323–353.

Welter, F. (2004), 'Institutionelle Einflüsse auf Gründerinnen und Unternehmerinnen', in M. Tchouvakhina (ed.), *Chefinnensache*, Heidelberg: Physica, pp. 33–69.

Welter, F. (2006), 'Mythos Unternehmenswachstum? Ein kritischer und reflektierender Blick auf Wachstumspade von KMU', in J.-A. Meyer (ed.), *Aufbruch und Wachstum von KMU in neue Märkte. Jahrbuch der KMU-Forschung und -praxis 2006*, Lohmar, Germany: Verlag Joseph Eul, pp. 19–36.

Welter, F. (2011), 'Contextualizing entrepreneurship – conceptual challenges and ways forward', *Entrepreneurship Theory and Practice*, **35** (1), 165–184.

Welter, F., C. Brush and A. de Bruin (2014), *The Gendering of Entrepreneurship Context*, IfM Working Paper 01/14, Bonn, Germany: IfM Bonn.

Wiepcke, C. and N. Pickard (2011), *Geschlechtergerechte Berufsorientierung in Schulbüchern*, Schwäbisch Gmünd, Germany: Institut für Gesellschaftswissenschaften der Pädagogischen Hochschule Schwäbisch Gmünd, accessed 3 March 2015 at https://www.ph-gmuend.de/deutsch/downloads/oekonomie/Wiepcke_schriftenreihe_Nr__3.pdf.

WIPO (World Intellectual Property Organization) (2008), *WIPO Intellectual Property Handbook*, 2nd edn, accessed 30 September 2014 at http://www.wipo.int/edocs/pubdocs/en/intproperty/489/wipo_pub_489.pdf.

## 4. Three faces of innovation: institutions, gender and entrepreneurship in Latin America
*Ruta Aidis*

## INTRODUCTION

Innovation is the lifeblood for most entrepreneurs and increasingly for most world economies. Disruptive innovations such as Facebook, Google and PayPal create jobs, markets and even industries, while other innovations bring about incremental change and improvements to existing markets. There also exists a gendered dimension to innovation. Jennings and Brush (2013) write that entrepreneurship is not a gender-neutral phenomenon, and the same can be said for innovation. Women have been innovating alongside men, yet their innovations have often remained unnoticed or discounted, often because the innovation has been less disruptive or focused on female-dominated activities such as services and household production. But historically, even when innovative activity by women has been disruptive, it has often been overlooked. This chapter takes a closer look at three highly successful innovative female entrepreneurs in Latin America. By exploring their business developments, we uncover some of the gendered impediments that exist for innovative women in the Latin American context. Some of the examples are universal, while others are clearly linked to the environment in Latin America.

One gendered characteristic in Latin America that is found in most countries worldwide regardless of the rate of women entrepreneurship development is that most women entrepreneurs operate in female-dominated sectors (Inter-American Development Bank, 2012,[1] p. 20). As a result, women entrepreneurs are more concentrated in sectors such as food and beverages, services, manufacturing and retail, while men tend to focus on less traditional sectors which require more innovation, such as the internet or software development (ibid.). Sector influences the type of innovative activity that occurs.

Are women in Latin America innovative? According to 2012 data from the Global Entrepreneurship Monitor (GEM), 24 per cent of female start-ups[2] in Latin America are 'innovative', introducing new products and/or services through their businesses (GEM, 2012). This places Latin American countries at the mid-range, with the US (36 per cent) at the upper end and developing Asia (17 per cent) at the lower end. The GEM data also indicate that the Latin American region boasts a relatively high degree of female entrepreneurship: 15 per cent of working-age females are engaged in total entrepreneurship activity (TEA)[3] compared to 19 per cent of working-age males. The highest female TEA rates are found in Ecuador (27 per cent) and Chile (19 per cent). However, these numbers are often inflated because of the high percentages of female entrepreneurs who are necessity driven, that is, starting businesses for economic survival (as is the case for 41 per cent of the female TEA rate in Ecuador), and also influenced by the high percentages of self-employed women working in the informal sector, estimated as 69 per cent in Brazil and 79 per cent in Mexico.[4] Other Latin American countries such as Colombia have both a high percentage of male and female TEA (26 per cent and 19 per cent respectively) and a high proportion of high-growth TEA (as measured by an expected increase of 20 or more employees in the next five years).

Our case study analysis is based on the experiences of three successful and innovative female entrepreneurs from Brazil, Colombia and Bolivia. Though this is arguably a small sample of a much broader phenomenon, nonetheless it provides some useful insights. In Brazil, we analyse the case of Leila Velez, co-founder and currently CEO of Beleza Natural – an innovative beauty institute chain. In Colombia, we analyse the case of Carolina Guerra, co-founder of Ingerecuperar, a hazardous waste treatment and recycling company. In Bolivia, we analyse the case of Maria Claudia Mendez, founder of Origenes Bolivia, which specializes in creating upmarket fashion and household accessories made from alpaca and other natural fibres. These three companies span three different countries as well as three different sectors: personal services (Beleza Natural), industrial services and recycling (Ingerecuperar) and manufacturing (Origenes Bolivia).

The case studies are based on interviews and secondary data collected on the three women entrepreneurs. Data were originally collected in 2012 and updated in 2015 to reflect any changes to the businesses. Existing data were verified, and supplemental information was gathered through semi-structured telephone and Skype interviews with Carolina Guerra and Maria Claudia Mendez in June 2012. A personal fact-checking interview was conducted with Leila Velez in June 2015.

This chapter is structured as follows. It first profiles the three female entrepreneurs and provides a useful background for the subsequent sections. There follows a description of institutional theory and how it pertains to the gendered realities encountered by female innovator entrepreneurs. The chapter then chronicles the gendered institutional impediments for innovation, as well as including some overall institutional constraints to innovation. The chapter goes on to focus on the role played by international awards and recognition for helping female innovator entrepreneurs overcome existing institutional impediments. Finally, this chapter ends with a discussion and conclusion.

## PROFILES OF THREE ENTREPRENEUR INNOVATORS: LEILA, CAROLINA AND MARIA CLAUDIA

### Leila Velez

> *I was very poor. I used to play with rich kids and see the way they lived and said, wow, life can be as good as that. Why can't I? I can find ways to make my life better and help my family and as many people as I can.*[5] (Leila Velez)

As is typical for most entrepreneurs, this success story began with a problem. For Leila and her partner Heloisa 'Zica' de Assis, the problem was managing their kinky hair in a natural way. In Brazil, as in many parts of the world, most women with kinky hair straighten their hair using large amounts of chemicals that actually damage hair. Leila's sister-in-law Zica was a hairdresser who recognized the need for a hair product that would enhance naturally curly hair's beauty rather than trying to change it through chemicals. She started experimenting with different treatments, trying them out on herself and Leila. After ten years of trial and error, Zica developed a unique hair treatment formula, which continues to form the flagship hair treatment for Beleza Natural's operations today.

During this time, Leila was learning first-hand about the fast food business. Together with her brother-in-law Rogerio, she started working at McDonald's when she was only 14 years old. Leila often jokes that she received a 'McDonald's MBA'.[6] Actually, both Leila and Rogerio learned a great deal from McDonald's in terms of managing large operations, building to scale, quality control and training processes. While working at McDonald's, they also became interested in becoming entrepreneurs themselves.[7]

Zica and her husband Jair, Leila and Rogerio formed the start-up team, and Zica created the novel hair treatment. Initially they started out by offering Zica's hair treatment from Zica and Jair's suburban home to family and friends. But within three months word spread and women were lining up, not deterred by the wait, for their proprietary service.[8] In response, the team patented Zica's hair treatment and opened their first rented salon in 1993. They named their business 'Beleza Natural', which from Portuguese translates as 'natural beauty'. Though the team clearly saw the potential market for their product, others were sceptical and not very supportive. As a result, from the beginning, they were 100 per cent self-financed.

Leila Velez and her partners at Beleza Natural utilized *incongruities*[9] in their innovative process. That is, they incorporated practices from other industries and adapted them to transform the beauty salon experience. In traditional beauty salons, clients typically develop a relationship with an individual hairdresser, not the salon. In contrast, Beleza Natural fosters a client's attachment to its brand, not the hairdresser. Beleza Natural has built its business based on McDonald's fast food approach by providing top-notch, affordable hair care, regardless of who is on shift. In addition, like McDonald's, it offers a set 'menu', in this case 30 haircut styles which have been carefully developed as ideal styles for kinky hair. As Leila Velez, Beleza Natural's CEO, comments: 'I have no shame in copying.'[10] They were also innovative in their market niche. Instead of creating an elite salon, Beleza Natural primarily made its target market low-income women, often from the bottom of the pyramid (BOP).[11] In addition, Beleza Natural's approach reaches far beyond hair care to focusing on empowering their female clientele as well as their 1400 employees.

Since the beginning, Beleza Natural has experienced exponential growth. Starting with only one hair salon in 1993, Beleza Natural operates over 29 salons and a cosmetics research lab, and produces a full line of hair care products. In 2012, Beleza's revenue was more than US\$30 million.[12]

## Carolina Guerra

Carolina Guerra, who grew up in Buga, Colombia, always wanted to be an entrepreneur. However, it took several years before Carolina saw the opportunity to start her own business. First, she studied materials engineering at Universidad del Valle (Valle University). After graduating with a bachelor's degree, Carolina ended up getting a job. The company she worked for needed to comply with Colombia's new environmental legislation for aluminium dross disposal.[13] Up until then, most companies creating aluminium dross wastes, which are typical for automobile production and food packaging, would simply dump the remaining dross into a landfill. A more 'acceptable' means to dispose of aluminium dross is incineration, but this solution creates another form of environmental hazard through airborne toxins.

Even though the solution did not yet exist in Colombia, Carolina and two of her male colleagues knew there had to be a more environmentally sound manner to dispose of dross. They decided to develop a solution themselves. After intensive research, they devised a method for neutralizing the hazardous effects of aluminium dross and actually recycling it, creating building materials suitable for use in construction.

Carolina left her full-time job and along with her two colleagues started Ingerecuperar in 2007. In Spanish, *inge* is an abbreviation for engineering and *recuperar* means recovery. The company's main focus is to engineer solutions for hazardous waste recovery. Carolina and her partners at Ingerecuperar in Colombia implemented *process innovation* by introducing an environmentally friendly procedure that not only neutralizes hazardous wastes but also recycles it into useful eco-materials. Initially Ingerecuperar developed a novel method for aluminium dross recycling. In fact, they actually purchase the dross from companies, since the recycled outcome, a form of cement used to manufacture building blocks, benches and fence posts, can be sold for a profit. Ingerecuperar is the first company in Colombia that obtained an environmental licence for aluminium dross recycling.

Although their recycling process was novel and environmentally friendly, their initial years of operation were not easy. Carolina recollects that her parents were initially sceptical about her choice to quit her good job in order to start her company. Luckily, Carolina's friends were very supportive of her new business. The start-up capital was enough to purchase the necessary machinery and other costs associated with re-cycling aluminium dross. However, for the initial two years of business, there was not enough income to provide the three founders with salaries. During that time, in order to reduce her personal expenses, Carolina continued to live with her parents.

Currently, Ingerecuperar is a growing business with a large vision for the future. More recently, Ingerecuperar has expanded its recycling operations to include other categories of hazardous waste, including incinerator ash, pipeline powder and lead-based wastes from battery production. The firm employs 15 full-time employees, and there is an almost a 50/50 division between employees working on recycling operations and those working in research and development. This reflects Ingerecuperar's continued emphasis on diversifying and expanding its activities to add additional hazardous waste solutions to its services. Carolina serves as director, and her partner and ex-colleague Eduardo heads the research and development group. Carolina's other partner and ex-colleague left the company and was replaced by Marta, a former environmental authority employee from Cali. Carolina, Eduardo and Marta form the partnership core and make all major decisions affecting Ingerecuperar's operations jointly. Though Ingerecuperar is a relatively small company, its operations are expanding: in its third year of operations, Ingerecuperar's revenue was approximately US$100 000, which more than tripled to approximately US$360 000 in 2012.

**Maria Claudia Mendez**

Maria Claudia Mendez did not start out as an entrepreneur.[14] Instead, after going to the US and receiving a master's degree in economics at the University of Texas, Maria Claudia returned to Bolivia and focused on getting a job in Bolivia's oil sector. In 2000, she was hired as a financial economic analyst by an engineering firm, the Hydrocarbon Super-intendency. This was no small feat given that, out of its 84 employees, Maria Claudia was only the third woman to be hired for a technical position; all the other women were secretaries, cleaners or service personnel. Initially elated about her new job, Maria soon noticed that she was treated differently from her male colleagues. She worked more hours than most of her male colleagues but earned the lowest salary in her division. Maria Claudia stuck it out for three years, but the situation did not improve. In 2003, she quit her job and began dreaming of having her own business.[15] Later that year, at 30 years of age, Maria Claudia used her personal savings to start Origenes Bolivia SRL.

Origenes Bolivia outsources its production to indigenous artisans mainly from the Mestizo, Aymara and Quechua ethnic groups in Bolivia. The vast majority of Origenes Bolivia's artisans are poorly educated women who work from their homes located on the outskirts of the capital city La Paz and El Alto. Given the non-existence of paid daycare in Bolivia, working from home provides many advantages for mothers, especially single mothers, to take care of their children while making an income. The artisans either hand-make the products or use hand-operated machines which require no electricity. The numbers of artisans working for Origenes Bolivia fluctuate from 35 to 100. From the beginning, Maria Claudia has been adamant she will not make use of child labour in any of her company's operations.

In terms of innovation, Maria Claudia addressed *changes in perception* with her company Origenes Bolivia by targeting a new market segment for hand-made apparel. She developed new designs and achieved a high level of quality for her apparel and household accessories that would have an upmarket appeal. Origenes Bolivia also expanded their market reach by adopting several avenues for sales. Initially, Origenes Bolivia's products were geared towards the export market, but in 2008 they expanded their operations to include two boutique shops in Bolivia. In addition to their own label, Origenes Bolivia also provide a private label service, manufacturing tailor-made products that suit their clients' needs and that are sold using their clients' label. Maria Claudia emphasizes Origenes Bolivia's unique marketing approach: it is not the only company in Bolivia that exports apparel and textiles made by indigenous artisans, but it is the only Bolivian company that simultaneously sells to the local and international markets and provides a private label service.

Maria Claudia plans to grow Origenes Bolivia further and is currently investing in company improvements such as software development, accounting and warehouse operations. She believes there are opportunities to expand in Europe (especially Northern Europe) and Japan and also regionally into the Brazilian market. Regrettably, the current political situation between Bolivia and the US is not suitable for further expansion into US markets.

## INSTITUTIONAL IMPACT ON GENDER AND INNOVATION

In every society, individuals are acting within the constraints and opportunities provided by the context. This context is made up of institutions that form the 'rules of the game' (North, 1990). Institutions do not affect all individuals in the same way. Rather, worldwide, institutions exhibit a gendered effect, since culture, customs, laws, traditions and beliefs grant privileges, denote acceptable behaviours and legally define an individual's rights and freedoms. There is a growing recognition of the gendered nature of institutions on female entrepreneurship development (Aidis, 2006; Aidis et al., 2007, 2013, 2014, 2015; Baughn et al., 2006; Jennings and Brush, 2013). As a result, many studies in the field of women's entrepreneurship have adopted an institutional lens (de Bruin et al., 2007). There is also increasing evidence that gendered restrictions affect women's abilities to start and scale their businesses (Aidis et al., 2015; Welter and Smallbone, 2011; World Bank, 2012).

In its *World Development Report 2012*, the World Bank identified discrimination against women as an example of institutional failure. For example, formal institutional failures can occur when laws and regulations discriminate against women, such as is the case where laws vest control over marital property in the hands of the husband (World Bank, 2012, p. 309) or where married working men with children receive a tax allowance, but their wives do not, so that working wives with children face higher taxes (ibid., p. 319). More subtle formal institutional failures can also occur when for example business credit programmes set up targeting male-dominated business sectors. Informal institutional failure occurs when gender roles, beliefs, norms and values are based on stereotypes but not on individual behaviours, talents and skills. Some social norms can be very persistent, such as the notion that 'a good wife' should be submissive to her husband (ibid., p. 172). The resilience of dysfunctional social norms may also stem from the difficulty of the potential gainers to credibly commit to compensate the losers after the change is made (ibid.).

A study by Women, Business and the Law[16] shows that more gendered legal restrictions result in fewer female-owned businesses (World Bank, 2013). Furthermore, in the US as in other parts of the world, women-owned businesses tend to grow less (in terms of revenue and employees) than businesses owned by men (Robb, 2014). The 2015 Global Women Entrepreneur Leaders Scorecard estimated the economic loss of the Gendered Business Growth Gap (Aidis et al., 2015). According to these estimations, there would be 5.8 million more jobs created in Brazil, 15 million more jobs in the US, and a whopping 74.4 million more jobs created in China in the next two years if women started growth-oriented businesses at the same rate as men (ibid., p. 7).[17] Though not addressed directly in the existing literature, it is implicitly understood that innovative activity, the key characteristic of entrepreneurs, is also impacted by the institutional environment.

Though in theory institutions are created to facilitate economic trans-actions, institutions can be maintained for long periods of time even if they are inefficient (DiMaggio and Powell, 1983; North, 1990). There are several reasons for these inefficient institutional outcomes. First of all, even when they clash with new formal rules, informal rules (such as norms, values and customs) have tenacious survival ability because they have become part of habitual behaviour (i.e. culture) and informal institutions provide a sense of stability (North, 1990). For example, verbal harassment of women (or catcalling) has not only been tolerated in Latin America, but also often seen by many as an integral part of the Latin American culture. Only recently has this gendered behaviour come under scrutiny in several Latin American countries, some of which have introduced measures to penalize catcalling. Argentina is deliberating legislation that would fine men up to US$775 for catcalling women. In

Peru, legislation has already been put in place that would penalize catcallers for up to 12 years in prison.

Second, informal institutions may change more slowly because of the influence of path dependence. Though the past cannot be used to neatly predict the future, pre-existing incentive structures in the environment can illuminate the direction in which institutions affect further economic development. This occurs because institutional change is usually incremental and is seldom discontinuous (North, 1990, p. 10). As a result, unproductive paths may persist for extended periods of time. For example in Latin America, women's role in family firms tends to be more limited because of their gender. Daughters generally do not inherit a share of the family firm unless their husbands are part of the firm. The shares inherited by daughters also tend to involve less lucrative parts of the family business, while wives tend to be in charge of the hospitality of the business and not with the day-to-day running of the family firm (Gupta and Levenburg, 2010).

Third, lock-in can occur as a result of a symbiotic relationship between existing institutions and organizations that have evolved as a consequence of the incentive structure provided to those institutions. Even when the formal rules change, organizations which benefited from the outdated informal rules and which would lose their benefits if they adopted new informal practices complementary to formal rule changes will continue to participate in detrimental informal rule practices in order to retain their position of power. An example of this is the influence of the 'old boys' network', especially in male-dominated industries such as mining, oil extraction, construction and other key sectors in many Latin American countries as well as worldwide (Aidis, 2016).

Fourth, when formal and informal institutions clash, as in the case where formal rules are changed but informal rules have not changed, non-compliant behaviours proliferate and can result in the formation of underground economies (Feige, 1997, p. 22). Even though in Latin America women enjoy de jure equal rights, in most countries there are still significant gendered gaps for access to education, finance and internet use, as well as few role models of women as successful entrepreneurs and innovators. These conditions combined limit women's entrepreneurial and innovative activities.

Informal institutions can also influence the 'stereotype threat'; that is, women are expected to be less able than men to perform a particular function (such as be a leader in politics or business, or be successful in scientific careers). Consequently, they will likely not perform as well as men because they lack a sense of self-efficacy or they will be less likely to develop aspirations for these roles. Thus, the social norm will be further confirmed and sustained, which can explain how norms can persist even without any legitimate foundation (World Bank, 2012, p. 173).

The types of innovations by women have been directly affected by the gendered constraints in the institutional environment worldwide that continues to limit women's access to fields and sectors deemed of 'high status' such as engineering, science and technology. As a result, women's innovations tend to occur in 'lower-status' realms related to women's care taking, home responsibilities and fashion. Innovations such as liquid paper (Bette Nesmith Graham), windshield wipers (Mary Anderson), square-bottomed paper bags (Margaret Knight) or, even more recently, Spanx (Sara Blakely) are trivialized because they are not considered 'high-tech', 'scientific' or 'innovative enough'. But even when women innovate in 'higher-status' fields, such as the creation of bulletproof material Kevlar by Stephanie Knight, their names are less celebrated and are quickly forgotten.

However, women entrepreneurs are not simply passive recipients of the institutional environment; rather, they can also contribute to institutional change. In other words, entrepreneurial behaviour can trigger institutional change, just as the institutional environment can impact behaviour (Welter and Smallbone, 2011, p. 114). By advocating the removal of gendered institutional barriers for women, successful women entrepreneurs such as those highlighted in this chapter can act as catalysts for institutional reform that supports women entrepreneurs and innovators.

In the following section, we explore some of the specific institutional impediments faced by innovative women entrepreneurs identified in our three case studies, such as gendered attitudes, access to finance and access to support and networks, as well as overall institutional impediments such as access to global markets and bureaucratic barriers.

## INSTITUTIONAL IMPEDIMENTS TO INNOVATION

### Gendered Attitudes

In a number of ways, Maria Claudia's personal entrepreneurship story is typical of that of many female entrepreneurs. Like Maria Claudia, female entrepreneurs often start their own businesses after coming up against the glass ceiling in their workplaces. This form of discrimination acts as an organizational push for women to start their own businesses (Hisrich and Brush, 1986). Initially elated about her new job, Maria Claudia soon noticed that she was treated differently from her male colleagues: she worked more hours than most of her male colleagues but earned the lowest salary in her division. Maria Claudia stuck it out for three years, but the situation did not improve. In 2003, she quit her job and began her own business in a female-dominated sector. What often is overlooked in cases such as Maria Claudia's is the tremendous loss of human capital and innovative potential that occurs when women exit male-dominated industries after experiencing on-the-job discrimination and instead abandon their skills developed and expertise gained to start their businesses in female-dominated sectors. This experience created the conditions for Maria Claudia to decide to start her own business. Her understanding of the Bolivian market, her desire to help local craftswomen and her international experience contributed to her focus on new markets for apparel and textiles.

Similarly, Ingerecuperar is not a purely female business but was started by Carolina Guerra and two of her male colleagues. It is the first and only company in Colombia to obtain an environmental licence. An environmentally focused business is more common among female than male entrepreneurs. Ingerecuperar's operations are in a male-dominated sector, one that is characterized by informality of operations. Initially, 'as a woman', Carolina says she was 'viewed as weak and vulnerable' and that she had to make additional effort in order to prove her credibility. Her male partners did not encounter this type of constraint. This indicates that women innovating in male-dominated industries such as engineering often need to redirect their efforts from their innovations to establishing credibility amongst male clients and peers.

**Access to Capital**

It is not uncommon for innovative start-ups to be self-financed, and all three cases highlighted here were self-financed. However, self-financing comes with hidden costs. Many women entrepreneurs self-finance the growth of their businesses, but this is one of the core issues that is likely to hinder growth (IFC, 2011, p. 39). Undercapitalization can lead to slow growth and, in many cases, result in business stunting or failure. Furthermore, many innovations are never pursued by women who do not have the personal circumstances, personal savings or support from an entrepreneurial team that would allow them to self-finance their initial business operations. For the three women in our case studies, boot-strapping and lack of external financing played a role in their business development.

In fact, Beleza Natural was not even able to open a bank account, and its initial start-up capital came from the sale of Leila's co-founder's

Volkswagen Beetle. What is striking is the fact that Beleza Natural was self-financed from its humble beginnings and throughout its phenomenal growth. This changed in 2013, when GP Investments bought one-third of Beleza Natural for approximately US$32 million. With this funding, Beleza Natural expects exponential growth by increasing the total number of salons to 120 over four years and $451 million in sales by 2018.[18] After enjoying tremendous success in Brazil's domestic market, Beleza Natural is also planning to expand internationally into the US market.

At Colombia-based Ingerecuperar, start-up capital totalled US$50 000 that was invested by Carolina and her two co-founders. These funds were enough to pay for the purchase of the necessary machinery and other costs associated with recycling aluminium dross, but for the first two years of operations the three founders were not able to pay themselves a salary. Carolina had to borrow her portion of the start-up capital from her parents and move back in with her parents in order to survive the first two lean years of operations. After two years, their revenue expanded enough for them to be able to pay themselves a salary, and their market visibility also increased, which allowed them to receive bank loans and angel financing.

Maria Claudia worked as a financial economic analyst for an engineering firm before starting her business. She received a good salary at her job and, upon quitting, was able to start her business solely using her personal savings. She was also able to set up a bank account. However, Maria Claudia describes how, when she went to the bank on a business-related matter, she would be designated the worst, least experienced clerks to handle her banking needs. As she was a woman, the bank did not view her as a 'legitimate entrepreneur'.

**Access to Networks**

Networking and networks in terms of both personal connections and business-related networks proved important for the entrepreneurs in our case studies. Personal networks were critical sources of support to boost morale during innovative business development, while business-related networks were important especially as a means to overcome limited resources. Cultivating client networks was a strategy used by some of our entrepreneurs to spur business growth, develop new products and services, and gain loyalty and trust.

Lack of a supportive business-related network had the greatest effect on Maria Claudia, most likely since she was a solo female entrepreneur, whereas Leila and Carolina were part of mixed-gender entrepreneurial teams. Maria Claudia recounts how, in 2005, only two years after starting

Origenes Bolivia, she was ready to close her business. As one of the few college-educated, opportunity-driven, high-impact solo female entrepreneurs in Bolivia, she felt lonely, helpless and frustrated. Most importantly, she had no peers who shared similar experiences and who could give her support. Luckily, the NGO Vital Voices,[19] which focuses on promoting women's economic empowerment, invited Maria Claudia to take part in the Fortune/US Department of State/Vital Voices mentoring programme.[20] There she learned the importance of women building bridges for other women to overcome existing gendered barriers. Most importantly, by sharing her experiences with the other participants, she realized that running a business is not always easy and that every entrepreneur faces her own set of difficulties. Maria Claudia returned to Bolivia full of inspiration to continue and grow Origenes Bolivia.

**Access to Markets and Globalization**

The ability to expand operations beyond domestic borders is a key factor for success for most high-impact entrepreneurs. An important issue raised in two of the case studies was the important role of market openness through free trade agreements for promoting exports to the US market. Maria Claudia identified exporting as her main strategy for generating a sustainable income. Logically, given its proximity and market size, Maria Claudia initially oriented Origenes Bolivia's exports to the US market. She actively sought US buyers by attending the largest US trade show in Las Vegas (the annual Magic fashion show). There, she was able to build a network of 50 US-based boutiques that purchased her merchandise. At the same time, she expanded Origenes Bolivia's exports to Canada, Europe, Japan, Korea and Mexico. Unfortunately, Origenes Bolivia's further expansion in the US market was prematurely curtailed in 2011 when the Bolivian government rejected an extension of the free trade agreement with the US. Paying duties on exports to the US essentially 'closed the door' to further Origenes Bolivia's US-destined exports. As a result, Origenes Bolivia had to reorient its business strategy to focus on expanding exports to Europe as well as domestic sales through its two boutique shops.

Ingerecuperar is developing its export strategy based on Colombia's free trade agreements with the US and South Korea. They believe both markets will provide opportunities to export the aluminium dross recycled building materials they produce, which are suitable for LEED[21]-certified pre-fab construction projects. Given the large domestic market in Brazil, Beleza Natural initially focused on domestic expansion, but globalization of its operations is the next logical step. As Leila Velez states, 'Our goal is to become the global reference in this segment, and to bring this concept to communities all over the world where there are a lot of people with kinky hair who face similar challenges.'[22]

**Bureaucracy as a Barrier to Innovation**

In all three countries, the female entrepreneurs experienced impediments, barriers and interference from 'the bureaucracy', who often act as the de facto 'gatekeepers' for innovative businesses. Leila feels there is tremendous potential and opportunity in Brazil, especially given it is a large market and booming economy. However, the Brazilian bureaucracy can be overwhelming. Since local officials did not believe that Beleza Natural's innovative hair treatment targeting 'bottom of the pyramid' clients would be profitable, Beleza Natural had to wait an entire year before they were given the green light to open their cosmetics factory.[23]

Ingerecuperar had to invest heavily in raising environmental awareness with Colombia's environmental authorities. Even though Colombia passed a law outlining the acceptable procedures for disposing of hazardous waste, Carolina found that it took a lot of effort on her part to educate the environmental authority specifically on the issues regarding hazardous wastes and recycling. In fact, the better part of Carolina's time and effort in the first two years of operations was spent raising awareness about environmental issues with the local Colombian environmental authority.

## INTERNATIONAL AWARDS AND TRAINING BOOST VISIBILITY

International awards and programmes played a pivotal role in increasing the credibility and visibility of successful entrepreneurs while providing broader benefits to their companies in terms of recognition as well as increasing their customer base. All three of our female entrepreneurs were recipients of international awards or training.

Maria Claudia was invited to participate in the Fortune/US Department of State/Vital Voices mentoring programme in 2005. As discussed above, this played a critical role in Maria Claudia's decision to continue in her business. Lack of support, and financial and emotional hardship brought Maria Claudia to the brink of closing her business only two years after starting it. The camaraderie, recognition, role models, mentorship and support she received by attending the Fortune/US Department of State/ Vital Voices mentoring programme inspired her not only to continue her

business but to initiate a mentorship training programme initially targeting female entrepreneurs in Bolivia.

Leila received a number of awards and recognition for her entrepreneurial pursuits, including being named Ernst & Young's Entrepreneur
of the Year in 2006 and receiving the High-Impact Female Entrepreneur
of the Year 2011 award from Veuve Clicquot.[24] These help Beleza
Natural gain credibility, recognition, and exposure to international networks as well as funders, so in 2005 Leila and her partners asked
Endeavor Global Inc.[25] for assistance. After they joined Endeavor's
entrepreneurship programme, Beleza Natural's revenues grew by 914 per
cent, and employment increased by 214.[26]

A large credibility boost came to Carolina when she was awarded
Cartier's Women's Initiative Award in 2011. This award helped increase
Carolina's credibility as a female entrepreneur working in a predominantly male-dominated sector. It attracted additional customers and
was followed by further recognition in Colombia of Carolina and her
business.

## DISCUSSION AND CONCLUSIONS: OVERCOMING GENDERED HURDLES TO INNOVATION

In this chapter, we explored the impact of gendered institutions on
innovation by women. Utilizing an institutional perspective, three case
studies from Latin America were profiled in order to uncover the
characteristics and gendered impediments faced by successful and innovative female entrepreneurs in Latin America. Although the gendered
institutional environment can negatively impact women from starting or
scaling a business, successful women entrepreneurs can also serve as
catalysts for institutional reform.

Barriers exist for both male and female entrepreneurs and innovators.
In this chapter, we identify some of the specific gendered impediments
that lead to institutional failure, creating further barriers for female
innovators. One such barrier presented is loneliness and lack of exposure
to peers or a supportive environment. This may initially seem like a
trivial issue, but as Maria Claudia's case shows it can stunt business
development and may deter innovative activities from taking place.
Another barrier illustrated by Carolina's case is that women innovators
who move beyond female-dominated sectors tend to need to allocate
increased time and effort to establish credibility amongst their male
peers. In addition, lack of credibility limits access to outside financing,
which can inadvertently exclude women who do not have personal

wealth or can bootstrap the first several years of their business (as Carolina did).

Maria Claudia, a well-educated solo female entrepreneur from Bolivia, exemplifies how gender discrimination in the workforce can act as a catalyst for a woman to start her own business. Working as a financial analyst, Maria Claudia hit the glass ceiling in the macho culture of the oil industry and quit. She started her own business using her own savings. She chose to start her business in a female-dominated sector (the retail trade). She almost closed her business through lack of a supportive environment. These are examples of gendered barriers faced by women introducing innovation. Though different, Leila and Carolina encountered similar barriers. Leila Velez and her three co-founders (two of whom were male) needed to bootstrap their business for many years before they were able to gain access to outside financing. What was striking is that, in all three cases, international recognition played a critical role in increasing the female innovator entrepreneur's visibility, credibility and ultimately access to resources domestically. In all three cases, there was very limited attention paid to these women entrepreneurs' achievements within their respective countries. In the end, international recognition served as a catalyst for domestic recognition.

This chapter illustrates that women entrepreneurs are making significant contributions to their countries' economies through their innovative activities. However, in Latin America, international organizations play a vital role in increasing the attention to and visibility of innovative women entrepreneurs, which in turn has led to domestic recognition and access to resources. Developing high-profile domestic awards programmes for innovative women entrepreneurs in Latin American countries could facilitate the increase of women who not only choose to become entrepreneurs but also have access to the resources needed to scale their businesses and unleash their innovative contributions.[27]

## NOTES

1. This study is based on quantitative and qualitative data collected by online surveys, face-to-face interviews and focus groups conducted across nine countries in Latin America and the Caribbean (Argentina, Brazil, Chile, Colombia, Costa Rica, Jamaica, Mexico, Peru and Uruguay).
2. Defined as 'Total Early Phase Entrepreneurial Activity' by the Global Entrepreneurship Monitor (GEM), and measured as the percentage of the 18- to 64-year-old population who are either nascent entrepreneurs or owner-managers of a new business (no more than 42 months old).

3.  TEA measures the percentage of the population of 18–64 years who are either nascent entrepreneurs or owner-managers of a new business (no more than 42 months old) (www.gemconsortium.org).
4.  Based on ILO data (2004–2010 data) sourced from Aidis et al. (2013).
5.  Endeavor Global (2012).
6.  Daniel (2011).
7.  Ruvolo (2011).
8.  Milken Institute (2012).
9.  According to Drucker, there are seven main sources of innovation: the unexpected; incongruities; process needs; industry and market structure; demographics; changes in perception; and new knowledge (Drucker, 1985).
10. Ruvolo (2011).
11. The bottom of the pyramid (BOP) is an economic term referring to the largest but poorest socio-economic group in the world, constituting more than 2.5 billion people who live on less than $2.50 a day. C.K. Prahalad and S.L. Hart's book *The Fortune at the Bottom of the Pyramid* (2005) illustrated the idea of targeting BOP clients as a viable business strategy.
12. Margulies (2012).
13. Traditionally, hazardous by-products produced during various industrial operations were simply dumped in landfills. However, this poses numerous environmental dangers, as well as risks for human health and welfare. To minimize environmental damage, increasingly national governments are introducing stricter regulations for the disposal of hazardous wastes. This was the case in Colombia in the mid- and late 2000s, when the government introduced new restrictions for the disposal of aluminium dross, a hazardous by-product of aluminium smelting.
14. In fact, she feels that being an entrepreneur is one of the most difficult jobs she has had in her life (*Nueva Empresa*, 2007).
15. Women who are blocked from 'climbing the corporate ladder' encounter the 'glass ceiling', which can act as an organizational push factor that can motivate women to leave their corporate positions to become entrepreneurs (Hisrich and Brush, 1986).
16. Calculations based on the Women, Business and the Law database, World Bank World Development Indicators database and World Bank Enterprise Surveys, based on 94 economies for which data are available (World Bank, 2013).
17. Estimates based on data sourced from the Global Entrepreneurship Monitor and United Nations Population Division for 2010–2012 (Aidis et al., 2015, p. 7). For a detailed discussion of the methodology, please refer to the methodology discussion section for the Global Women Entrepreneur Leaders Scorecard available on www.dell.com/gwelscorecard.
18. Sciaudone (2014).
19. Vital Voices is a US-based NGO started in 1997 that focuses its activities for women in three main areas: human rights, public and political leadership, and economic empowerment. It boasts an international staff and team of over 1000 partners, pro bono experts and leaders, including senior government, corporate and NGO executives, who have trained and mentored more than 12 000 emerging women leaders from over 144 countries in Africa, Asia, Eurasia, Latin America and the Caribbean, and the Middle East. These women have returned home to train and mentor more than 500 000 additional women and girls in their communities (http://www.vitalvoices.com).
20. The International Women Leaders Mentoring Partnership brings young business-women from around the world to intern with some of the most powerful women. CEO Ann Moore and the US State Department, working with embassies around the world, nominate the interns. Vital Voices, an international non-profit organization

chaired by Melanne Verveer (formerly Hillary Clinton's chief of staff when she was first lady), helps administer the programme. In 2006, 17 women from 14 countries participated.

21. Leadership in Energy and Environmental Design (LEED) is an internationally recognized green building certification system.
22. Ruvolo (2011).
23. Milken Institute (2012).
24. Veuve Clicquot, a premium champagne house in France, created its annual Business Women Awards in 1972. The High-Impact Female Entrepreneur of the Year award is a more recent addition created in partnership with Endeavor and the Endeavor Entrepreneur Summit.
25. Endeavor is a non-profit organization headquartered in New York that promotes 'high-impact entrepreneurship' in emerging markets. Endeavor founder and CEO Linda Rottenberg describes Endeavor as 'venture capital without the capital', since Endeavor primarily focuses on providing training, mentoring and support from a network of business leaders, finance and organizational experts, and successful entrepreneurs (Margulies, 2012).
26. Endeavor Global (2012).
27. WeGROW is a recent regional initiative launched by the Inter-American Development Bank to support growth-oriented women entrepreneurs in Latin America (http://www.fomin.org/en-us/home/knowledge/developmentdata/wegrow.aspx).

# REFERENCES

Aidis, R. (2006), *Laws and Customs: Entrepreneurship, Institutions and Gender during Economic Transition*, SSEES Occasional Book Series, London: University College London, School of Slavonic and East European Studies.

Aidis, R. (2016), 'Business and occupational crowding: Implications for female entrepreneurship development and success', in M.C. Diaz Garcia (ed.), *Women Entrepreneurship in Global and Local Contexts*, forthcoming.

Aidis, R., F. Welter, D. Smallbone and N. Isakova (2007), 'Female entrepreneurship in transition economies: The case of Lithuania and Ukraine', *Feminist Economics*, **13** (2), 351–377.

Aidis, R., J. Weeks, L. Szerb, Z. Acs and A. Lloyd (2013), 'The 2013 Gender-GEDI Index: Executive report', accessed at www.dell.com/dwen.

Aidis, R., J. Weeks, L. Szerb, Z. Acs and A. Lloyd (2014), 'The 2014 Gender-GEDI Index: Executive report', accessed at www.dell.com/dwen.

Aidis, R., J. Weeks and K. Anacker (2015), 'The Global Women Entrepreneur Leaders Scorecard 2015: From awareness to action', Report, ACG Inc.

Baughn, C., B. Chu and K. Neupert (2006), 'The normative context for women's participation in entrepreneurship: A multicountry study', *Entrepreneurship Theory and Practice*, **30** (5), 687–708.

Bruin, A. de, C. Brush and F. Welter (2007), 'Advancing a framework for coherent research on women's entrepreneurship', *Entrepreneurship Theory and Practice*, **31** (3), 323–339.

Daniel, J. (2011), 'Endeavor Entrepreneurs share success stories at Dell Women's Entrepreneur Network Event', accessed at http://www.endeavor.org/blog/dell-womens-entrepreneur-network-2011.

DiMaggio, P. and W. Powell (1983), 'The iron cage revisited: Institutional isomorphism and collective rationality in organizational fields', *American Sociological Review*, **47**, 147–160.

Drucker, P. (1985), *Innovation and Entrepreneurship: Practice and Principles*, New York: Harper & Row.

Endeavor Global (2012), 'Our entrepreneurs: Leila Velez', accessed at http://www. endeavor.org/entrepreneurs/leila-velez/97.

Feige, E. (1997), 'Underground activity and institutional change: Productive, protective and predatory behavior in transition economies', in C. Tilly, J. Nelson and L. Walker (eds), *Transforming Communist Political Economies*, Washington, DC: National Academy Press, pp. 21–34.

GEM (Global Entrepreneurship Monitor) (2012), 'Women entrepreneurs report', accessed at www.gemconsortium.org.

Gupta, V.N. and N. Levenburg (2010), 'A thematic analysis of cultural variations in family businesses: The CASE project', *Family Business Review*, **23** (2), 155–169.

Hisrich, R. and D. Brush (1986), 'Women and minority entrepreneurs: A comparative analysis', in J. Hornaday, E. Shills, J. Timmons and K. Vesper (eds), *Frontiers of Entrepreneurship Research*, Dordrecht, Netherlands: Kluwer, pp. 566–587.

IFC (International Finance Corporation) (2011), 'Strengthening access to finance for women-owned SMEs in developing countries', accessed at http://www.ifc.org/wps/wcm/connect/a4774a004a3f66539f0f9f8969adcc27/G20_Women_Report.pdf?MOD=AJPERES.

Inter-American Development Bank (2012), 'WEGrow: Unlocking the growth potential of women in Latin America and the Caribbean', Ernst & Young, accessed at http://idbdocs.iadb.org/wsdocs/getDocument.aspx?DOCNUM=38671934.

Jennings, J. and C. Brush (2013), 'Research on women entrepreneurs: Challenges to (and from) the broader entrepreneurship literature?', *Academy of Management Annals*, **7** (1), 663–715.

Margulies, P. (2012), 'Linda Rottenberg's high impact endeavor', *Strategy and Business*, **66**, Spring, accessed at http://www.strategy-business.com/article/12106?gko=8b1a9.

Milken Institute (2012), Panel video: Game changing entrepreneurs, accessed 30 April 2012 at http://www.milkeninstitute.org/events/gcprogram.taf?function=detail&eventid=gc12&EvID=3420.

North, D. (1990), *Institutions, Institutional Change and Economic Performance*, Cambridge, UK: Cambridge University Press.

*Nueva Empresa* (2007), 'Origenes: Nuestra jefe es el consumidor final', *Nueva Empresa*, 3 December, p. 3.

Prahalad, C.K. and S.L. Hart (2005), *The Fortune at the Bottom of the Pyramid*, Upper Saddle River, NJ: Prentice Hall.

Robb, A. (2014), 'Gender-gaps still a big issue for startups', CBS Commentary, accessed at http://www.cnbc.com/2014/11/19/.

Ruvolo, J. (2011), 'Bye Brazilian blowouts: The next big Brazilian hair trend is Beleza Natural', *Forbeswoman*, 23 January, accessed at http://www.forbes.com/sites/julieruvolo/2012/01/23/bye-bye-brazilian-blowouts-the-next-big-brazilian-hair-trend-is-beleza-natural/.

Sciaudone, C. (2014), 'Gisele Bundchen not a model for Beleza Natural hair salon', *Bloomberg News*, 22 May, accessed at http://www.bloomberg.com/news/2014-05-22/gisele-bundchen-not-a-model-for-beleza-natural-hair-salon.html.

Welter, F. and D. Smallbone (2011), 'Institutional perspectives on entrepreneurial behavior in challenging environments', *Journal of Small Business Management*, **49** (1), 107–125.

World Bank (2012), *World Development Report 2012: Gender Equality and Development*, accessed at http://siteresources.worldbank.org/INTWDR2012/Resources/7778105-129969996858/7786210131593622006/Complete-Report.pdf.

World Bank (2013), *Women, Business and the Law Report 2014*, accessed at http://wbl.worldbank.org/reports.

# 5. Self-employed women's everyday innovations in East Africa

## Malin Tillmar

## INTRODUCTION

In public debate and among laypeople, it is commonly thought that innovations are made of metal (see Utbult, 2007), or are at least technological and product-driven (Blake and Hanson, 2005). As several chapters in this book point out, however, that is a misconception that has gendered consequences. To clarify what innovation is, I use the *Oxford Handbook of Innovation* definition: 'Invention is the first occurrence of an idea for a new product or process, while innovation is the first attempt to carry it out into practice' (Fagerberg et al., 2005, p. 4). This definition distinguishes between two requirements, both of which must be fulfilled for a specific change to be regarded as an innovation. The first require-ment is the first occurrence of an idea. The second requirement is that this idea is put into practice, in one way or another. It should be noted that the definition does not include connotations of whether the products are goods or services, nor in which sector, industry or organizational form they are carried out. However, most attention is given to product innovation in the form of goods. There is an obvious risk that this bias may cause the economy to miss out on the many advantages of innovation that we fail to even perceive, let alone encourage and support.

In addition, innovation research has traditionally focused on the manufacturing sectors, paying only limited attention to innovations and innovativeness in other private (see Barras, 1986; Gallouj and Weinstein, 1997; Miles, 2005) and public (Earl, 2002; Mulgan, 2007; Potts and Kastelle, 2010; Windrum and Koch, 2008) sectors, for example in services. Service innovations and organizational innovations are not commonly included in mainstream innovation surveys (see the European CIS, and also the Canadian innovation survey, SIBS, and its US equivalent, BROS). A consequence of this focus on the manufacturing sectors is that it makes men appear to be more innovative than women (Ljunggren et al., 2010). The gender of the innovator in itself affects who is perceived and recognized as innovative (Nyberg, 2009). Nyberg holds that women's innovations are made invisible as a result of the male gender labelling of innovation as a concept, and its links to technology. Amble (2010), Kvidal and Ljunggren (2012), Lindberg (2010) and Ljunggren et al. (2010) have drawn similar conclusions. The emerging research field of gender and innovation (see Alsos et al., 2013) is increasingly shedding light on the dimensions involved in the ongoing gendering of innovation along several dimensions: *gender labelling of the industry*; the *gender of the innovator*; and the *operationalization of the concept of innovation* (Nählinder et al., 2015). Actively seeking low-technology innovation and recognizing structural factors affecting innovation are important features in the research agenda called for by Alsos et al. (2013). The authors call not only for research treating gender as a variable (i.e. more studies on women innovators) but also for research focusing on the gendered process of innovations and the gendered discourse of innovation. By reporting from qualitative case studies of women's everyday innovations in low-tech sectors in a non-western context, this chapter sets out to follow that research agenda. The conclusions and implications carry significance from all three perspectives.

As argued by Nählinder et al. (2015), an inherent problem in the operationalization of the concept has been that the term 'innovation' has been used in questionnaires. As a result, innovative people who do not identify themselves as such or do not reflect upon their activities in those terms do not report innovations. The idea that an innovation is some radical shift, for example in technology, leads to innovations being under-reported (ibid.). A more inclusive concept is 'everyday innovations' (Farmer and Butte, 2014). Here, I use the term to highlight that innovations can also be smaller changes that take place on an everyday basis, in order to handle everyday business life.

Mainstream views on innovation have been challenged not only by increased gender awareness, but also by the changing global conditions in terms of competitiveness and the rise of emerging markets. Some countries, such as India and China, are already something more than sources of cheap labour, but the pace of this global rise is yet to be seen. The contextual influence on innovation has been recognized though the term 'frugal innovation', meaning simple products developed in and for contexts with more basic living conditions, or 'reverse innovation' (Govindarajan and Ramamurti, 2011), implying also the transfer of such innovation for exploitation in the more 'developed' western context. The literature that is emerging often focuses on strategies for western multinational corporations and still suffers from the above-discussed bias towards male-labelled product innovations, such as in the ICT or automobile industries (see Aschmoneit and Janevska, 2013).

One of the emerging markets which has rocketed to attention in the last few years is the African market (see for example the relevant issues of *The Economist* and *Time Magazine*, 2011, 2012; Bjerström, 2013; Rylander, 2014). The Afro-pessimism which dominated the 1980s and 1990s has turned into an optimism, although with caution. On average, economic growth in Africa in 2014 was expected to be above 5 per cent (Rylander, 2014). The middle class is growing, democratic development is positive in most countries, the Asian influence is growing, and world relationships are hence changing. Yet there are reasons for caution regarding the economic development on global, continental and national levels. For example, owing to corruption, distrust in government, a low tax basis and unemployment, considerable faith is placed in the private sector and in SMEs. As in many corners of the world, women's entrepreneurship is expected to solve multiple problems, such as unemployment, economic growth and gender equality (see Ellis et al., 2007a, 2007b).

Thus, from an empirical standpoint too, the situation merits in-depth studies of women entrepreneurs and their innovations in Sub-Saharan Africa. This chapter reports from the three largest countries in the East African Community (EAC): Kenya, Tanzania and Uganda. The EAC, like the EU, has both political and economic goals. The cooperation currently includes a customs union and a common market, while reintroducing a common currency is under political debate. On average, the GDP per capita in the region is US$727, with Kenya taking the lead (East African Community, 2013). Economic growth is, however, faster in Tanzania. Conditions differ greatly between rural and urban contexts and based on the level of education and class. This chapter reports from a broad interview study of middle-class SME owners in urban (capital city) settings.

Empirical studies of the everyday situation and the innovativeness of female entrepreneurs in the emerging markets of East Africa is still lacking. It is my contention that such studies are needed both to better support the development of such markets and to better understand the phenomenon of innovation, and how it is gendered and contextually dependent.

In this chapter, I therefore argue that mainstream perspectives on innovation are not only gender-biased, in several dimensions, but also context-biased and ethnocentric. The aim is to shed light on the innovativity that is exercised, even required, by women SME owners in emerging economies simply to sustain the livelihood of themselves and their families. In the process, the aim is to shed light on the context dependence of how innovations occur and what is in fact innovative.

## METHODOLOGY

This chapter reports from interviews conducted for a project regarding gender perspectives on SME cooperation and development. The project has gathered extensive interview data with female and male entrepreneurs, as well as NGO representatives, from Tanzania, Kenya and Uganda. Innovativeness in various dimensions has been striking among the interviews with the women entrepreneurs. In this chapter, I have chosen four cases that illustrate a variety of innovations.

This research has been inspired by an interactive research approach (Svensson and Aagaard Nielsen, 2006), and has been conducted in collaboration with the Tanzanian Chamber of Commerce, Industry and Agriculture (TCCIA) and the Canadian NGO Enablis, and in dialogue with local researchers. Since the research questions deal with sensitive and informal issues, a suitable research design is to build primarily on informal interviews and dialogues with entrepreneurs in combination with participant observation. The TCCIA and its partner organization Tanzania Women Chamber of Commerce (TWCC) in Tanzania, Enablis and Moi University in Kenya, and Makerere University Business School (MUBS) in Uganda have greatly facilitated access to informants or interviewees by providing me with access to their networks.

It is my contention that female-owned micro-businesses in the informal sector (Kinyanjui, 2008; Pedersen, 2001; Snyder, 2000) have been the focus of previous studies, but that less attention has been given to slightly more formalized micro-businesses which have employed only a few people. The border between the formal and the informal sector is not clear cut (Lindell, 2010), and to reach the primary target group of interviewees I searched for those who claimed to have registered their businesses and had around 2–15 employees. Still, the reader should be aware that the number of employees is a relative measure, and that there is also a question of formally and informally 'employed' (Lindell, 2010). Owing to the widespread practice of diversification, it was not possible to focus on one or a few industries. I took my point of departure in food-processing businesses, and extended the snow-ball method not only to the processing of natural products (cosmetics, fabric, batik and jewellery making), but also to retailing, computer services and consultancies. The interviewees in the project as a whole are spread along the class dimension, with the exception of the poorest so-called 'petty traders', who will not have any employees. When it comes to practical, and female-labelled, household work such as cleaning and cooking, it is common practice in most households to engage young 'house-girls' with less economic resources as assistants, in exchange for salary and/or some pocket money and food and shelter, depending on the economic situation. The cases selected for this chapter are centred in the growing educated lower middle class.

When conducting the interviews, I was in all three countries accompanied by local master's students who assisted me in booking the interviews and guiding me around the town. My ability to speak Kiswahili was a great advantage for two main reasons. First, being white creates a power distance to people in these contexts. Speaking the local language contributed greatly to reducing this distance and accessing richer information. Second, the loss of information which occurs through using an interpreter could be avoided. Twelve interviews were conducted with women entrepreneurs in Dar es Salaam, Tanzania, ten with people within the same category in Kampala, Uganda, and twelve in Nairobi and Eldoret, Kenya. In the descriptions in this chapter, the interviewees have been given fictive names. In addition to interviews with entrepreneurs, representatives from a number of support organizations were interviewed: TCCIA, TWCC, Tanzania Women Lawyers Association (TAWLA), Small Industries Development Organization (SIDO) and Private Sector Development Fund (PSDF) in Tanzania and Uganda, Enablis in Tanzania and Kenya, representatives from the universities of Dar es Salaam, Moi, Nairobi and Makerere, and Uganda Women Entrepreneurs Association Limited (UWEAL). The interviews were conducted during field trips from March 2012 to April 2014. Representatives from TCCIA, Enablis, Moi University and Makerere University are key informants, who were interviewed continuously. As to the interaction with those active in the field, I conducted a half-day interactive follow-up workshop at TCCIA in February 2013, and at Enablis Tanzania I made a key-note speech in order to give and receive feedback after the empirical studies. The adequacy of the empirical findings was confirmed on both these occasions.

## VARIETIES OF INNOVATIONS BY EAST AFRICAN WOMEN

To illustrate the innovativeness that takes place, and that is at times even required, among self-employed women in East Africa, I will present four examples below. The cases illustrate the variety of innovations that exist.

First, a product innovation from Uganda is described, followed by a service innovation from the same country. Organizational, or process, innovations from Tanzania and Kenya then follow.

### Red Wine Kampala-style: Product Innovation for the Ugandan Market

Pamela is employed full time in a state institution in Uganda. She recently graduated with an MBA and runs three businesses. She has five children between 18 and 12 years old, and her husband is a public servant who is 'very busy, moving around a lot'. To supplement her incomes in order to cover school fees and improve the standard of living, she started a poultry business 12 years ago, breeding chickens and selling broilers and eggs. A few years later, she started growing mushrooms at the family *shamba* (small farmplot by a rural or semi-urban residence).

The business that brings in the most money is, however, the wine business, started in 2009. '*I don't have to work too much for this.*' Red wine is considered a high-status drink, and is often consumed at weddings and other functions. The wine is sold in big jugs and plastic containers. Pamela sells it to colleagues and contacts, whom she finds through her government employment. The wine business gives her more profit per month than her government salary. When asked about the conditions for growing grapes, and the production process, Pamela gives me a clever smile and laughs. '*No, no, I make it from pineapple.*' She buys large quantities of slightly overripe pineapple from specific suppliers at the larger markets, and colours it with hibiscus plants from her *shamba*.

Hibiscus plants are used in traditional medicine by the local medicine men. Making alcoholic beverages from different crops and plants is common practice around the globe, but this use of hibiscus plants to colour the wine is also seen as a new combination by the local entrepreneurship researchers at Makerere University. When there are no flowers available, Pamela burns sugar to get the red colour, but she says the taste is different. The product is very popular on the local market. It looks like red wine from grapes. It was only when tasting that I could see that this was another, quite different, product. Apparently, this new combination has found a local market.

Pamela collects orders for wine during a month, and then buys the pineapple, harvests the hibiscus and calls in her children for a full day of wine production, once a month. The profit is used for school and university fees for the children.

## Staying at Home and Providing Privacy: Service Innovation Caused by Gendered Restraint in Uganda

Fatma was a bank officer when her husband advised her to give up her job, since she did not give the family enough time. Instead, she went to work in her husband's engineering firm and was awarded an MBA at the university in 2006. Since then, she has been struggling with different micro-level projects alongside her work for the engineering firm. Her path has been lined with challenges related to internal cooperation, collaborators and market relations. Many women in Uganda are faced with the choice between their business and their marriage, Fatma explains. For her, the priority is clear:

> *You have to know exactly what you want. That is a challenge … For me, I know what I want. I want to be married; it's our tradition. I think if I get a business opportunity that really conflicts with my husband's interests, I wouldn't do it … because I know what makes me happy; I know what I want. So I'm really sitting down with him and explaining my business. We talk and we discuss. If he doesn't like it … I cannot do it … because in the culture here most men want you to be home; you should have less money than them. So you have to do it tactfully. Of course, I cannot do business he doesn't like.*

The boundary of Fatma's business life is thus set by what her husband agrees to. She is part of his engineering and construction business, but they do not always agree on strategic decisions. It is a very male-dominated sector and she feels *'a bit left out'*. Hence, she has started a trading business, with his permission. She trades in clothing and fabrics. Cultural taboos have, however, led to her husband not agreeing to Fatma travelling to stay overnight either abroad or within the country. When sending friends, family or others to buy goods for her, she has faced many challenges, including being cheated and receiving substandard products. Selling the goods has also posed a challenge. A shop in town would have been the best option, but her husband does not allow that. In his opinion, women trading in town are not 'good women' and are frowned upon or seen as looking for a man. For this reason, husband and wife agreed to sell via intermediaries who were friends of the husband. In this instance, trust-related problems occurred and money was lost.

All these obstacles have led Fatma to make the decision to go into trading in second-hand clothes. These are not substandard quality, and are delivered directly to Uganda via wholesalers. Normally, these clothes are then re-sold in chaotic marketplaces, where she is not allowed to go. Being a middle-class woman, Fatma has, however, made an analysis of how the growing middle class wants to look, that is, more and more

American or perhaps European. It is status to be able to say: 'I got this from my cousin in the US.' But it is definitely not status to be seen browsing around in the market for second-hand clothes. Fatma says: *'So I give them the comfort of my home.'* This way, her business can be home-based and hence in line with the organizational requirements set up by her husband. She currently has a solid clientele who call her regularly to hear if she has received a new delivery of clothes. The clients visit her house to use the fitting room and the discretion that her home provides.

### Single Woman on the Bus to the Bush: Organizational Innovation in a Tanzanian Context

Karen resigned from her full-time job in 2007 to realize her vision of organic poultry with a community development component. She had partnered with her sister-in-law, who was in finance. Karen entrusted her sister-in-law with her savings, which were used for registering the business and obtaining the required licences and permits. Unfortunately, the cooperation between the two partners broke down. Karen explained that her sister-in-law was not interested in the organic or the development parts of her project, which were the basis for Karen's commitment. So her sister-in-law pulled out, leaving Karen unemployed with no funds. While searching for a new interested partner, who could also contribute funding, Karen had to take on consulting work to support herself and her children. The consequences on her life were profound: *'So I worked long hours. And that cost me my marriage, of course. My husband did not want to support me.'*

The story of how Karen eventually found a new business partner, the legal documents needed and access to land is a long one. The strategy was to let go and move on, avoiding listening to discouraging advice. What has been particularly challenging for Karen has been breaking the gender barriers in her society. She explains:

> *Most people, when I talk to them about my project, they think that this is a male project, and that sometimes, you know, it makes me feel bad because they think that I am crazy ... And even the financiers, they would challenge you because you are a woman. How can you run a business like that?*

In the Tanzanian context, large-scale poultry is a male-gender-labelled business. It is fairly profitable. Karen argues that you normally need good contacts in the upper echelons of decision-making boards to have access to the industry. She has had a lot of trouble finding the information needed, and she argues that such information travels in male networks.

Furthermore, a poultry farm requires a lot of technical equipment, for hatching, milling and processing as well as quality control. Access to land is one of the biggest problems for women in East Africa. Karen has land now, but the challenges are not over: *'But the land is still a challenge because it does not have water. So I have to dig boreholes. You know, it's all male issues. And when they look at me they say, "Oh, you're too soft. How can you go on living in the village?"'*

In the Tanzanian context, what Karen did was something new. She went to live and work in the bush. And she did it alone, as a single woman, despite massive resistance. Normally, poultry farming is organized differently, in groups of males. Karen wanted to empower rural women and their community through her project. But this also meant that she had to board the bus by herself and go to the village. She narrates this very clearly in her own words:

> *And this is organic. You cannot have an organic farm in an urban area, so they would ask you: 'How would you manage to go on living in the bush as a woman?' So, it's like ... People think that it's only males who can manage to do that, and I try to prove them wrong. The very first time I went there, I boarded the bus and I went there on my own. And I managed to convince the village team and ... you know, so that I could purchase land from them, and I did. I purchased about 500 acres of land.*

To take on the tasks Karen does, the way she does it, as a woman, is clearly something new in the context. As we will come back to, it is hence an example of how it is innovative to challenge gendered organizing and division of labour.

## Moving Forward with and around the Husband: Organizational Innovation in Kenyan Family Culture

Two years ago, Laila was the Kenya marketing manager for a large multinational corporation. Domestic responsibilities made the long working hours and many days away from her young family impossible to handle, so she resigned from her job and started her own consultancy firm. Being used to a high tempo in the corporate world, she describes the first year as a struggle against under-stimulation and frustration coupled with the joys and relief of having time for her children, herself and the household. Her company became the solution to the equation. Because of her ambitions, it needed to be a limited company, which, according to Kenyan law requires more than one shareholder. Laila's husband and brother-in-law signed the papers, but did not put in any funds or effort at all. She says:

> *He ignored it. I think even the signing of that paper for me to register was to humour me, like to oblige, so the first year was really difficult because at that time I was running everything. I was the consultant. I was the office messenger. I was the communications specialist. I was the mother. All those things. And then I had come from my high-energy corporate world.*

To manage her situation, she decided to get a 'real' business partner as well, a woman. Now she is sharing an office and facilities with this woman, and they are co-consulting for each other's businesses. This was a necessary organizational solution because of her household responsibilities. Laila says:

> *There is the key scenario where husbands are fathers ... by name, to pay school fees and to be seen, but beyond that the woman takes on the responsibility of bringing up the children, so, if you are running such a ship and you have another ship called the business, one is bound to sink if you have to pay full attention to the other. That's why for women the support system is really important. You need a support system of people you can call, people you can work with, people that can pick up the ball if it falls on the business side as you are holding the ball on the family side.*

For cultural reasons, many East African women are not allowed to travel and stay outside the home overnight. Laila thinks it depends on the level of education and exposure and on the relationship as such. Her husband has not objected explicitly to her business trips. There is a risk that he might, but Laila is careful not to bring up the issue:

> *Let's say there is always the unspoken. That is resentment, or unexplained anger, but I can take that, as we are relating as grown-ups. If we have an issue we will discuss and solve it, so if he hasn't mentioned it I will assume there is no issue ... If I open up the can and say 'Oh, I think there is an issue. Can we talk about it?' then chances are he will say 'I am not OK with you going.' Then what will I do, because I have to go, I have committed to my client, but I cannot go if my husband says 'Don't go.' So it is best not to say.*

Still, she has to say when she will be travelling in good time, and make sure that all the necessary arrangements are made around the household and the children. She notifies the home help, gives her extra money and a bigger budget, and notifies her friends that she will be away and that the home help will call them if there is any problem. She prepares her children in every way possible, including explaining which of her friends will come and help them if there should be any problem while she is away. Laila explains that for this reason she is a member of many women's groups (*chamas*), which include both financial 'merry-go-round' arrangements and social support.

*So for me this is social networking. I have women friends that I'm close to, and most often they are the ones I call when I am going away for business, and tell them 'Hey, how is your week next week? I am away. Check home.' My children know them. They have developed a trust-based relationship. If they are sick, it wouldn't be like they are strangers. It would be 'Aunty Becky will come and Aunty Becky is taking you to the hospital.'*

However, within these groups people are on different levels. For her business, Laila also needs networks where she can receive, for example, financial and legal advice. Such networks are not as easy for women to access spontaneously. Laila is seeking support from an international NGO for such matters. That way, she has also succeeded in finding enough networks and access to advice for such matters. Her major problem has been having the support system in place to be able to organize her dual responsibilities. Now, towards the end of her third year as an SME owner, things are falling into place. Her bank account is starting to look good. Her upcoming challenge is that her husband, contrary to the position at the beginning, is starting to show an interest not only in the business but also in the bank account. She is happy that she previously made sure his shares in the company are the minimum that was required.

Laila's case shows how much innovative organizing in everyday life is required even to enable women's entrepreneurship and SME ownership in these contexts.

## DISCUSSION

The cases narrated illustrate not only the gendering but also the context-specificity of what kinds of innovations are needed, what kinds of innovation find a market, and what an innovation actually is. In this section, I will discuss such issues based on the cases.

Making red wine from pineapple and hibiscus flowers certainly seems innovative from a western perspective. It is almost a textbook case of a new combination, à la Schumpeter. Because we are used to viewing tangible goods as innovations, the example is fairly straightforward. To my knowledge and that of my local colleagues, this kind of red wine is new not only from the western perspective but also in the local context, yet the combination is perhaps more surprising to a westerner. In East Africa, alcohol is often produced locally in different forms from different crops. The characteristic of the local market in East Africa, which is more frequently beer-drinking, with wine being rarer and signalling status, is, however, the specific condition which gave the innovation a segment of the market.

Home-based sales of second-hand clothes to the middle class could be regarded as both a service innovation and a process innovation. To our knowledge, the idea and the exploitation of it is novel. And it works well. At the same time, it is a process innovation which solves Fatma's problem of wanting to engage in high-profit trading while keeping within the limits set by her husband. The case clearly shows an innovation which is invisible (see Nählinder et al., 2015; Nyberg, 2009). In fact, the very business idea, from both service and organizational innovation perspectives, is that it is supposed to be invisible! Nevertheless, it is very innovative, and deserves to be recognized as such.

In Karen's organic poultry farming, there are process innovations in the business model which build on the existing entrepreneurship and organic thinking among rural women. Still, what was considered most innovative in the local context was the new combination of 1) a single woman, 2) a title deed for rural land, 3) travelling alone to the rural areas and 4) conducting male-labelled work. Crossing the gender boundaries was thus the new idea, which in itself can be seen as organizational innovation (Blake and Hanson, 2005).

The fourth case, Laila's multiple organizational processes to manage both a family and a high-profile business, illustrates how innovative strategies in everyday life are required for women to handle the patriarchy in which they are embedded. Laila's ideas, and their realization, seem newer to western eyes than they probably would to East African eyes. Doing business in cooperation, and engaging the social network to be able to do so, is a common occurrence. In Laila's case, however, it is used more strategically for business purposes, and it is unusually well articulated. As a phenomenon, however, a similar organizational innovation is a prerequisite for women's entrepreneurship in many parts of the world, except perhaps in countries such as the Scandinavian ones, where high-quality, low-cost public childcare is readily available. Still, I argue that these are organizational innovations important for economic and social development, and hence requiring due attention.

Above, I noted that crossing the gender boundaries is in itself an innovation. Since gender boundaries differ between countries (as well as between tribes and other ethnic groups), what may or may not be regarded as an innovation is thus highly context-dependent (see Alsos et al., 2013). Karen's travelling to the villages, for example, is seen as more innovative through an East African cultural lens than through a western, while Laila's organizing seems more innovative to our western eyes than perhaps to East African eyes.

# CONCLUSIONS

Here, I argue that recognizing the creativity of women who, like Pamela, Karen, Fatma and Laila, invent new products, services or processes and implement them in their organizations is vital. That is not only from a feminist perspective, that is, for reasons of visibility and recognition of the contribution to the economy and society of women in an emerging market such as the East African, but also for our theoretical and common understanding of what innovation is. This understanding has long been biased towards technology and industry production, hence overlooking mundane innovativeness in everyday lives, service sectors and many women's innovations. It is thus vital to broaden the discourse on innovation (see Alsos et al., 2013; Doloreaux and Parto, 2005; Pettersson and Lindberg, 2013). On a practical level, when supporting innovations through various measures globally, nationally, regionally and locally, we should ask ourselves if we should ignore everyday innovations of the narrated kind. Perhaps that is so (if we assume that we could live without them, or that they will continue happening anyway), but I argue that such a political decision should in that case be an informed one, and not based on lack of knowledge or unconscious gender-blindness.

To date, research on innovation and gender has tended to focus on western contexts. As stated in the introduction, there have been studies on frugal and reverse innovation, for example in technology-intensive sectors, which recognize the role of emerging markets and developing countries. However, these have not had a focus on gender as a variable, nor the gendering process, nor the discourse perspective (see Alsos et al., 2013).

With these four selected cases I have wished to illustrate the innovative capacity and innovative behaviour existing among East African women, but also, by taking a gender perspective (Brush et al., 2009; West and Zimmerman, 1987), to highlight that this innovation is made invisible in the simultaneous construction of gender and innovation. In the innovation processes described, gender is constructed and re-constructed (see Brush et al., 2009). As an example, the gendered consequences for Fatma's business are re-produced by her entrepreneurship by the fact that she remains at home within the control of her husband. However, gender is also re-negotiated through her innovations in ongoing dynamic process, as she still pursues her own passion and is economically empowered.

This study and analysis has reinforced the importance of recognizing the context-specificity of innovation (see Alsos et al., 2013). It is not only the preconditions for various forms of innovation that are context-dependent, but also the very definition of what is new. There is a classic debate in mainstream innovation studies about 'new to the firm' and 'new to the world'. This discussion, however, is about the definition of the scope of the significant 'world', that is, the relevant context. With the markets in East Africa emerging and being increasingly incorporated in the world economy, this definition is likely to change not only in East Africa, but also in, for example, China, the US and the EU.

The innovativeness that, for gendered reasons, is required for women in Africa to even run their businesses is evident from the extensive empirical material in the project I am reporting from. The cases of Fatma and Laila both illustrate the process innovations which are required for women to even engage in entrepreneurship.

Yet all innovations are made invisible along all three dimensions discussed by Nählinder et al. (2015). First, the innovations are made by women. Second, the innovations often take place in female-labelled and female-dominated sectors. Third, they are not captured in the statistics as a result of the measurement methods, since they are often organizational or process innovations that are hard to measure, rather than a newly constructed technological product. However, I argue that an equally important reason for the invisibility is the context in which they are carried out. Given the changing global economic landscape, including the growth of developing economies and emerging markets such as the East African, the lack of knowledge of the contextual landscape of and for innovations may become an increasing problem. There is innovative capacity as well as contextual obstacles, which the globe cannot afford to neglect. I therefore argue that academia and theory development need to maintain the pace and remove both their blindfolds, the androcentric and the ethnocentric.

### A Note on Further Studies

Needless to say, there is thus a need for further empirical studies on everyday innovations made by women and men in emerging markets, with both gender as a variable and a feminist theoretical perspective (see also Alsos et al., 2013). The same applies to studies on how the gender dimension can, in various ways, in fact support innovations as such (see Fogelberg Eriksson, 2014), and how crossing gendered borders and division of labour may be regarded as organizational innovation. Finally, let us note that the cases narrated in this chapter are taken from a middle-class context. Everyday innovations naturally also take place at the grass-roots levels in all contexts, not least in the emerging markets.

These should also be analysed and understood from an innovation perspective.

## REFERENCES

Alsos, G., E. Ljunggren and U. Hytti (2013), 'Gender and innovation: State of the art and a research agenda', *International Journal of Gender and Entrepreneurship*, **5** (3), 236–256.

Amble, N. (2010), 'Innovasjonsordet og kvinnene: Status, utfordringer og kunnskapshull', in E. Ljunggren, G.A. Alsos, N. Amble, R. Ervik, T. Kvidal and R. Wiik (eds), *Gender and Innovation: Learning from Regional VRI-projects*, NF Report 2/2010, Bodø, Norway: Nordland Research Institute, pp. 42–66.

Aschmoneit, M. and D. Janevska (2013), 'Closing the gap between frugal and reverse innovation: The case of the Tata Nano', Master's thesis, SMIO programme, Linköping University, Sweden.

Barras, R. (1986), 'Towards a theory of innovation in services', *Research Policy*, **15** (4), 161–173.

Bjerström, E. (2013), *Det Nya Afrika*, Stockholm: Svante Weyler Bokförlag.

Blake, M.K. and S. Hanson (2005), 'Rethinking innovation: Context and gender', *Environment and Planning A*, **37** (4), 681–701.

Brush, G.G., A. de Bruin and F. Welter (2009), 'Gender-aware framework for women's entrepreneurship', *International Journal of Gender and Entrepreneurship*, **1** (1), 8–24.

Doloreaux, D. and S. Parto (2005), 'Regional innovation systems: Current discourse and unresolved issues', *Technology in Society*, **27** (2), 133–153.

Earl, L. (2002), *Innovation and Change in the Public Sector: A Seeming Oxymoron*, Ottawa: Statistics Canada.

East African Community (2013), *Facts and Figures*, Report, accessed at www.eac.int.

Ellis, A., M. Blackden, J. Cutura, F. MacCulloch and H. Seebens (2007a), *Gender and Economic Growth in Tanzania: Creating Opportunities for Women*, Directions in Development: Private Sector Development, Washington, DC: World Bank.

Ellis, A., J. Cutura, N. Dione, I. Gillson, C. Manuel and J. Thongori (2007b), *Gender and Economic Growth in Kenya: Unleashing the Power of Women*, Washington, DC: World Bank.

Fagerberg, J., D. Mowery and R. Nelson (2005), *Oxford Handbook of Innovation*, Oxford, UK: Oxford University Press.

Farmer, T.M. and X. Butte (2014), 'Everyday innovation', *Human Capital* (American Society for Training and Development), 8 February.

Fogelberg Eriksson, A. (2014), 'A gender perspective as trigger and facilitator of innovation', *International Journal of Gender and Entrepreneurship*, **6** (2), 163–180.

Gallouj, F. and O. Weinstein (1997), 'Innovation in services', *Research Policy*, **26** (4/5), 537–556.

Govindarajan, V. and R. Ramamurti (2011), 'Reverse innovation, emerging markets, and global strategy', *Global Strategy Journal*, **1** (3–4), 191–205.

Kinyanjui, M.N. (2008), 'From home to jua kali enterprise spaces: Entrepreneurship and female gender identity', *International Journal of Small Business*, **5** (3–4), 401–411.

Kvidal, T. and E. Ljunggren (2012), 'Implementing "a gender perspective" in an innovation programme: More innovation or ambivalence and uncertainty?', in S. Andersson, K. Berglund, E. Gunnarsson and E. Sundin (eds), *Promoting Innovation Policies, Practices and Procedures*, Stockholm: Vinnova, pp. 111–130.

Lindberg, M. (2010), 'Samverkansnätverk för innovation: En interaktiv och genusveten-skaplig utmaning av innovationspolitik och innovationsforskning', Dissertation, Luleå University of Technology, Sweden.

Lindell, I. (ed.) (2010), *Africa's Informal Workers: Collective Agency, Alliances and Transnational Organizing in Urban Africa*, Uppsala, Sweden: Nordic Africa Institute.

Ljunggren, E., G. Alsos, N. Amble, R. Ervik, T. Kvidal and R. Wiik (2010), *Gender and Innovation: Learning from Regional VRI-projects*, NF Report 2/2010, Bodø, Norway: Nordland Research Institute.

Miles, I. (2005), 'Innovation in services', in J. Fagerberg, D.C. Mowery and R.R. Nelson (eds), *The Oxford Handbook of Innovation*, Oxford, UK: Oxford University Press, pp. 433–458.

Mulgan, G. (2007), 'Ready or not? Taking innovation in the public sector seriously', *NESTA's Provocation*, 3 April.

Nählinder, J., M. Tillmar and C. Wigren-Kristoferson (2015), 'Towards a gender aware understanding of innovation: A three dimensional route', *International Journal of Gender and Entrepreneurship*, **7** (1), 66–86.

Nyberg, A.-C. (2009), 'Making ideas matter: Gender, technology and women's invention', Dissertation, Department of Human Work Sciences Division of Gender and Innovation, Luleå University, Sweden.

Pedersen, P.O. (2001), 'East African microenterprises negotiating social space: An introduction', in P.O. Alila and P.O. Pedersen (eds), *Negotiating Social Space: East African Micro Enterprises*, Asmara: Africa World Press.

Pettersson, K. and M. Lindberg (2013), 'Paradoxical spaces of feminist resistance: Mapping the margin to the masculinist discourse', *International Journal of Gender and Entrepreneurship*, **5** (3), 323–341.

Potts, J. and T. Kastelle (2010), 'Public sector innovation research: What is next?', *Innovation: Management, Policy and Practice*, **12** (2), 122–137.

Rylander, S. (2014), *Afrika vänder*, Lund, Sweden: Historiska Media.

Snyder, M. (2000), *Women in African Economies: From Burning Sun to Boardroom*, Kampala: Fountain Publishers.

Svensson, L. and K. Aagaard Nielsen (2006), 'Action research and interactive research', in K. Aagaard Nielsen and L. Svensson (eds), *Action Research and Interactive Research: Beyond Practice and Theory*, Maastricht, Netherlands: Shaker Publishing.

Utbult, M. (2007), *Måste innovationer vara av metall? Att tänka om och skapa nytt i kommuner, landsting och regioner*, Stockholm: SKL [Swedish Association of Local Authorities and Regions], Trygghetsfonden, Vinnova [Sweden's innovation agency].

West, C. and D. Zimmerman (1987), 'Doing gender', *Gender and Society*, **1** (2), 125–151.

Windrum, P. and P. Koch (2008), *Innovation in Public Sector Services*, Cheltenham, UK and Northampton, MA, USA: Edward Elgar.

# 6. Gendered understandings of innovation in nursing and entrepreneurship: an exploratory study in the Portuguese context

*Selma Martins, Emília Fernandes and Regina Leite*

## INTRODUCTION

Research on innovation has frequently been associated with masculinity and male professional or organizational contexts. This innovation–masculinity association has been the major reason why women come upon several difficulties when they enter, make a career in or expect to be recognized as competent in such innovation contexts. In fact, within innovation contexts, women are considered as exceptions or aliens that do not fit the masculine norm (Wikhamn and Knights, 2013).

Entrepreneurship has been one of the masculine territories where innovation is celebrated and used to characterize the success of an entrepreneurial project (Bruni et al., 2004). The literature tends to explore the gender inequalities and devaluation of women and their enterprises in the entrepreneurial practice (Kelly, 2014). However, innovation is rarely considered and fully explored in the research related to gender and entrepreneurship (Alsos et al., 2013). This applies to the area of nursing entrepreneurship in particular. Nursing has been historically and symbolically very feminized and inscribed by the femininity. Despite the transformations we are currently witnessing in the nursing profession, such as the number of male nurses entering the field, it is still considered a female-dominated domain (Latimer, 2000; McDonald, 2013).

Following the financial crises and the high unemployment rate, Portugal and particularly the health care sector started witnessing an unprecedented rise in new entrepreneurial projects. These projects have allowed certain professional areas such as nursing practice to explore new ventures. In recent years, we have seen a constant increase in the number of private entrepreneurial projects in nursing care services.

The present chapter aims then to explore: 1) how innovation is constructed within this new occupation that is signified by a gender paradox; and 2) how such construction can be a barrier or an opportunity to gender equality and women's emancipation in this professional, private business context.

Therefore, for the purpose of this chapter, innovation is considered as the production of new ways of signifying and creating professional practices, resulting in a rearrangement of gender relations and working practices in the organizational settings (Wikhamn and Knights, 2013). In other words, innovation is here understood as a discourse (Alsos et al., 2013). Based on this, and bearing in mind what Jones and Spicer (2005) wrote about entrepreneurship, innovation can be described as an 'empty signifier' open to different meanings related to particular organizational and work contexts.[1] In this chapter, we believe that discourses of innovation can be differently constructed and mobilized depending on the political, economic and social contexts considered. Specifically, we intend to analyse the innovation practices in 'service delivery' of entrepreneurship in nursing care and the possible operationalizations of innovation, through its relation with new gendered meanings such as 'caring' and 'nurturing', traditionally associated with nursing. With this in mind, we aim to explore how innovation can be redefined and legitimized through a discourse of femininity, and how such a new gendered understanding of innovation can contribute to gender equality in such a specific entrepreneurial context.

In order to accomplish this, we have conducted 18 semi-structured interviews with nursing professionals who have started their own businesses in nursing care. The interviews revealed a clear link between the 'act of care' and the 'ability to innovate', in this case concerning a new and differentiated way of providing nursing services. The expression 'out of the box' was applied, since these services add something to what was already being provided in the nursing area. We refer to innovative services that are based on a new kind of relationship that favours care and proximity above all else, with a client who is also qualified as 'a patient'. Furthermore, the expression 'out of the box' emerged here associated with the opportunity of using all the technical nursing skills in a more autonomous and articulated way in order to respond to the patients' needs. Finally, being 'out of the box' also meant being in a constant process of learning in their new work environment, which calls for new uses and new meanings in terms of their skills and experiences as nursing professionals. This is true for both men and women interviewees, although one might expect the latter to be at an advantage. In fact, the innovation in the practice of entrepreneurship in nursing care services appears associated mainly with the 'so-called natural strengths, such as "listening", sharing, building relationships' (Kamberidou, 2013, p. 1). Nevertheless, interviewees disassociated such meanings from femininity and inscribed them exclusively in an 'innovative' and gender-neutralized way of doing business in the field of nursing. So, if on the one hand we can assume that entrepreneurship in nursing can be understood as a form of 'claiming' that innovation can be constituted by femininity, on the other hand an attempt is being made by both female and male interviewees to neutralize and disconnect such meanings from femininity when describing their practices as entrepreneurs in nursing.

In view of the above, it is our aim to highlight how innovation is constructed in this new occupation that derives from the association between nursing and entrepreneurship and how such a new conception can be understood as a way of reproducing or transforming the gender asymmetries in such work contexts. The chapter starts with a brief literature review focusing on innovation, gender, nursing and entrepreneurship. We then present our methodology by explaining the interviewing method, describing our participants and the content analysis used. After this, we present the content analysis of the interviews' qualitative material. Finally, we discuss our findings and present some conclusions.

## INNOVATION, GENDER, NURSING AND ENTREPRENEURSHIP

In a report of the International Center for Research on Women, Malhotra et al. (2009, p. 4) argue that 'Innovation systems are defined by the relationships between all of the actors, ideas and processes needed for innovations to be created, adopted and diffused.' Based on such a definition, the authors seem to be claiming for a holistic version of innovation that is not exclusively associated with technology and particular economic and organizational settings. However, in the mainstream literature, the practice of innovation is often related to engineering and industry innovation, and defined through an abstract language related to new arrangements of products, processes and systems of organization (Alsos et al., 2013; Poutanen and Kovalainen, 2013). Innovation is also related to creativity. It is such creativity, stimulated by the formal practices and management tools and a result of the individual motivation, that allows the development of new products and ways of organizing, which are considered meaningful and a novelty in the work contexts (Bharadwaj and Menon, 2000). Nevertheless, the main aim of such innovative practice is always to gain competitive advantage in today's unstable and/or new markets, and as a means to guarantee economic growth (Alsos et al., 2013).

When we adopt a gender perspective to reflect on those systems of meanings that constitute the dominant discourse of innovation, it becomes clear that gender is always turned invisible and a neutral positioning is often assumed, whether we are thinking about academic research or about the practical reality of organizations (Alsos et al., 2013). Such neutrality is generally assumed despite recognizing that innovation contexts are expressly masculinized (Lohan and Faulkner, 2004) and the subjects considered to best represent the ideal innovator are men (Alsos et al., 2013; Wikhamn and Knights, 2013). In this sense, the gendered association with men or masculinity circumscribes and prescribes what and who must be considered as (de)valued when we think about innovation. Based on this, we can state that masculinity seems to define what innovation means and who can be an innovator. Masculinity is not however put in question when a gender-neutral positioning in relation to innovation is assumed. This gendered condition of innovation and its neutrality end up discriminating against and devaluing women in the innovation contexts, since women are perceived as less innovative and less prepared to perform successfully an innovative professional practice (Alsos et al., 2013; Wikhamn and Knights, 2013). Poutanen and Kovalainen (2013) show how, in the male-dominated chemical industry, the gendered process of segregation occurs at the micro-level of product innovation, defined as 'the process of invention, and innovation leading to a new product' (2013, p. 262–263). The authors analyse the gendered practice of a token female innovator in a hegemonic masculine engineering culture and the power relations between her and her male colleagues. Their study shows how innovation is constantly gendered through the relations of those involved in it, the types of products that are created, and its relationship to specific industrial cultures.

Kelan (2008) concludes that despite the tendency to value a certain femininity in the rational work areas of innovation by emphasizing social and emotional skills, as in the case of information communication technology (ICT) work, the ideal worker is still described as male. This research shows how such contexts depend on service work and the relationship with customers, and 'being good with people' (Kelan, 2008, p. 58). In this sense ICT workers tend to re-appropriate conventional feminine meanings such as emotions and social skills to define the ideal worker. However, the emphasis on emotionality does not necessarily imply that such work contexts are becoming more feminine, as argued by

Kelan: 'The rise of emotions and their often feminine connotation tell us little about who profits from enacting certain behaviour' (2008, p. 53). The author comes to the conclusion that the genderization of emotions tends to vary according to the discourse contexts that are considered by the ICT workers. In other words, in spite of the fact that the interviewees formulated a discursive construction of women as socially competent, when considering whether more women should work in ICT they did not find any resemblance between women and the ideal worker. This ideal is preserved as gender-neutral and viewed as something that can be enacted by everyone.

This gendered picture does not seem to be really different when we consider the new approaches to innovation processes, like open innovation, addressed in some recent studies. The research conducted by Wikhamn and Knights (2013) in the automotive industry shows that this new paradigm of innovation does not seem to play a very successful role in the legitimation of women as workers and innovators. This remains true even when the concept of open innovation values conventionally feminine meanings like collaboration and intuition. Such meanings tend to be re-appropriated by a masculinity inscribed in rational control and competition (Wikhamn and Knights, 2013). The authors confirmed how a new way of doing innovation that could enhance women's participation (as a result of the above-mentioned proximity between open innovation and femininity) is instead contributing to the preservation of a masculine managerialism.

According to the previous studies, it becomes clear how gender, as a social and cultural construction, defines the way we understand innovation and the relations of power and inequality between men and women in these work contexts. That is why Alsos et al. (2013) in an article focusing on gender in innovation emphasize the need to go further on the relation between those two concepts, by exploring how professionals define innovation and the extent to which such definitions are gendered. The aim is to develop an interpretative analysis of how gender is constructed through 'negotiations and practices', with a focus on femininity and masculinity (2013, p. 243).

The gender relations inscribed in innovation have become more complex with the emergence of new professional combinations that enact simultaneous contradictory gendered meanings. We believe that this may be the case for nursing professionals who decide to become entrepreneurs in nursing care.

Historically and symbolically, the nursing profession has been seen as a women's occupation, inscribed in a femininity related to care and nurturing (Evans, 1997; McDonald, 2013; Padilha et al., 2006). However, as McDonald (2013) reminds us, the number of men in nursing has notably increased. Men tend to gain rapid access to higher positions in nursing management, and make an effort to preserve their association with masculinity using four principal strategies. The author summarized male nurses' strategies as follows: 1) distancing themselves from women; 2) preserving traditional masculine values (e.g. having pride in one's work, doing a proper job, pursuing a career, being true to oneself, being assertive, being blatant and challenging authority); 3) relabelling the occupation by bringing more male characteristics to nursing; 4) redefining masculinity coherently with their occupations (McDonald, 2013, pp. 563–564). This strategy of distancing nursing practices from the feminine meanings is also present in the need to legitimate the 'authenticity' of such a profession. This presupposes valuing technical and medical care to the detriment of social care (Latimer, 2000). Moreover, it seems that research (Wilson, 2002) and the academic journals of nursing seem to be interested in exploring the relation between gender and innovation (Alsos et al., 2013). Despite the changes and emerging tendencies occurring in nursing, this profession is still considered female-dominated and closely linked to femininity (Heikes, 1991; Latimer, 2000).

On the contrary, entrepreneurial practice is defined by a certain masculinity inscribed in a psychological individuality that is traditionally associated with men and that can be called the entrepreneurial mentality (Bruni et al., 2004). In this masculine conception, entrepreneurship appears associated with risk, autonomy and obstinacy, and is presented as a way of fostering innovation and creating new jobs in a capitalist system (Alsos et al., 2013; Perren and Jennings, 2005). Under this discourse of entrepreneurship, innovation emerges as an important and somewhat overlapping construct. And this may well be the reason why the figure of the entrepreneur becomes associated with the archetypes of the explorer, adventurer and inventor (Ahl, 2004; Bruni et al., 2004; Ogbor, 2000).

As a result, and as with innovation, women tend to persist as the 'other' of this social and cultural construction (Ahl and Marlow, 2012), the marginal gender that does not correspond to the ideal personal and individual profile of an entrepreneur. Although women were always present in the narratives of entrepreneurship, albeit in secondary and supporting roles, the main figure of entrepreneurship is the male entrepreneur (e.g. Guerreiro, 1996). In a way, women's presence and relation to business and entrepreneurial contexts are paradoxical. While recognizing that the enterprise activity depends heavily on them, women are neither described nor perceived through the label of 'entrepreneur'. This 'fault' can also be extended to their enterprises, which are perceived as less valued, related to economic sectors of low income, and not innovative enough (Anna et al., 2000).

In the literature on entrepreneurship and gender, the poststructuralist feminists are now exploring the ways female entrepreneurs resist and reinscribe such masculine norms that constrain their practices, and question their legitimacy as entrepreneurs in their organizational and business daily lives (Lewis, 2013).

The presumed close relation between innovation and entrepreneurship has been appropriated and used in a Portuguese political discourse that emphasizes the need (of individuals) to invest in innovative entrepreneurial projects (Programa Estratégico para o Empreendedorismo e Inovação, 2014). There is a belief that Portuguese society will be able to overcome the financial crises and high unemployment rate with the help of entrepreneurial initiatives and innovation, particularly in the health care sector. We have witnessed the rise of new entrepreneurial projects following such discourse that have allowed certain professional areas (e.g. nursing) to explore new ventures. In recent years, new private entrepreneurial projects in the area of nursing care services have emerged and seem to be growing steadily.

Taking all this into consideration, we intend to explore how such new arrangements between contradictory gendered occupations – entrepreneurship and nursing – can produce new gendered understandings of innovation. Specifically, we are interested in exploring how, in a context of gender paradox, it is possible to redefine the meaning of an 'innovative act' in business and how such an act can be legitimized through femininity. In this sense, our research focus is on the gendered construction of innovation. Such an aim is particularly important in the sense that research has not truly explored the simultaneous relations between gender, entrepreneurship and innovation. The paucity of studies is evident, particularly in the relationship between innovation and gender, even in the entrepreneurship field (Alsos et al., 2013). Alsos et al. (2013) suggest that maybe it is because the 'person' is usually 'absent' from innovation process research. 'When people are not visible in the discourse, gender easily becomes invisible' (Alsos et al., 2013, p. 237). It is however important not to forget that individuals are above all social and cultural beings, and all processes are always gendered by the system of meanings or discourses that society and organizations use to define them. Basically we agree with Poutanen and Kovalainen's (2013) concern that it is important to explore the micro-contexts of innovation, and this can be achieved by bringing the persons as innovators and their innovation stories into research.

We hope that our research will contribute with new insights to the understanding of innovation, specifically in terms of new barriers put in place to women who are professionally active in innovative contexts. We also expect to further develop a neglected area by focusing on the relations between gender, innovation and entrepreneurship, looking specifically at the entrepreneurial practices in nursing care.

## METHODOLOGY

Considering our aims and the exploratory nature of the study, we decided to conduct our research through the use of a qualitative methodology. The qualitative methodology intends to understand the meanings and significances that people attribute to their experiences. It is not concerned with the numerical composition of the sample and its representativeness, since its main purpose is to deepen the understanding of a particular social group and an organization (Pope and Mays, 2006), which is in line with the objectives of the present study.

This methodology assumes an inductive thought which advocates study and knowledge from personal experiences. Qualitative methodology also pays special attention to the relationship between researchers and researched in the sense that both have an active participation in this process and are mutually influenced, without forgetting the importance of cultural context (Pope and Mays, 2006; Silverman, 2011).

In order to fulfil the aims outlined above, we interviewed nurse entrepreneurs from northern Portugal face to face, using a semi-structured script. Face-to-face interviews have been the main technique of qualitative research, despite the expenditure of time, since it allows a communication synchronized in time and space, leading to a spontaneous response on the part of the interviewee (Opdenakker, 2006). It should be noted that all interviews were fully transcribed. Oliver et al. (2005) reported that the transcript of the interview is a fundamental aspect in qualitative research, since it influences the way participants are understood, the information that is shared and the conclusions obtained.

In this sense, we conducted 18 semi-structured interviews among nursing professionals who had started a business with the aim of analysing the innovative practices in 'service delivery' and its possible relation to the gendered meanings of 'caring' and 'nurturing' associated with nursing practice. We were particularly interested in exploring the meaning of 'innovative act' in the nursing care business and how such an act was gendered.

The interviews took place from November 2012 to August 2013. Most occurred in the workplaces of the study's participants, with an average duration of 46 minutes. The group of interviewees comprised 11 men and 7 women, with ages between 30 and 39 years; most of them were married and had children. Their businesses were located in the north of Portugal; they had been working for one to five years in the activity and employed 2–38 individuals. First, we collected the contact details of nurse entrepreneurs through information gathered on the internet, from the Portuguese Health Regulation Authority and from the Nurses' Council. Subsequently, we asked the first nurses interviewed to refer other nurses who might fit the research aim. The names and contacts of other nurse entrepreneurs were provided using the snowball sampling technique (Noy, 2008). According to Noy (2008), this technique can enhance our social knowledge as a result of the quality of the interactions established, and has emerged as a way of gaining access to new participants and as a means of enriching the group of participants in the study.

At a later stage, we proceeded to the content analysis, by categories, of the material obtained. The content analysis aims at describing the situations and their interpretation regarding the context, with the purpose of providing knowledge, new perspectives, a representation of facts and a practical guide to action (Elo and Kynga, 2008). To Hsieh and Shannon (2005) analysis by categories is, within the various techniques of content analysis, the most used in practice. According to them, 'in conventional content analysis, coding categories are derived directly from the text data' (p. 1277). It should be noted that to conduct the content analysis of interviews we resorted to NVIVO software because, as noted by Mays and Pope (1995), computer software can be used as a facilitator of content analysis of the transcribed interviews.

## FINDINGS

### Thinking and Acting 'Out of the Box' in Entrepreneurship versus 'Entrepreneurship in Nursing Service'

In the interviews with the Portuguese entrepreneurs in nursing services, both women and men tend to use the expression 'out of the box' to define innovation, in the sense of 'developing something beyond what is usually done' (Interview 6, female entrepreneur). However, the term 'innovation' seems to be associated with different entrepreneurial practices which are defined through different meanings. When interviewees were describing entrepreneurship in general, innovation was considered synonymous with such practices and described through various meanings such as 'creativity' and 'proactivity' related to the individual figure of the entrepreneur. Innovation 'is to think about new strategies, to do the same task better. Essentially, it is to be creative and being [pause] and be proactive, trying to do more and better every day' (Interview 14, female entrepreneur).

Another main meaning that is associated with innovation when related to entrepreneurship in general is that it is immediately and almost exclusively related to an economic activity ruled by the market, and a way of guaranteeing competitive advantage in that market. 'Something innovative is, above all, an analysis, we could say a market analysis. We feel that there is a gap in something ... one way of entering the market and behaving differently, doing something new, different and that places us in a good position in the market' (Interview 13, male entrepreneur).

This system of meanings can also be found in the mainstream definitions of entrepreneurship (e.g. Casson et al., 2009; Davidsson, 2004; Rauch and Freese, 2007) and innovation (Bharadwaj and Menon, 2000). Such meanings seem to be culturally related to a masculine entrepreneurial mentality (Bruni et al., 2004) that celebrates certain symbolic individual attributes and profit as the main goal of innovation and entrepreneurship.

Nevertheless, our interviewees, both men and women, presented such meanings as gender-neutral. In a way, the use of those meanings and their neutralization allow these nursing professionals to signify and legitimize their new entrepreneurial activity and assume the positioning of 'innovators'. The legitimization of the interviewees in this new territory comes from their knowledge and ability to use the dominant discourse about innovation and entrepreneurship, consequently presenting themselves as able to occupy their new position in the entrepreneurial context.

However, the content of the meanings used to define innovation and entrepreneurship changes when the interviewees define themselves as entrepreneurs in nursing care. The innovation now turns out to assume a relational and emotional dimension, which had been omitted in their first definitions of innovation in entrepreneurship in general, and which is emphasized to the detriment of the economic and technical dimensions.

> We are always searching for innovation ... We have to look at the human being in a holistic way and not only in a commercial way ... When we started our business, there were already other companies which provided nursing services at the patient's home. We tried to do what the others do, but in a different way, with a different nature, and this is why we felt motivated to start the company ... I used to say, as a joke, that anyone can administer an injection. However, the way we give the injection to the patient, the way we

receive the patient before giving the injection, the way we talk to him after the injection, and the way we give all the instructions before and during the dosing may really make the difference, because the act of injection is always the same for all the patients and the technique learned at the universities is the same for everyone. (Interview 13, male entrepreneur)

This dimension is particularly relevant to enhance innovative behaviour in work teams. The relational and collaborative environment seems to be a critical condition to foster creativity. In a sense, the relation of such a dimension to innovation resembles the values inscribed in the open innovation process, which are openness, trust and collaboration, which Wikhamn and Knights (2013) also related to a discourse of femininity. 'I think that what distinguishes us [in terms of innovation] from others is the unique work relational abilities that we create ... We created three training courses in Portugal from scratch, with our team, and we were really innovators' (Interview 1, male entrepreneur).

Our findings from the interviews allow us to identify a link between the 'act of care' and the 'ability to innovate', related here to a new and differentiated way of providing nursing services. In this new act of innovation nursing values seem to be emphasized to the detriment of the entrepreneurial mentality. It seems that this system of meaning is embedded in the 'vocational' feminine tradition of nursing (Latimer, 2000), re-signifying what can be understood as being innovative in entrepreneurship. So the innovative practices in the 'service delivery' and related to the 'act of care' seem to be the key to the entrepreneurial success. And success means here the satisfaction of the patient, and consequently the satisfaction of the work teams.

We cannot dissociate our company from the nursing service delivery. That's what we are used to as nurses; that's what we have been trained to do. I think that this little bit of 'humanity' and the way we take care of the patients in the services we provide allow us to make the difference. It is not the 'feeling' of business [in economic terms] but the 'feeling' of care. And this is what we intend to pass on to our nursing team. I know that this is a business, but the prevalent feeling must be: do the best for the patient to guarantee his/her satisfaction and then maintain this satisfaction. (Interview 18, male entrepreneur)

Within this concept of innovation the abstract language disappears and the relational and emotional concerns emerge and become even more explicit when interviewees relate it to the quality of care. This special link between innovation and care becomes very explicit in one of the narratives of the interviewees that compares such a way of caring with 'art' to illustrate the uniqueness of such an act: 'The name [of the company] was carefully selected and it was not due to chance. After 20 years as a nurse, I still argue that the 'art of care' is the most important one. That is the reason why we chose the English word 'CARE' to name our company' (Interview 13, male entrepreneur).

However, and as concluded by Kelan (2008) in her research on ICT workers, such meanings traditionally linked to femininity are not presented as gendered or as more suitable to the female entrepreneurs in nursing care. Once again, the gendered nature of this new conception of innovation linked to the entrepreneurial act is neutralized. Moreover, the male interviewees are the ones who reinforce such meanings in the innovative act of entrepreneurship in nursing services and use them to define themselves as entrepreneurs.

In the following section we will further explore the relations between innovation and the act of care, and the focus of such attention: the patient. We will also explore another dimension that appears as a complement to the first one: autonomy (of exploring and deciding) in nursing services.

### Service Delivery, Patients and the Art of Care: A New Gendered Way of Thinking and Doing Innovation?

As stated before, the innovative act in nursing services entrepreneurship has as a first aim to guarantee the quality of health and life of the client. However, the interviewees never used the word 'client', continuing to prefer the word 'patient'. This allows them to deny a mainly economic approach to their business and an instrumental and market-driven relation to their patients.

Moreover, the centre of this innovative act is no longer the entrepreneur as described in the mainstream entrepreneurship literature. Inscribed in an instrumental and individualistic perspective, the traditional protagonist of the successful stories of entrepreneurship is always the individual, with his (usually it is a man) ability to innovate and his personal attributes that allow him to build up his business and make a profit. This new perspective on entrepreneurship puts the client-patient at the centre of the innovative act. It is an altruistic perspective that values emotions, communication, health education, and a holistic view of the service. Furthermore, interviewees recognized that it is only through the caring act that they can innovate, since innovation opportunities in areas of a more technical nature are scarce.

> We do not have many areas where we can innovate. Working in the health service [pause] actually means taking care of others, taking care of someone

who needs us. Innovating depends on that. In my case, innovation came with the need to help mothers in the breastfeeding process, and I wanted to have a space that allowed me to receive mothers, talk to them and help them. (Interview 14, female entrepreneur)

Consistent with previous research (Kelan, 2008; McDonald, 2013; Wikhamn and Knights, 2013), both female and male entrepreneurs tend to neutralize this new conception of innovation. However, when we focus specifically on nursing activity where innovation emerges and in relation to whom, we can say that there is a tendency to gender such innovative practices and subjects by female entrepreneurs. When discussing this topic in the interviews, women tend to reinforce the importance of care as a way of innovating, by referring to its potential in a gendered activity such as maternity and in relation to a very particular gendered position: mothers. We suggest that, if this new way of innovating in entrepreneurship based on care is considered as gender-neutral, their particular relations with the practice and with the clients are deeply gendered by women. New ways of innovation in nursing entrepreneurship are offered to improve the lives of babies and mothers, protecting and nurturing them in this particular gendered moment related to the core of femininity. These businesses are intended to provide differentiated nursing practices concerning maternity (antenatal and postnatal) and infant care practices, such as (breast)feeding, changing, bathing and sleeping. Despite being a happy occasion in most cases, women's transition to motherhood can also be a stressful time, especially for first-time mothers. Recognizing the potential for developing new and more effective ways of improving maternity services, some entrepreneurs in nursing have built their business around these practices. 'As far as I am concerned, the mothers that I could help I would help. So, from my experience, I tried to do better [primary maternal services]. The idea to create a business was born here' (Interview 17, female entrepreneur).

On the contrary, men tend to emphasize activities and patients that are not immediately gendered, such as health education, or that are assumed as gender-neutral, such as disaster victims: 'The hospital did everything; the hospital did everything, but did not answer to all the needs of the populations, especially in the case of the disaster victims' (Interview 16, male entrepreneur). 'We entrepreneurs in nursing … develop what we can call [pause] health education. When assisting a person we are always trying to make sure that the patient understands what we are doing and what we are saying' (Interview 9, male entrepreneur).

The expression 'out of the box' has also been associated with the opportunity of using all the technical and relational skills in nursing in a

more autonomous and articulated way. Both male and female entrepreneurs described the use of a greater autonomy in the way they
delivered the health services to clients or patients. Such autonomy is
perceived as allowing them to go further in their professional activity.
Autonomy is then considered a way of enhancing such services to the
benefit of their patients and their professional growth: 'First of all I could
implement my ideas in the relationship with the patient without having to
ask A, B or C, "May I do this?"' (Interview 1, male entrepreneur).

We suggest that autonomy, considered a masculine attribute of the
entrepreneurial mentality (Bruni et al., 2004), is here put at the service of
the feminine values (taking care of the patients). The relations between
those feminine meanings and innovation in nursing care entrepreneurship
are reinforced by both male and female interviewees, without the
interviewees making any specific reference to the gendered nature of the
innovation act.

The different ways of constructing meanings associated with the two
forms of entrepreneurship – (general) entrepreneurship versus entrepreneurship in nursing care – are summarized in Table 6.1.

In this sense, we argue that individuals in a new occupation, entrepreneurs in nursing care, reinscribe innovation in the femininity but
detach such femininity from women by neutralizing it. Moreover, men
claim such a feminine system of meanings as part of their identity as
entrepreneurs, as with the ICT workers in Kelan's (2008) research. This
also became visible in the study of McDonald (2013), where men
re-appropriated the feminine discourse to describe their practice and
identities as male nurses. In this regard, such new gendered understandings of the innovative act can serve to bring about a rethinking of the
emergence of alternative masculinities in opposition to the masculine
entrepreneurial mentality.

Nevertheless, we cannot claim that this new occupation inscribed in a
'feminine' innovation can serve to facilitate the association of women
with innovation or to foster women's entry to and participation in such
particular entrepreneurial contexts (Kelan, 2008; Wikhamn and Knights,
2013). The reason why we cannot make such an argument is that, in a
way, such femininity is not here considered as more suitable for women,
even if we presuppose that women are at an advantage because such
gender signification comes associated mainly with the 'so-called natural
strengths, such as "listening", sharing, building relationships' of women
(Kamberidou, 2013, p. 1).

*Table 6.1    Innovation gendered meanings*

| Entrepreneurship | Entrepreneurship in nursing care 'out of the box' |
|---|---|
| Economic approach of the individual | Holistic approach of the individual |
| The client and profit as focus of attention | The patient as focus of attention |
| Creativity related to technical issues | Creativity related to unique work relational abilities based on effective and empathetic communication versus technical and medical care issues |
| Activity strongly related to the economic perspective (economic aspects come first) | Activity strongly related to social, emotional and relational aspects |
| 'To do more and better' | 'The art of care' |
| A way of entering the market or a market approach | Altruism devaluing a fast return on investment |
| The 'feeling' of business versus the 'feeling' of care | The 'feeling' of care versus the 'feeling' of business |
| Profit | Patient satisfaction and promoting health education |
| Focus on individual attributes of the entrepreneur | Focus on dealing with patients' fragilities and their particular needs (e.g. disaster victims and maternity services) |
| Ambition and proactivity as main values of the entrepreneur | Value in entrepreneurs' autonomy based on a personal view of the patients' needs |

## DISCUSSION AND CONCLUSION

In this chapter, we have explored how innovation is gendered in an occupation that is signified by a gender paradox: entrepreneurship in nursing care. We were particularly interested in exploring how innovation is constructed in particular settings and how such constructions are gendered. We believe that exploring the gendered system of meanings associated with innovation also allows us to understand the situations of discrimination and privilege of professionals in such contexts.

Based on a content analysis of the qualitative materials from interviews with female and male entrepreneurs, we have identified different meanings associated with the innovative act in entrepreneurship. One of the meanings emphasizes an abstract, individualistic and economic act that can be inscribed in a masculine entrepreneurial mentality (Bruni et al., 2004), although presented as gender-neutral by the participants. Another meaning highlights a relational, emotional and caring act associated with nursing services delivery, and having as its central focus the client-patient. This latter can be understood as inscribed in the social and traditional feminine values, although the participants also presented such innovative acts as gender-neutral.

The first interpretation combined innovation and entrepreneurship and emerged in the entrepreneurial narratives of the interviewees as not having any relation to their particular professional lives. It is a sort of normative prescription of an ideal that must be followed to be innovative in entrepreneurship in general. It seems that the subjects used such a way of defining innovation in entrepreneurship to legitimize their right to be recognized as innovators and entrepreneurs. This claim is usual in the newcomers or/and minorities who arrive in a professional and organizational context where they are understood as 'others' (e.g. Gill, 2014; Lewis, 2013). Contrary to Kelan's findings, the general idea of innovation is constructed through a masculinity that is nevertheless neutralized (Kelan, 2008).

In a sense, the participants can be considered as 'new' types of entrepreneurs who are also proclaiming themselves to be innovative. The neutralization of gender is also a strategy that allows participants to reinforce such recognition. In addition, it reveals a lack of gender awareness that this definition of innovation and entrepreneurial mentality produces a particular (masculine) ideal of an innovator (Alsos et al., 2013) and of an entrepreneur (Ogbor, 2000).

The subversion of this group of participants is then in re-signifying and legitimizing the innovation act in entrepreneurship through their association with nursing and its feminine values, thus jeopardizing the economic, instrumental and individualistic dominant masculine discourse about entrepreneurship and innovation.

This new conception of innovation in nursing entrepreneurship, although never explicitly revealed as feminine, helps both female and male entrepreneurs to define their daily practices in the entrepreneurial contexts and is the main reason for starting their businesses. That is achieved by the 'altruistic' dimension of their entrepreneurial business – the reinvention of new ways of relating to the client-patient – and by exploring forms of caring and communicating in the nursing services. And even autonomy is perceived as being put at the service of the nursing entrepreneurial practices in what concerns relations with the patients. Additionally, the entrepreneurs rejected the idea of relating their innovative practice exclusively to an economic aim.

According to the female and male entrepreneurs interviewed, and based on this new version of innovation, to 'do something different from the usual' is to do 'femininity' even if it is not acknowledged as such.

Emotions and social competences are discussed as if they have nothing to do with gender. The gender neutralization of such feminine meanings allows participants to detach them from a close relation to women, thus enabling all entrepreneurs in this particular context to be innovative, as found in previous research (Kelan, 2008; McDonald, 2013).

From our point of view, and taking into consideration other studies (Kelan, 2008; McDonald, 2013), such gender neutralization has different implications for female and male entrepreneurs in nursing care. For male entrepreneurs this neutralization allows them to re-appropriate such meanings without acknowledging that they become more 'feminine'. Moreover, as literature about males in female-dominated occupations (e.g. Lupton, 2000) reminds us, neutralizing femininity in the innovation act related to nursing entrepreneurship can be a strategy used by males to preserve their 'masculinity', even if this means openness to the constitution of alternative masculinities.

On the other hand, women cannot refer to the femininity of innovative acts because traditionally female-dominated occupations and practices constructed by femininity tend to be socially devalued (Reskin, 1988). Perhaps women neutralize femininity in order to maintain the value of this new innovation act in this new professional occupation. For this reason, the relation between femininity and the innovation act concerning entrepreneurship in nursing care does not mean that women will have more opportunities in the new occupation. As Kelan (2008) argues, women who enter masculine professions continue to be considered above all as women and are always perceived as gendered professionals.

A potential change in the system of meanings related to innovation with the incorporation of femininity does not seem to be enough to alter the power relations between men and women in this context, and to produce equality and openness to difference and diversity. The logic of gender seems always to value masculinity, even if this discourse is now changing and re-appropriating new meanings and feminine contents that are transformed into gender-neutral.

In order to gain more insight into the gendered power relations in innovative and entrepreneurial contexts, we argue that more research is needed to explicitly explore gender in the life stories of female and male entrepreneurs and their understandings of the innovation act. The success of entrepreneurship in nursing requires a nursing workforce that is properly educated, trained and supported to deliver innovative services. The present chapter provides several meanings associated with innovation, gender, nursing and entrepreneurship. Such meanings can be used by educators and trainers to stimulate reflection and discussion on entrepreneurial (gendered) attributes and their impact on gender (in)equality.

## NOTE

1. Influenced by a Lacanian perspective, Jones and Spicer (2005) conceptualize entrepreneur/ship as a multiple practice that is impossible to 'trap' in a stable meaning in the sense that such meaning would always be dependent on the social and economic discourses operating in a particular context. Such impossibility led the authors to name entrepreneur/ship as an empty signifier.

## REFERENCES

Ahl, H. (2004), *The Scientific Reproduction of Gender Inequality: A Discourse Analysis of Research Texts on Women's Entrepreneurship*, Malmo, Sweden: Copenhagen Business School Press.

Ahl, H. and S. Marlow (2012), 'Exploring the dynamics of gender, feminism and entrepreneurship: Advancing debate to escape a dead end?', *Organization*, **19** (5), 543–562.

Alsos, G.A., E. Ljunggren and U. Hytti (2013), 'Gender and innovation: State of the art and a research agenda', *International Journal of Gender and Entrepreneurship*, **5** (3), 236–256.

Anna, A.L., G.N. Chandler, E. Jansen and N.P. Mero (2000), 'Women business owners in traditional and non-traditional industries', *Journal of Business Venturing*, **15** (3), 279–303.

Bharadwaj, S. and A. Menon (2000), 'Making innovation happen in organizations: Individual creativity mechanisms, organizational creativity mechanisms or both?', *Journal of Product Innovation Management*, **17** (6), 424–434.

Bruni, A., S. Gherardi and B. Poggio (2004), 'Entrepreneur-mentality, gender, and the study of women entrepreneurs', *Journal of Organizational Change Management*, **17** (3), 256–268.

Casson, Mark, Bernard Yeung, Anuradha Basu and Nigel Wadeson (eds) (2009), *The Oxford Handbook of Entrepreneurship*, Oxford, UK: Oxford University Press.

Davidsson, Per (2004), *Researching Entrepreneurship*, New York: Springer.

Elo, S. and S.H. Kynga (2008), 'The qualitative content analysis process', *Journal of Advanced Nursing*, **62** (1), 107–115.

Evans, J. (1997), 'Men in nursing: Issues of gender segregation and hidden advantage', *Journal of Advanced Nursing*, **26** (2), 226–231.

Gill, R. (2014), '"If you're struggling to survive day-to-day": Class optimism and contradiction in entrepreneurial discourse', *Organization*, **21** (1), 50–67.

Guerreiro, Maria das Dores (1996), *Famílias na Actividade Empresarial. PME em Portugal*, Oeiras, Portugal: Celta Editora.

Heikes, J. (1991), 'Where men are in the minority: The case of the men in nursing', *Sociological Quarterly*, **32** (3), 389–401.

Hsieh, H.-F. and S.E. Shannon (2005), 'Three approaches to qualitative content analysis', *Qualitative Health Research*, **15** (9), 1277–1288.

Jones, C. and A. Spicer (2005), 'The sublime object of entrepreneurship', *Organization*, **12** (2), 223–246.

Kamberidou, I. (2013), 'Women entrepreneurs: "We cannot have change unless we have men in the room"', *Journal of Innovation and Entrepreneurship*, **2** (6), 1–17.

Kelan, E. (2008), 'Emotions in a rational profession: The gendering of skills in ICT work', *Gender, Work and Organization*, **15** (1), 49–71.

Kelly, Louise (2014), *Entrepreneurial Women*, vols I–II, Santa Barbara, CA: Praeger.

Latimer, Joanna (2000), *The Conduct of Care: Understanding Nursing Practice*, Oxford, UK: Wiley-Blackwell.

Lewis, P. (2013), 'The search for an authentic entrepreneurial identity: Difference and professionalism among women business owners', *Gender, Work and Organization*, **20** (3), 252–266.

Lohan, W. and W. Faulkner (2004), 'Masculinities and technologies: Some introductory remarks', *Men and Masculinities*, **6** (4), 319–329.

Lupton, B. (2000), 'Maintaining masculinity: Men who do "women's work"', *British Journal of Management*, **11** (1), 533–548.

Malhotra, A., J. Schulte, P. Patel and P. Petesch (2009), *Innovation for Women's Empowerment and Gender Equality*, Washington, DC: International Center for Research on Women.

Mays, N. and C. Pope (1995), 'Qualitative research: Rigour and qualitative research', *British Medical Journal*, **311** (6997), 109–112.

McDonald, J. (2013), 'Conforming to and resisting dominant gender norms: How male and female nursing students do and undo gender', *Gender, Work and Organization*, **20** (5), 561–579.

Noy, C. (2008), 'Sampling knowledge: The hermeneutics of snowball sampling in qualitative research', *International Journal of Social Research Methodology*, **11** (4), 327–344.

Ogbor, J.O. (2000), 'Mythicizing and reification in entrepreneurial discourse: Ideology-critique of entrepreneurial studies', *Journal of Management Studies*, **37** (5), 605–635.

Oliver, D.G., J.M. Serovich and T.L. Mason (2005), 'Constraints and opportunities with interview transcription: Towards reflection in qualitative research', *Social Forces*, **84** (2), 1273–1289.

Opdenakker, R. (2006), 'Advantages and disadvantages of four interview techniques in qualitative research', *Forum: Qualitative Social Research*, **7** (4), accessed 27 January 2015 at http://www.qualitativeresearch.net/index.php/fqs/article/view/175/392.

Padilha, M.I.C.S., H.H. Vaghetti and G. Brodersen (2006), 'Género e enfermagem uma análise reflexiva', *Revista de Enfermagem*, **14** (2), 292–300.

Perren, L. and P.L. Jennings (2005), 'Government discourses on entrepreneurship: Issues of legitimisation, subjugation, and power', *Entrepreneurship Theory and Practice*, **29** (2), 173–185.

Pope, C. and N. Mays (2006), 'Qualitative methods in health research', in Catherine Pope and Nicholas Mays (eds), *Qualitative Research in Health Care*, 3rd edn, Malden, MA: Blackwell, pp. 1–10.

Poutanen, S. and A. Kovalainen (2013), 'Gendering innovation process in an industrial plant – revisiting tokenism, gender and innovation', *International Journal of Gender and Entrepreneurship*, **5** (3), 257–274.

Programa Estratégico para o Empreendedorismo e Inovação (2014), 'O que é o programa +e+i?', accessed 27 January 2015 at http://www.ei.gov.pt/index/.

Rauch, A. and M. Frese (2007), 'Let's put the person back into entrepreneurship research: A meta-analysis on the relationship between business owners' personality traits, business creation, and success', *European Journal of Work and Organizational Psychology*, **16** (4), 353–385.

Reskin, B. (1988), 'Bringing the men back in: Sex differentiation and the devaluation of women's work', *Gender and Society*, **2** (1), 58–81.

Silverman, D. (2011), *Qualitative Research*, 3rd edn, London: Sage.

Wikhamn, B.R. and D. Knights (2013), 'Open innovation, gender and the infiltration of masculine discourses', *International Journal of Gender and Entrepreneurship*, **5** (3), 275–297.

Wilson, M. (2002), 'Making nursing visible? Gender, technology and the care plan as script', *Information Technology and People*, **12** (2), 139–158.

# PART III

# GENDER AND INNOVATION IN AN ORGANIZATIONAL CONTEXT

# 7. Eyes wide shut: differential influences of gender on innovation in organizations

*Shruti R. Sardeshmukh and Ronda M. Smith*

## INTRODUCTION

Women are becoming an increasingly important market force as consumers and purchasing decision makers (Hewlett et al., 2013b). Organizations can better understand the needs of this increasingly powerful customer group by leveraging an under-utilized source of innovative ideas, their female employees. DeTienne and Chandler (2007) found that women were more likely to undertake the learn–innovate sequence whereby an individual 'identifies a customer need that is not being adequately met and develops a product that represents a significant innovation to that which currently exists in the market' (p. 369). Recognizing women's ideas and developing women to take on senior management positions can therefore be very important for innovation. Not surprisingly, Dezsö and Ross (2012) find that organizations that have at least one woman in the top management team have innovation-intensive strategies and also perform better than organizations with all-male top management. Similar research suggests that, when inputs from female employees are encouraged, organizations are more likely to come up with better and more innovative ideas (Hewlett et al., 2013b). It is clear that such innovations can be very important for existing corporations; in fact, they are critical for the growth and survival of organizations (Baumol, 2002), especially when we recognize the real 'power of the purse' (Hewlett et al., 2013b) among today's women.

It is a fact that women form nearly half of the total labour force in many developed countries (Catalyst, 2014; USDOL, 2010; WGEA, 2014), yet they are underrepresented as innovators (Ranga and Etzkowitz, 2010). Not only are women often clustered in industries that are considered non-innovative (Ranga and Etzkowitz, 2010), but in many cases they are invisible in their employing organizations such that their ideas may not even be heard (Cooper, 2012). Hewlett et al. (2013a) report that, without leadership attending to the entire context and the process of innovation, women are substantially less likely to win support for their ideas. Ignoring the innovative ideas originating from a large proportion of employees can hinder the organization's ability to innovate and stay competitive in the dynamic business environment. This limited perspective is akin to operating with one eye closed, thereby seeing less than half the picture.

Several structural and social barriers exist to women driving and championing their innovative ideas in organizations. As Runco et al. (2010, p. 353) eloquently stated,

> For much of human history, women and men have been allowed very different levels of access to resources, education, and financial support that are necessary for creative performance. This has led to an expectation that men should blaze valuable new trails, but significantly less opportunity for women to do the same. (Runco et al., 2010)

We also know that women are consistently underrepresented in the science, technology and innovation domains (Huyer and Hafkin, 2012). While there are conscious efforts to address this gender imbalance in the science, technology, engineering and mathematics (STEM) fields, there are similar yet unaddressed issues in innovation processes within business organizations.

While the focus on innovation may differ across different industries and public versus private sector organizations, there is an increasing acknowledgement that innovation is a key capability for all organizations in surviving, adapting and creating a competitive advantage in the dynamic work environment (Anderson et al., 2004, 2014; Zhou and Shalley, 2003). Female employees have the potential to contribute substantially to organizational innovation if their ideas are channelled and implemented effectively. Consistent with the goals of this Handbook, we adopt a diversity perspective, emphasizing how gender diversity contributes to coming up with innovative ideas. Once generated, these ideas need to be implemented for the innovation to materialize. As Kuratko (2014) explains, a culture represented by the open sharing of information, and a nurturing environment which allows innovative employees to reach their full potential is important for the organization. If the existing HR policies are not effective in channelling ideas from nearly half the workforce, women in particular, it clearly points towards the business case for incorporating gender-conscious initiatives designed to encourage and incorporate innovative ideas generated by female employees. There is a clear need to identify practices and processes to encourage women's innovative ideas. To address this issue, we draw on research literature from innovation, gender theory and diversity management. We then identify some of the barriers women face in the different stages of the innovation process, and suggest gender-conscious diversity management practices to mitigate the innovation barriers faced by women.

## INNOVATION

Kanter (1984, p. 52) defined innovation as 'the process of bringing any new problem-solving idea into use'. West and Farr (1990) defined workplace innovation as 'the intentional introduction and application within a role, group or organisation of ideas, processes, products or procedures, new to the relevant unit of adoption, designed to significantly benefit the individual, the group, the organisation or wider society' (p. 9). More specifically, innovation in the organizational context has been recognized to involve both the 'development and [the] implementation of new ideas' (Garud et al., 2013; Van de Ven, 1986).

More recently, Anderson et al. (2014) argued that 'Creativity and innovation at work are the process, outcomes, and products of attempts to develop and introduce new and improved ways of doing things. The creativity stage of this process refers to idea generation, and innovation refers to the subsequent stage of implementing ideas toward better procedures, practices, or products' (p. 1298). Based on these definitions, we follow accepted definitions of innovation as a process whereby new and useful ideas are implemented in the organizational context and composed of two distinct stages – idea generation and idea implementation (Mumford et al., 2002).

Research on creativity and innovation indicates that a multitude of factors including individual, team-level and organizational factors influence idea generation in organizations. Individual factors such as personality traits, motivation and psychological states as well as stress and well-being all influence idea generation behaviours (Anderson et al., 2014). We also know that the task context factors, such as job complexity, routinization and job requirements, and social context factors, such as leadership, supervision, social networks and justice perceptions, have an influence on both idea generation and idea implementation (Anderson et al., 2014).

While the research is clear on the key role of employees as the drivers of creativity and innovation (Zhou and Shalley, 2011), there is less research on how the gender of the individuals involved influences the process of innovation in organizations. Innovation is a gendered concept, in the sense that there is a prominent masculine discourse (Alsos et al.,

2013; Wikhamn and Knights, 2013), and conventional images of innovators are typically male. In fact, Ranga and Etzkowitz (2010) articulate that there is an 'implicit, socially constructed assumption that women are less innovative than men as a function of traditional gender relations, that men-dominated industries/sectors are more innovative than women-dominated ones, all rooted in a social perception of technology that is more often associated to men than to women' (p. 3).

Pettersson and Lindberg (2013) point out three key features of masculine discourse on innovation: 1) gender issues are not central to the process and outcomes of innovation; 2) innovation networks and policies continue to be dominated by men; and 3) innovations are usually described in terms of technology and machines, which are male domains, rather than in terms of relationships and services. While the entrepreneurship literature has focused on individuals as the key concepts in the entrepreneurship process, the innovation literature has not paid enough attention to the role of the individual innovator, which reinforces the assumption of male dominance in the innovative sphere (Ranga and Etzkowitz, 2010; Nählinder, 2010). This clearly points to the need for understanding the role of gender in the innovation process.

Extant research suggests there are beneficial effects of gender diversity on innovation. For example, laboratory research has demonstrated the positive effect of gender diversity on decision making (LePine et al., 2002), and tapping women employees for ideas can improve the success of product innovation substantially (Hewlett et al., 2013b). Poutanen and Kovalainen (2013) detail through a narrative how product innovation was actually gendered by the innovator in a manufacturing plant in the chemical industry. By the nature of the innovator being female, and a token player in a male-dominated organization, she was able to recognize and exploit an opportunity to innovate an existing product manufactured by the company, one that the men were likely to have never conceptualized. This individual case study is highly insightful into the potential for women in innovation.

Alsos et al. (2013) propose a framework for a state-of-the-art research agenda on the topic in which they defined innovation in terms of perception from three different perspectives: innovation as 'outputs'; innovation as a 'process'; and the 'discourse' associated with public policy development. In this chapter, we investigate how gender influences the processes within each stage of the innovation, giving attention to the factors that either accelerate or inhibit these processes at the individual and/or the organizational level.

## STAGES OF INNOVATION

### Idea Generation: The Influence of Social Roles, Capabilities and Motivation

Idea generation is the first stage of the innovation process, whereby the individual employees within an organization come up with ideas through a creative process (Mumford, 2000). Innovative ideas come from the need to solve work-related problems or incongruities and discontinuities that individual employees come across during the course of work (Kanter, 1989). Such creativity among employees is driven by expertise and knowledge (Amabile, 1998; Mumford, 2000), creative thinking skills (Amabile, 1998) and intrinsic motivation (Amabile, 1998, 2000). We also know that employee innovation is highly influenced by employees' attitudes and motivation (Amabile and Kramer, 2011). Ford (1996) argued that factors such as sense-making processes, motivation, knowledge and skills influence whether or not employees will participate in creative activities and thereby generate or suggest ideas. While the area of gender and innovation is under-researched, in the next few paragraphs we investigate the factors which might point to the differences between idea generation among men and women employees.

Recall that expertise and knowledge, or human capital, is important for idea generation. Individual differences (including exposure to life experiences) influence ideation, and whether opportunities get recognized and by whom (Shane, 2000). Research in entrepreneurial contexts suggests that human capital varies between men and women, such that they actually utilize different conceptual and cognitive sequences for identifying opportunities (DeTienne and Chandler, 2007). Based on gender roles, women may also make different occupational and educational choices, highlighting the point that women can bring a new knowledge base and can be a new untapped source of ideas. Further, since idea generation is driven by not just the education and work experiences but also life experiences and perspective, women can bring to the table a new set of ideas even if they have similar educational and occupational backgrounds. Tapping this underexplored source of ideas, women as innovators can benefit organizations. Unfortunately, women may also face certain disadvantages, which may impede ideas generated by women. To explore this, we use the framework of social role theory.

### Social roles
Social role theory (Eagly et al., 2000) articulates that the difference in behaviours of men and women can be traced back to the different social

roles undertaken by men and women. Traditionally, women have been underrepresented in the workforce in general, and therefore under-represented in work-related activities associated with creative processes and idea generation. This was because there were fewer opportunities for women to undertake idea generation processes in the work domain. In fact, men still continue to have better career alternatives and resources to undertake work-related creativity and idea generation tasks (Runco et al., 2010). We also know that social roles affect work–family conflict and contribute to a lot of work pressure for individuals. Women continue to be responsible for the lion's share of household work, even when they work full time outside the home. Expressing new ideas in the work environment may require challenging the status quo. In turn, it may also increase the overall work load in the short term, thereby impacting well-being, creating barriers to workplace idea generation for women.

Gender role expectations also hinder the way women's ideas may be expressed. Research shows that women and men do not differ in the innovativeness of their ideas (Alsos et al., 2013; DeTienne and Chandler, 2007), yet women differ from men such that, in an environment where a woman may have to compete and negotiate for her idea to be heard, she may be less likely to present ideas in the first place. Innovation and idea generation are by definition unpredictable and can upset the status quo (Kanter, 1984). This requires agentic behaviour to put forth one's ideas and advance them in competition with other alternatives. Research on negotiation (Kulik and Olekalns, 2012) as well as leadership (Eagly et al., 2003) has demonstrated that gender-role-incongruent behaviour on the part of women often receives a backlash. We also know that entrepreneurial behaviour to put forth one's ideas involves confident, competent agentic behaviour, which can clash with gender role expect-ations and generate a backlash. In fact, we know that women need to use gender-role-consistent influence tactics, while men may use both agentic and communal influence tactics (Smith et al., 2013). Idea generation is not an easy process for an individual, and the costs to the employees are rarely captured in the research on innovation (Janssen et al., 2004). For example, resistance to one's innovative ideas may create interpersonal conflict (Janssen, 2003). In such contexts, women who use agentic tactics to promote their ideas may get a stronger backlash, as they get punished for taking on male roles (Ranga and Etzkowitz, 2010), which may also have an impact on the social support which women employees value (Foss et al., 2013). When women have to express and pitch their ideas in a competitive context, they may underestimate their ideas and experience self-doubt and lower self-efficacy; they may also adopt an accommodat-ing style whereby they may back down and therefore not fully express their ideas (Kray et al., 2001, 2002). Alternatively, they may diminish their agentic behaviour by using disclaimers and hedges, downplaying the importance of their ideas (Reid et al., 2009), which may hinder the ideas getting noticed.

## Development of capabilities

Women also experience fewer developmental opportunities in the workplace, which may hinder the development of expertise. Past research has clearly demonstrated that women are less likely to have access to opportunities to gain experience in key business roles and other similar developmental experiences (Ohlott et al., 1994). Ohlott et al. (1994) found that, while women experience the same obstacles to work advancement as men, they do not have access to the same types and amount of support to overcome these obstacles, leading to lowered motivation and increased stress, resulting in lower idea generation and expression behaviours. The traditional career patterns of continuous employment do not accommodate motherhood, further penalizing women in terms of advancement (Ranga and Etzkowitz, 2010). Therefore, we argue that in traditional organizational structures women experience obstacles in acquiring the key knowledge base and lack the necessary support to overcome them, creating impediments to their development in organizations.

## Motivation

Motivation is a core component driving creativity and idea generation processes in organizations. Traditionally, women identify more closely with family roles and men identify with the role of work. In other words, traditional gender role orientation indicates that men seem to demonstrate more work centrality and women seem to demonstrate more family centrality (Livingston and Judge, 2008). We know that work role centrality is strongly influenced by socialization processes (Mannheim, 1993). The more salient the role to the individual, we can argue that the more motivated an individual is to contribute creatively to that domain, indicating that the creative potential of women is traditionally less likely to be expressed in the work role, reducing the motivation for women to apply their creative thinking skills in work roles.

Women face greater challenges when they express their ideas, further reducing their motivation. Given the barriers they face, women may need more encouragement than men to advance their ideas within the corporate hierarchy (Tharenou et al., 1994). In fact, successful women who can push forth their ideas may have to use the strategy of getting informal male support ahead of the meetings, and even let go of some if not all of the credit for the ideas (Ranga and Etzkowitz, 2010), all of which can dampen the motivation to participate in the innovation process fully.

Research by Khazanchi and Masterson (2011) on employees and supervisors in a creative context in India suggests that supervisors in organizations have the ability to influence idea generation behaviours, and the organizational context influences how safe it is to promote ideas once generated. They concluded that organizational justice, specifically informational justice, influences employees' perceived organizational support and therefore employees feel safer sharing their ideas upward. In turn, organizations that can establish trust through honest and transparent communication with employees can expect employees to be more likely to contribute to idea generating discussions.

Innovative ideas are a unique product of an individual's experience, problems and perspective; as women's work, and hence perspective, continues to be undermined in the workplace, so are their ideas. Research suggests that, when ideas are put forth and presented, women's ideas may not even be heard (Cooper, 2012). Further, if traditional work structures are not receptive to ideas generated by women, it may lead creative female employees to restore psychological balance by withdrawing from the idea generation process (Farmer et al., 2003) and further reducing the intrinsic motivation for generating ideas in the work domain (Amabile, 1998). In addition, contributions by women to innovative ideas often go unrecognized (Ranga and Etzkowitz, 2010), further reducing their motivation. As a result, while women may be equally abled (e.g. to generate the same number of ideas), they may not be equally heard (e.g. not all their innovative ideas get expressed let alone captured for consideration and further implementation) or feel equally valued. Such practices call for organizations to reconsider the opportunities within their organizational policies and day-to-day practices to increase trust via organizational justice in all its forms: procedural, distributive, interactional and informational (cf. Colquitt and Rodell, 2011).

***Proposition 1:*** *While individual, task, social and contextual factors all influence idea generation, gender may also impact the process of idea generation such that women's idea generation is hindered by social role expectations in several ways.*

While it is clear that women's ideas can bring forth unarticulated approaches and new avenues, it is not very clear that the ideas generated by women will get captured for implementation. In the next few paragraphs we identify challenges to women in terms of idea implementation.

## Idea Implementation: The Role of Social Networks, Social Capital and Champions

Idea implementation is a key stage in the innovation process, to the extent that innovation is defined as 'the implementation or adoption of new, useful ideas by people in organizations' (Amabile, 1998; Amabile et al., 1996). Without implementation of the generated ideas, there is no innovation.

Research has also found that, while the idea generation process is influenced more by the individual and task characteristics, the implementation of innovative ideas is a function of group and organizational characteristics (Axtell et al., 2000). Innovation implementation is an inherently social process, and West and Hirst (2003, p. 297) state that 'innovations commonly involve changes to an array of processes, and are rarely the result of the activity of one individual. Thus, for an innovation to be implemented effectively, teamwork and cooperation are essential.' Participative decision making, supportive peers, supervisory support and autonomy within work roles translate into greater implementation of ideas (Amabile, 1998). In their article on gender and innovation, Foss et al. (2013) state that 'there is a need for a broader understanding of the factors that facilitate or hamper employees in implementing new ideas' (p. 313). In other words, developing an understanding of the factors that enhance or hamper employee idea implementation can also help us better understand gender-specific factors that hinder women's ideas being implemented.

It is well articulated that diversity can spur creative potential in teams, but it can also stymie implementation (Ancona and Caldwell, 1992; Williams and O'Reilly, 1998), as diversity in a group may impact the social dynamics of that group. This indicates that we need to take into account the social dynamics, including social networks and social capital, to understand the process of innovation implementation.

### Social networks and social capital

In this context, we investigate the role of a social capital perspective. While social capital is defined in many ways, in essence it captures the value of an individual's connections with resource-filled others (Borgatti and Foster, 2003). In other words, social capital involves social networks that can be accessed for resources, and such networks are very important for implementation of innovation. In fact, Obstfeld (2005) argues that such social network activity is the key to an individual's engagement with the innovation. The social capital may exist at individual, organizational or even regional level. In this chapter, we focus on the social capital of individuals within an organization and use the definition by Payne et al. (2011): 'Assets and resources made available through social relationships that an individual can use to their personal benefit' (p. 497). In general, the more diverse the social contacts, or the less constrained the networks, the greater is the social capital for the individuals such that individuals can get access to more diverse and unique information through these networks. Individuals with diverse networks can also bridge structural holes, thereby coordinating and accessing otherwise inaccessible resources (Burt, 1998).

Social capital is generated through an individual's social networks. The principle of homophily (McPherson et al., 2001) suggests that people with similar characteristics tend to form network ties. Not surprisingly, social networks are highly gendered, and women tend to have less constrained networks such that they have more women in their networks than men. When the professions are male-dominated, just the lack of numbers may hinder women's social networks with colleagues as well as supervisors, as it limits the informal interactions (Koberg et al., 1998).

Further, we know that women are often 'outsiders' and lack the necessary legitimacy through their own social networks (Burt, 1998) in the sense that women are often clustered at the lower end of the hierarchy, with substantially less presence in the upper echelons of the organization (Dezsö and Ross, 2012). In the business, technology and general organizational hierarchy, 'women are regarded as the second sex' (Rönnblom and Keisu, 2013, p. 352). Further, the returns to social capital are different for women than for men (Burt, 1998). Women benefit more from developing closer network ties with contacts on the higher rungs of the hierarchy, as it can allow them to 'borrow' social capital, yet homophily makes it difficult for women to develop close ties with higher-status male network contacts. We argue that a lack of social capital may hinder the implementation of ideas generated by women. When women do indeed attain the higher status in the network, they may experience the disadvantages of tokenism (Kanter, 1977).

**Role of champions**

Closely related is a notion of idea champions. Innovation research and best practices have long suggested that idea champions play a key role in the implementation of new ideas. Chakrabarti (1974) defined the role of champions as the role of 'selling the idea to the management and getting the management sufficiently interested in the project' (p. 58). Such champions 'are required to turn a new idea into a concrete new project' (Burgelman, 1983, p. 232) to garner support (Howell and Higgins, 1990) and are articulated to be a 'critical contributor to successful innovation' (Kelley and Lee, 2010).

Innovative ideas also involve changes to existing structures, processes and practices. The status quo is comfortable to many, and some may tend to lose resources or power as a result of innovative ideas, which may create resistance to the implementation of the innovative ideas (Ford and Sullivan, 2004). To overcome obstacles to implementation of the novel ideas, an individual may need to engage the support of idea champions in higher or more influential ranks within the organization. While it is natural that not all ideas that are generated find a path to implementation, research has shown that women and minorities are less likely to win senior management endorsement for their ideas, thus reducing the chance of their innovative ideas being implemented (Hewlett et al., 2013a).

The challenge then becomes: where do individual employees find champions for their ideas? Champions often tend to be supervisors or managers who use their 'power and influence to help ... navigate the complex socio-political maze inside their corporations' (Day, 1994, p. 150). Social capital generated through network ties can help individuals find champions for implementing their ideas. However, the outsider status of women (Burt, 1998) may restrict their access to finding champions for implementing their ideas.

The social network challenges for women are even more intensified when the idea generator is a woman who attempts to gain champions from a higher rung in the hierarchy. Women may have to advance their ideas in the face of other competing ideas for implementation, and, as we outlined before, such competitive agentic behaviour can generate a backlash against women. Further, a shortage of women available in senior management positions may force women to seek a male champion for their ideas. This dynamic may create more barriers than having a same-gendered champion in pursuit of innovation in the workplace, thereby further hindering the implementation of ideas generated by women in the organization.

**Proposition 2:**   *Inadequate social capital may hinder the implementation of ideas generated by women, such that women's social networks, which lack social capital, hinder their access to idea champions and reduce the implementation chances for women's ideas.*

## DIVERSITY MANAGEMENT PRACTICES

Management policies, in particular HR policies and processes, can therefore indicate the organization's commitment to employee-driven innovation. We know that HR practices play an important role in developing a culture that promotes creativity, idea generation and innovation. Such HR policies also need to take into account the gendered perspective on innovation. Therefore, we draw on the literature on diversity management practices and suggest gender-blind and gender-conscious human resource policies to foster innovation in organizations.

To encourage women's input into idea generation and idea implementation, the organizations need to adopt what Thomas and Ely call an 'Integration-and-Learning Perspective' (Ely and Thomas, 2001; Thomas and Ely, 1996). An Integration-and-Learning Perspective is characterized by the organizations' appreciation of 'the insights, skills, and experiences employees have developed as members of various cultural identity groups [, which] are potentially valuable resources that the work group can use to rethink its primary tasks and redefine its markets, products, strategies, and business practices in ways that will advance its mission' (Ely and Thomas, 2001, p. 240). From such a perspective follow diversity management practices implemented in the organization (Kulik, 2014). Yang and Konrad (2011b) define diversity management practices as 'the set of formalized practices developed and implemented by organisations to manage diversity effectively among all organisational stakeholders'. These practices encompass broad aspects of HR practices, including recruitment and selection, training and development, performance management, and compensation.

Konrad and Linnehan (1995) distinguish between identity-blind and identity-conscious HR practices. Identity-blind practices emphasize elimination of discrimination by being blind to demographic group membership and applying HR practices equally across all groups. Identity-conscious practices, on the other hand, explicitly and formally include demographic group identity in HR decisions in addition to the identity-blind practices.

Kulik (2014) distinguishes between identity-blind and identity-conscious practices for an organization developing a mentoring programme. For example, an organization may develop a gender-blind mentoring programme for the junior staff of either gender to advance into management positions. On the other hand, a gender-conscious mentoring programme will involve a targeted programme for the female junior staff; such a programme would involve training and tactics to address the challenges faced by women. We also know that identity-conscious diversity management can be more effective for achieving diversity outcomes (Konrad and Linnehan, 1995).

In the context of innovation, organizations may implement general practices which pertain to the inclusion of a diversity of ideas and voices coming from various ranks, perspectives and positions within an organization, and they may be applicable across different groups. While such an organizational climate for innovation and flexibility (Patterson et al., 2005) can foster innovation, it is important to understand whether the openness is accessible to women. In other words, employee involvement practices (Yang and Konrad, 2011a) which reach out to marginalized employees, including women, are critical to making sure that women get access to key knowledge flows. However, if identity-blind employee involvement practices will not effectively mitigate the challenges encountered by women in participating fully in the innovation process, it may be necessary to incorporate the gender-conscious practices that can help women overcome the different biases they experience in the process of idea generation and implementation. We argue that identity-conscious practices (Konrad and Linnehan, 1995) when adopted by organizations will encourage and support the development of ideas presented by women and further encourage idea generation and innovation.

## DISCUSSION

Both the idea generation and the idea implementation stages are critical to organizational innovation. They are also closely linked in the sense that implemented ideas come from the pool of generated ideas. The idea generation and idea implementation stages are clearly linked, yet there is little research that takes a holistic perspective on the innovation process incorporating both the stages (Anderson et al., 2014). There are strong reasons for encouraging employees to generate more ideas. Beyond that, Diehl and Stroebe (1987) found that the quality and quantity of submitted ideas were closely related in brainstorming research, suggesting that by encouraging employees to generate more ideas it can in effect also improve the motivation for participating as well as the quality of ideas. On the other hand, having one's ideas ignored may be demotivating, creating dissatisfaction among the employees. This chapter indicates that women consistently face disadvantages in the idea generation and implementation phases, indicating that the disadvantages are cumulative, and removing the innovation barriers for women can be very beneficial for the organization. Women are often clustered at the bottom of the hierarchy. They also form a large number of boundary employees in service industries, as they interact with the customers. We also know that women entrepreneurs are more likely to come up with innovations that satisfy customer needs (DeTienne and Chandler, 2007), indicating that women can be a formidable source of 'bottom-up' innovation. Such 'bottom-up' innovations, those coming from the lower levels in organizations, tend to be more fundamental and radical (Granovetter, 2005), indicating that there is a strong business case for encouraging innovative ideas by female employees.

The consequences of silencing women's ideas go beyond the outcome of missing out on opportunities for innovation. Silencing women's ideas may discourage women from being engaged with their work roles and make for unhappy employees. Further, the organization may lose the resource if the employee leaves the organization because her voice is not heard (Withey and Cooper, 1989).

While the innovation processes are clearly gendered (Alsos et al., 2013; Ranga and Etzkowitz, 2010), the innovation landscape is changing. With the advent of global teams and information and communication technology (ICT), the gender of the person in the team is becoming less important, levelling the field for women to put forth their ideas and implement them. Innovation is no longer just about product and process innovation, but it also includes innovation in services (Ranga and Etzkowitz, 2010). In addition there is a movement towards greater emphasis on collaborative open innovation processes, rather than the more traditional, agentic, solo innovator models (Wikhamn and Knights, 2013), suggesting that feminine approaches have an important role to play in the innovation process. The changes in the innovation landscape and the increasing power of the purse indicate that women will become increasingly important players in the innovation domain. Therefore, gender-conscious HR policies will be very important for organizations that want to harness the innovative potential within their female employees.

## RECOMMENDATIONS

Based on the diversity management literature on gender-conscious policies, we offer the following recommendations for organizations:

- Provision of channels and processes to express ideas. Research indicates that women thrive on opportunities for mastery but do not seek competition (Kanfer and Ackerman, 2000), suggesting that creating a safe and supportive environment for idea capturing can help channel creative ideas by women in the workplace. Empirical support also shows that co-worker support is important for women during the idea generation stage (Foss et al., 2013). Therefore, through the design of supportive 'ladders' to channel their innovative ideas, and provision of organizational support through diversity management, women may be encouraged to advance new ideas for the organization.

- Gender-conscious team formation. A traditional option in organizations is to use participative management techniques, forming a committee or a problem-solving team to address an issue or generate solutions to a problem. The forming of such committees or teams in itself can raise concerns about who was or wasn't included. When possible, such groups should be gender-balanced. Depending on the culture of the organization, when people speak up, their identity and role in the organization may automatically be attached to the idea, so that the idea is evaluated in the context of whom the idea came from as opposed to the idea being assessed on its own merits. An option of course is to solicit ideas from employees anonymously so that the identity of the person suggesting it is unknown. In circumstances when this is not feasible, techniques such as using computer-mediated communication tools (Pissarra and Jesuino, 2005) or variations of the nominal group technique may allow for more anonymity, or at least reduce the association of specific ideas with individual participants (cf. Paulhus and Yang, 2000).

- Women's innovation network (WIN) role models, networking and support groups. Diversity management practices that encourage the development of 'affinity groups', in our context women's innovation networks, can lead to better outcomes for women (Yang and Konrad, 2011a). The outcomes of such networking can provide women 'with the tools, insights and more importantly, the support into organisational life' to advance in the organization (Hersby et al., 2009). For example, lean in circles (http://leanincircles.org/) provide peer support for women who want to take on new challenges, and such or similar networks within the organization can help women by information sharing as well as peer support. It can also create opportunities for networking with women across the hierarchy, and further develop women's networks to enhance their social capital. In addition, while the traditional discourse in the innovation literature is masculine, a strong connectivity among women innovator networks can promote the inclusion of 'mother-hood', a metaphor representing the household (Brush et al., 2009) in the innovation discussion. Finally, such networks can exemplify the need for grit and persistence to drive the innovative ideas to completion, and provide support for women (Dhaliwal, 2010).

- Mentoring and idea champion programmes. Mentoring is an excellent developmental tool that can help women advance within organizations (Ragins, 1999). The same tool can be used to channel female employees' innovative ideas by actively developing senior champions for women innovators. The literature on gender and mentoring has consistently highlighted that women do not always get access to high-quality mentors (Ragins and Cotton, 1991). Women may not be able to access women mentors, as the number of women in senior leadership positions continues to be small (Dezsö and Ross, 2012). Yet access to male mentors may not be a setback for encouraging women's innovative ideas. In fact, high-powered male mentors can help provide better sponsorship for advancement (Ragins and Kram, 2007; Sosik and Godshalk, 2000). These mentors can also undertake the role of idea champions and create opportunities for women's ideas to get noticed and implemented. Such mentoring can create social capital for female protégés (Burt, 1998) and provide them with the legitimacy they need to advance their ideas. This is consistent with the finding by Hewlett et al. (2013a) that support from senior leadership can indeed provide channels for the implementation of women's innovative ideas. Therefore, developing gender-conscious mentoring and idea champion programmes can help channel female employees' innovative ideas.

## CONCLUSIONS

Pursuit of innovation requires that organizations not just take into account the diversity of the individuals involved but also embrace a broader perspective of valuing novel ideas and new approaches towards problem solving.

Bringing together the diversity and innovation literature, we contribute to both the gender and the innovation literature in several ways. First, by exploring the ways gender may influence the activities in the process of innovation we highlight an important but often overlooked resource and capability within organizations, that is, female employees. Second, by recommending identity-conscious practices for capturing and nurturing innovative ideas, we offer a means by which to be more inclusive of all employees, especially women, in the workplace. By exploring the structures and processes in organizations, we address the call for research in gender and innovation (Alsos et al., 2013). Finally, identity-conscious HR policies have been primarily developed in the area of diversity management and targeted to human resources practitioners. By extending this conversation to the innovation audience, we not only deepen the HR conversation, but also have the potential to reach many male-dominated professions in the operational areas of business, including the sciences.

We have argued that, to encourage idea generation and idea implementation by women, it is not enough to include women in the process (e.g. tokenism); rather it is important to develop and foster organizational practices that involve organizational structures and communication channels that facilitate women's involvement as well as the full consideration of their respective ideas in the innovation process. In an effort both to influence our academic understanding of the role of gender in innovation and to address the needs in practice, our discussion here has focused on the processes involved in innovation within organizations as well as some organizational strategies addressing diversity management practices that could be useful to organizations desiring to enhance the role of women in their innovation processes.

# REFERENCES

Alsos, G.A., E. Ljunggren and U. Hytti (2013), 'Gender and innovation: State of the art and a research agenda', *International Journal of Gender and Entrepreneurship*, **5** (3), 236–256.

Amabile, T.M. (1998), 'How to kill creativity', *Harvard Business Review*, **76** (5), 76–87.

Amabile, T.M. (2000), 'Stimulate creativity by fueling passion', in Edwin A. Locke (ed.), *Basic Principles of Organizational Behavior: A Handbook*, Oxford, UK: Blackwell, pp. 331–341.

Amabile, T.M. and S.J. Kramer (2011), 'The power of small wins', *Harvard Business Review*, **89** (5), 70–80.

Amabile, T.M., R. Conti, H. Coon, J. Lazenby and M. Herron (1996), 'Assessing the work environment for creativity', *Academy of Management Journal*, **39** (5), 1154–1184.

Ancona, D.G. and D.F. Caldwell (1992), 'Demography and design: Predictors of new product team performance', *Organization Science*, **3** (3), 321–341.

Anderson, N., C.K.W. De Dreu and B.A. Nijstad (2004), 'The routinization of innovation research: A constructively critical review of the state-of-the-science', *Journal of Organizational Behavior*, **25** (2), 147–173.

Anderson, N., K. Potočnik and J. Zhou (2014), 'Innovation and creativity in organizations: A state-of-the-science review, prospective commentary, and guiding framework', *Journal of Management*, **40** (5), 1297–1333.

Axtell, C.M., D.J. Holman, K.L. Unsworth, T.D. Wall, P.E. Waterson and E. Harrington (2000), 'Shopfloor innovation: Facilitating the suggestion and implementation of ideas', *Journal of Occupational and Organizational Psychology*, **73** (3), 265–285.
Baumol, William J. (ed.) (2002), *The Free-market Innovation Machine: Analyzing the Growth Miracle of Capitalism*, Princeton, NJ: Princeton University Press.
Borgatti, S.P. and P.C. Foster (2003), 'The network paradigm in organizational research: A review and typology', *Journal of Management*, **29** (6), 991–1013.
Brush, C.G., A. de Bruin and F. Welter (2009), 'A gender-aware framework for women's entrepreneurship', *International Journal of Gender and Entrepreneurship*, **1** (1), 8–24.
Burgelman, R.A. (1983), 'A process model of internal corporate venturing in the diversified major firm', *Administrative Science Quarterly*, **28** (2), 223–244.
Burt, R.S. (1998), 'The gender of social capital', *Rationality and Society*, **10** (1), 5–46.
Catalyst (2014), 'Statistical overview of women in the workplace', accessed 4 March 2015 at http://www.catalyst.org/knowledge/statistical-overview-women-workplace.
Chakrabarti, A.K. (1974), 'The role of champion in product innovation', *California Management Review*, **17** (2), 58–62.
Colquitt, J. and J. Rodell (2011), 'Justice, trust and trustworthiness: A longitudinal analysis integrating three theoretical perspectives', *Academy of Management Journal*, **54** (6), 1183–1206.
Cooper, R. (2012), 'The gender gap in union leadership in Australia: A qualitative study', *Journal of Industrial Relations*, **54** (2), 131–146.
Day, D.L. (1994), 'Raising radicals: Different processes for championing innovative corporate ventures', *Organization Science*, **5** (2), 148–172.
DeTienne, D.R. and G.N. Chandler (2007), 'The role of gender in opportunity identification', *Entrepreneurship Theory and Practice*, **31** (3), 365–386.
Dezsö, C.L. and D.G. Ross (2012), 'Does female representation in top management improve firm performance? A panel data investigation', *Strategic Management Journal*, **33** (9), 1072–1089.
Dhaliwal, S. (2010), 'Training women to win', *International Journal of Gender and Entrepreneurship*, **2** (3), 287–290.
Diehl, M. and W. Stroebe (1987), 'Productivity loss in brainstorming groups: Toward the solution of a riddle', *Journal of Personality and Social Psychology*, **53** (3), 497–509.
Eagly, Alice H., Wendy Wood and Amanda B. Diekman (2000), 'Social role theory of sex differences and similarities: A current appraisal', in Thomas Eckes and Hanns M. Trautner (eds), *The Developmental Social Psychology of Gender*, New York: Psychology Press, pp. 123–174.
Eagly, A.H., M.C. Johannesen-Schmidt and M.L. van Engen (2003), 'Transformational, transactional, and laissez-faire leadership styles: A meta-analysis comparing women and men', *Psychological Bulletin*, **129** (4), 569–591.
Ely, R.J. and D.A. Thomas (2001), 'Cultural diversity at work: The effects of diversity perspectives on work group processes and outcomes', *Administrative Science Quarterly*, **46** (2), 229–273.
Farmer, S.M., P. Tierney and K. Kung-McIntyre (2003), 'Employee creativity in Taiwan: An application of role identity theory', *Academy of Management Journal*, **46** (5), 618–630.
Ford, C.M. (1996), 'A theory of individual creative action in multiple social domains', *Academy of Management Review*, **21** (4), 1112–1142.
Ford, C. and D.M. Sullivan (2004), 'A time for everything: How the timing of novel contributions influences project team outcomes', *Journal of Organizational Behavior*, **25** (2), 279–292.
Foss, L., K. Woll and M. Moilanen (2013), 'Creativity and the implementation of new ideas: Do organizational structure, work environment and gender matter?', *International Journal of Gender and Entrepreneurship*, **5** (3), 298–322.

Garud, R., P. Tuertscher and A.H. Van de Ven (2013), 'Perspectives on innovation processes', *Academy of Management Annals*, **7** (1), 775–819.

Granovetter, M. (2005), 'The impact of social structure on economic outcomes', *Journal of Economic Perspectives*, **19** (1), 33–50.

Hersby, M.D., M.K. Ryan and J. Jetten (2009), 'Getting together to get ahead: The impact of social structure on women's networking', *British Journal of Management*, **20** (4), 415–430.

Hewlett, S.A., M. Marshall and L. Sherbin (2013a), 'How diversity can drive innovation', *Harvard Business Review*, **91** (12), 30–30.

Hewlett, S.A., M. Marshall and L. Sherbin (2013b), 'How women drive innovation and growth', *HBR Blog Network*, accessed 4 March 2015 at https://hbr.org/2013/08/how-women-drive-innovation-and/.

Howell, J.M. and C.A. Higgins (1990), 'Champions of technological innovation', *Administrative Science Quarterly*, **35** (2), 317–341.

Huyer, S. and N. Hafkin (2012), 'National assessments on gender equality in the knowledge society: Gender in science, technology and innovation', Women in Global Science and Technology, accessed 4 March 2015 at http://wisat.org/data/documents/GEKS_-Synthesis-Nov2012.pdf.

Janssen, O. (2003), 'Innovative behavior and job involvement at the price of conflict and less satisfactory relations with co-workers', *Journal of Occupational and Organizational Psychology*, **76** (3), 347–364.

Janssen, O., E. van de Vliert and M. West (2004), 'The bright and dark sides of individual and group innovation: A special issue introduction', *Journal of Organizational Behavior*, **25** (2), 129–145.

Kanfer, R. and P. Ackerman (2000), 'Individual differences in work motivation: Further explorations of a trait framework', *Applied Psychology*, **49** (3), 470–482.

Kanter, R.M. (1977), *Men and Women of the Corporation*, New York: Basic Books.

Kanter, R.M. (1984), 'SMR forum: Innovation: Our only hope for times ahead?', *MIT Sloan Management Review*, **25** (4), 51–55.

Kanter, R.M. (1989), 'Swimming in newstreams: Mastering innovation dilemmas', *California Management Review*, **31** (4), 45–69.

Kelley, D. and H. Lee (2010), 'Managing innovation champions: The impact of project characteristics on the direct manager role', *Journal of Product Innovation Management*, **27** (7), 1007–1019.

Khazanchi, S. and S.S. Masterson (2011), 'Who and what is fair matters: A multi-foci social exchange model of creativity', *Journal of Organizational Behavior*, **32** (1), 86–106.

Koberg, C.S., R.W. Boss and E. Goodman (1998), 'Factors and outcomes associated with mentoring among health-care professionals', *Journal of Vocational Behavior*, **53** (1), 58–72.

Konrad, A.M. and F. Linnehan (1995), 'Formalized HRM structures: Coordinating equal employment opportunity or concealing organizational practices?', *Academy of Management Journal*, **38** (3), 787–820.

Kray, L.J., L. Thompson and A. Galinsky (2001), 'Battle of the sexes: Gender stereotype confirmation and reactance in negotiations', *Journal of Personality and Social Psychology*, **80** (6), 942.

Kray, L.J., A.D. Galinsky and L. Thompson (2002), 'Reversing the gender gap in negotiations: An exploration of stereotype regeneration', *Organizational Behavior and Human Decision Processes*, **87** (2), 386–410.

Kulik, C.T. (2014), 'Working below and above the line: The research–practice gap in diversity management', *Human Resource Management Journal*, **24** (2), 129–144.

Kulik, C.T. and M. Olekalns (2012), 'Negotiating the gender divide: Lessons from the negotiation and organizational behavior literatures', *Journal of Management*, **38** (4), 1387–1415.

Kuratko, D.F. (2014), *Entrepreneurship: Theory, Process, Practice*, 9th edn, Mason, OH: South-Western Cengage Learning.

LePine, J.A., J.R. Hollenbeck, D.R. Ilgen, J.A. Colquitt and A. Ellis (2002), 'Gender composition, situational strength, and team decision-making accuracy: A criterion decomposition approach', *Organizational Behavior and Human Decision Processes*, **88** (1), 445–475.

Livingston, B. and T. Judge (2008), 'Emotional responses to work–family conflict: An examination of gender role orientation among working men and women', *Journal of Applied Psychology*, **93** (1), 207–216.

Mannheim, B. (1993), 'Gender and the effects of demographics, status, and work values on work centrality', *Work and Occupations*, **20** (1), 3–22.

McPherson, M., L. Smith-Lovin and J.M. Cook (2001), 'Birds of a feather: Homophily in social networks', *Annual Review of Sociology*, **27** (1), 415–444.

Mumford, M.D. (2000), 'Managing creative people: Strategies and tactics for innovation', *Human Resource Management Review*, **10** (3), 313–351.

Mumford, M.D., G.M. Scott, B. Gaddis and J.M. Strange (2002), 'Leading creative people: Orchestrating expertise and relationships', *Leadership Quarterly*, **13** (6), 705–750.

Nählinder, J. (2010), 'Where are all the female innovators? Nurses as innovators in a public sector innovation project', *Journal of Technology Management and Innovation*, **5** (1), 13–29.

Obstfeld, D. (2005), 'Social networks, the tertius iungens orientation, and involvement in innovation', *Administrative Science Quarterly*, **50** (1), 100–130.

Ohlott, P.J., M.N. Ruderman and C.D. McCauley (1994), 'Gender differences in developmental job experiences', *Academy of Management Journal*, **37** (1), 46–67.

Patterson, M.G., M.A. West, V.J. Shackleton, J.F. Dawson, R. Lawthom, S. Maitlis, D.L. Robinson and A.M. Wallace (2005), 'Validating the organizational climate measure: Links to managerial practices, productivity and innovation', *Journal of Organizational Behavior*, **26** (4), 379–408.

Paulhus, P.B. and H.C. Yang (2000), 'Idea generation in groups: A basis for creativity in organisations', *Organizational Behavior and Human Decision Processing*, **82** (1), 76–87.

Payne, G.T., C.B. Moore, S.E. Griffis and C.W. Autry (2011), 'Multilevel challenges and opportunities in social capital research', *Journal of Management*, **37** (2), 491–520.

Pettersson, K. and M. Lindberg (2013), 'Paradoxical spaces of feminist resistance: Mapping the margin to the masculinist innovation discourse', *International Journal of Gender and Entrepreneurship*, **5** (3), 323–341.

Pissarra, J. and J.C. Jesuino (2005), 'Idea generation through computer-mediated communication: The effects of anonymity', *Journal of Managerial Psychology*, **20** (3/4), 275–291.

Poutanen, S. and A. Kovalainen (2013), 'Gendering innovation process in an industrial plant – revisiting tokenism, gender and innovation', *International Journal of Gender and Entrepreneurship*, **5** (3), 257–274.

Ragins, Belle R. (1999), 'Gender and mentoring relationships: A review and research agenda for the next decade', in Gary N. Powell (ed.), *Handbook of Gender and Work*, Thousand Oaks, CA: Sage, pp. 347–370.

Ragins, B.R. and J.L. Cotton (1991), 'Easier said than done: Gender differences in perceived barriers to gaining a mentor', *Academy of Management Journal*, **34** (4), 939–951.

Ragins, Belle R. and Kathy E. Kram (eds) (2007), *The Handbook of Mentoring at Work: Theory, Research, and Practice*, Thousand Oaks, CA: Sage.

Ranga, M. and H. Etzkowitz (2010), 'Athena in the world of techne: The gender dimension of technology, innovation and entrepreneurship', *Journal of Technology Management and Innovation*, **5** (1), 1–12.

Reid, S.A., N.A. Palomares, G.L. Anderson and B. Bondad-Brown (2009), 'Gender, language, and social influence: A test of expectation states, role congruity and self-categorization theories', *Human Communication Research*, **35** (4), 465–490.

Rönnblom, M. and B.I. Keisu (2013), 'Constructions of innovation and gender (equality) in Swedish universities', *International Journal of Gender and Entrepreneurship*, **5** (3), 342–356.

Runco, Mark A., Bonnie Cramond and Alexander R. Pagnani (2010), 'Gender and creativity', in Joan C. Chrisler and Donald R. McCreary (eds), *Handbook of Gender Research in Psychology*, New York: Springer, pp. 343–357.

Shane, S. (2000), 'Prior knowledge and the discovery of entrepreneurial opportunities', *Organizational Science*, **11** (4), 448–469.

Smith, A.N., M.B. Watkins, M.J. Burke, M.S. Christian, C.E. Smith, A. Hall and S. Simms (2013), 'Gendered influence: A gender role perspective on the use and effectiveness of influence tactics', *Journal of Management*, **39** (5), 1156–1183.

Sosik, J.J. and V.M. Godshalk (2000), 'The role of gender in mentoring: Implications for diversified and homogenous mentoring relationships', *Journal of Vocational Behavior*, **57** (1), 102–122.

Tharenou, P., S. Latimer and D. Conroy (1994), 'How do you make it to the top? An examination of influences on women's and men's managerial advancement', *Academy of Management Journal*, **37** (4), 899–931.

Thomas, D.A. and R.J. Ely (1996), 'Making differences matter: A new paradigm for managing diversity', *Harvard Business Review*, **74** (5), 79–90.

USDOL (United States Department of Labor) (2010), 'Women in the labor force in 2010', accessed 4 March 2015 at http://www.dol.gov/wb/factsheets/Qf-laborforce-10.htm.

Van de Ven, A.H. (1986), 'Central problems in the management of innovation', *Management Science*, **32** (5), 590–607.

West, Michael and James Farr (1990), 'Innovation and creativity at work: Psychological and organisational strategies', in Michael A. West and James L. Farr (eds), *Innovation and Creativity at Work: Psychological and Organizational Strategies*, Chichester, UK: Wiley, pp. 3–13.

West, M.A. and G. Hirst (2003), 'Cooperation and teamwork for innovation', in M. West, D. Tjosvold and K. Smith (eds), *International Handbook of Organizational Teamwork and Co-operative Working*, Chichester, UK: Wiley, pp. 297–319.

WGEA (Workplace Gender Equality Agency) (2014), 'Gender workplace statistics at a glance', accessed 4 March 2015 at https://www.wgea.gov.au/sites/default/files/Stats_at_a_Glance.pdf.

Wikhamn, B.R. and D. Knights (2013), 'Open innovation, gender and the infiltration of masculine discourses', *International Journal of Gender and Entrepreneurship*, **5** (3), 275–297.

Williams, K.Y. and C.A. O'Reilly (1998), 'Demography and diversity in organisations: A review of 40 years of research', in Barry M. Staw and L.L. Cummings (eds), *Research in Organizational Behavior*, Greenwich, CT: JAI Press, pp. 77–140.

Withey, M.J. and W.H. Cooper (1989), 'Predicting exit, voice, loyalty and neglect', *Administrative Science Quarterly*, **34** (4), 521–539.

Yang, Y. and A.M. Konrad (2011a), 'Diversity and organisational innovation: The role of employee involvement', *Journal of Organizational Behavior*, **32** (8), 1062–1083.

Yang, Y. and A.M. Konrad (2011b), 'Understanding diversity management practices: Implications of institutional theory and resource-based theory', *Group and Organization Management*, **36** (1), 6–38.

Zhou, J. and C.E. Shalley (2003), 'Research on employee creativity: A critical review and directions for future research', in Joseph Martocchio (ed.), *Research in Personnel and Human Resource Management*, Oxford, UK: Elsevier, pp. 165–217.

Zhou, J. and C.E. Shalley (2011), 'Deepening our understanding of creativity in the workplace: A review of different approaches to creativity research', in Sheldon Zedeck (ed.), *APA Handbook of Industrial and Organizational Psychology*, Vol. 1: *Building and Developing the Organization*, Washington, DC: American Psychological Association, pp. 275–302.

# 8. Innovation in public care

*Nina Amble in cooperation with Paula Axelsen and Liv Karen Snerthammer**

## INTRODUCTION

The large cohorts of children born after the Second World War, 'the baby-boomers', are becoming 'a grey tsunami' in need of care, a need estimated to peak in 2040 (Gjefsen et al., 2014). In Norway, the majority of the staff in elderly care work part-time. This is a challenge, because: 1) a patient receives a disproportionate number of staff to relate to; 2) the staff receive a fragmented work environment and an income that it is impossible to live on; and 3) the managers have to lead too many employees with small jobs. Innovation is one of the means for solving this problem (NOU, 2011). In this chapter we address the following research question: how could a traditional part-time-dependent rota work system be challenged by the concept of innovation in order to create new pioneering working schedules based on full-time[1] positions? This expression and use of words contains a priority, namely to those who want to work full-time ahead of those who only want to work a little bit more, for example 60 per cent. Full-time in this context is 35.5 work hours per week.

The empirical basis for this chapter is an action research project in nursing and care work funded by the Norwegian Labour and Welfare Administration (NAV) and the Norwegian Agency for Lifelong Learning (VOX). The project, the Rota System as Innovation, focuses on the use of the concept of 'innovation' for the purpose of improving the shift system within health care organizations, in which 80 per cent of the employees are women. Nursing and care work are typically women's work, and it is common to organize the working hours into a six-week rota system. Experience shows that small part-time positions in a rota system are the starting point of unwanted part-time work, too small or too insecure a workload, and dissatisfaction at work (Vabø, 2006). This creates fragmentation for employees and users, which is impaired with lost learning opportunities, such as for mastery in work (Amble, 2014; Kirkevold and Engedal, 2008). With this understanding in mind, the main objective of the project was to develop sustainable work time arrangements which provided organizational cohesion and minimized the need for part-time positions and temporary staff. At the same time, it was important that the solutions should not increase the costs of operation.

Forty-six per cent of Norwegian women work part-time (Nicolaisen, 2013). In Norwegian municipal elderly care, only 35 per cent of the employees hold a full-time position (Moland and Bråthen, 2012), while by comparison 90 per cent in this service in Finland work full-time, which is defined as 37.5 hours per week (Lehto and Sutela, 2009). Moreover, part-time work is the single largest contributor to unequal income between men and women, leaving Norwegian women to live on 60 per cent of men's economic resources.

Part-time work can be either voluntary or involuntary, and there is a common understanding that involuntary or unwanted part-time positions in nursing and care work, with an unwanted low workload, are written into one's employment contract (Fasting, 2013; Ingstad, 2011; Moland and Bråthen, 2012). Employees with unwanted part-time work are often found in work organizations with an ongoing challenge regarding vacant shifts, vacant positions and a great demand for temporary workers. In the case where an employee with unwanted part-time contractual work reports an almost satisfactory workload and income, this may be due to the opportunity to work extra shifts (Fevang et al., 2004; Nicolaisen, 2013). However, this is an unsatisfying work situation, because the employee is not guaranteed a desired permanent workload and a desired income in the long term. It also represents considerable uncertainty for workers in terms of when and how they should work. In the opposite situation, when despite vacant shifts the workload is not satisfactory, this is because mandatory rest after a working Sunday and a vacant shift collide, which is a situation regulated by the Work Environment Act (Amble, 2008; Moland, 2013).

In this chapter, we want to show how it is possible to resolve such uncertainty and collisions, and how the word 'innovation' itself contributed to this:

1.   We describe how new, innovative work shift arrangements were developed in an action research project within two health care organizations in Norway.
2.   We show how the concept of innovation filled these processes with new content, and how this enables change.

The chapter is organized as follows. First, we introduce the background and context of the project. Next, we present some theoretical notions on innovation in the public sector, and gender and innovation, including the tradition and challenges of using the concept in the public sector. Subsequently, we present the research design and why we chose such an interactive methodology. Thereafter, we describe the two selected sub-projects, what we did and learned, and how the choice of definition and innovations came about in the rota system. After this, we discuss our findings in light of current theory and understanding in this area.

## BACKGROUND

Improvement projects in women's service work, whether private-, municipality- or state-driven, often have a negative perspective on problems such as 'sick absence', 'reducing unwanted part-time work', 'a bad work environment' and so on. In a talk at a conference, my suggestion was the following: why not use the concept of innovation to open up discussions, and explore whether some definitions for innovation could be relevant in working with human beings and care work? A councillor, a woman from a Norwegian municipality, was inspired by the idea and took the initiative to develop a project combining *innovation* and *the work time system in nursing and care work*, hoping to give such a development project a positive, energetic perspective.

The results reported in this chapter are from this larger Rota System as Innovation project, which included two municipalities and a regional health authority, with three hospitals situated in the Agder region in Southern Norway. We report the findings from one of the four municipal sub-projects and one of the two hospital sub-projects. The project started in 2011 as part of a national initiative to reduce unwanted part-time work, and was completed in January 2014. The project was a tri-partite project involving staff and representatives from labour unions, management and policymakers.

### The Arena for Innovation: The National Context

The idea of autonomy and employee-driven processes is not new in Nordic work life (Enehaug, 2014; Gustavsen et al., 2010; Hartikainen et al., 2010; Hvid, 2009; Karasek and Theorell, 1990; Trist, 1981). Although the countries represent differing national conditions regarding employment and competitiveness, research shows that what is referred to as the 'Nordic model' represents a mind-set, framework and practice of organizational learning and cooperation that Nordic companies and workplaces can take advantage of in striving to be more innovative (Aasen et al., 2013; Eikeland, 2012a, 2012b; Gustavsen et al., 2010).

Part-time work is primarily done by women, although women in male occupations tend to work similarly to men, as well as men in women's occupations working full-time (Abrahamsen, 2002; Magnussen and Svarstad, 2013). National statistics show that Norwegian women work 30 hours a week, whereas men work 37.5. This indicates that on average Norwegian women have a six-hour workday, but it is important to note that the hours are unevenly distributed. Part-time work is not just a phenomenon in relation to women with young children and toddlers, as recent studies indicate that young women increasingly work full-time while middle-aged women stay in part-time work (NOU, 2012).

There are many good reasons for both women and men to reduce their work hours, such as being a parent to young children, the desire to live a simpler life disengaged from the consumer society, or religious beliefs and practices which traditionally connect women to the family and men to employment. In Agder work life has been characterized by shipping and industrial jobs, and the region has been wealthy. The Agder region, which scores lowest on gender equality in Norway, has a female population that can be divided into two groups: modern women and a large group of religiously active women who are more conservative than religiously active women elsewhere in Norway (Magnussen, 2013). The two factors of religion and wealth might explain how part-time work and an unequal position between men and women are more apparent in Agder than in the other regions of Norway (Olsen et al., 2013). This regional context provides the platform and boundaries for investigating the innovations with regard to work schedules. Thus, what is innovative in Agder does not have to be innovative elsewhere in Norway. For instance, Finnmark has a totally different history, and to a greater degree has a full-time work culture that is similar to the Finnish work culture (Lehto and Sutela, 2009; Moland, 2013).

The rota system is the shift arrangement in the ward, that is, continuous work in which employment is divided into day, evening and night shifts. What makes shift work a rota system is the varying workload throughout the day, which in turn affects the number of employees at work on the three different shifts. In shift work, which is typical for men's work in the industry, there are fixed teams that work together on all three shifts with the same work tasks and workload in all shifts (continuous production). On the contrary, women's work typically has a varying number of people on each shift to meet a different workload or different work tasks throughout the day (e.g. helping patients to get up and get dressed in the morning and serve them breakfast, while only being present if help is needed in the night).

In Norway, there is an ongoing and unresolved political discussion related to what is more stressful, shift work or rota work (NOU, 2008). Currently, working hour placement outside the normal workday triggers additional payments. This favours men's shift working, while the drawback associated with a variation in teams and less rhythm in work – typical for women's rota work – is not compensated in the same way. Women in municipal care work have an 80 per cent higher absenteeism rate than the men in the same sector (PAI/KS, 2015). It is customary to explain women's high absenteeism in terms of a time bind, and we also believe it is relevant to draw attention to the rota system and to the conditions necessary for creating a good work environment in women's work.

## The Arena for Innovation: The Work Environment

The Norwegian sociologist Anne Lise Ellingsæter (2007) uses the concept of *time welfare* (Abrahamsen and Kalleberg, 1986) to describe how the workload and working hours do not necessarily say everything about the stress and pressure of work, and how the personal experience of the time also affects our personal well-being (Ellingsæter, 2007). In this way, work time becomes a multidimensional social category that is complex, contradictory and difficult to measure. Good time management is therefore dependent on work organization – in relation to the experience of rhythm, intensity, predictability, opportunity for mastery and autonomy in the work community (Amble, 2013).

According to Testad (2010), the number of carers per patient has never been higher in the Norwegian health care system than it is today, but it is debated as to whether the increase has occurred within administrative work rather than within care work. This has led to using the terms 'cold' and 'warm' hands, in which the increase in warm hands – those that give care and touch the receivers – is smaller than the increase in cold hands in the offices. The horizontal cohesion, the 'glue' in the work organizations, can thus be reduced in two ways: through the classical specialization of 'one woman, one function' and through design principles that 'isolate' the individual through reduced opportunities for horizontal contact in the work community (Nielsen and Nielsen, 2006; Vabø, 2007). People have neither the need nor the opportunity to talk together, nor do they want to help each other at work (Amble, 2013). Part-time positions support such developments, as it is believed that one can maintain quality in service when one allows the service provider to specialize in a few patients, though in reality it reduces the horizontal cohesion within the work community. This idea is supported by the recent Norwegian

PIAAC[2] study, in which women in health care and social care scored below the Norwegian average in terms of basic skills in reading, mathematics and problem solving, as this is linked to reduced learning opportunities and cooperation at work (Bjørkeng, 2013).

As in most Western countries the Norwegian management system in the health care sector is influenced by the New Public Management (NPM) (among others, Hvid and Kamp, 2012; Kamp and Hvid, 2012; Røvik, 2010; Vabo and Vabø, 2014). Many perceive this as a management system based on standardization, a 'taylorized' perspective on work taken from the model of businesses manufacturing goods. Nordic studies of the warm hands show that the NPM and its key ideas still leave room and a need for the use of vocational discretion (Vabø, 2007), that is, judgements which require soft skills and social competence. In her doctoral dissertation, Testad (2010) documents that the employee's sense of management, and possibilities for mastery and autonomy in work are the main contributors to the variation in the carer's health and well-being. Consequently, part-time positions together with leadership and management negatively affect the employee's health and well-being in nursing and care work. A new shift work scheme contains key factors that can – as our project intended – provide cohesion and a better work environment and create regenerative work (Kira, 2006).

## INNOVATION IN THE PUBLIC SECTOR

Many argue that the pace of change in the workplace is now higher than ever, and that work has gained new intensity (Eikeland, 2012a; Gustavsen et al., 2010; Oinas et al., 2012; Vabo and Vabø, 2014). Planned development and change contribute to this intensity. These planned processes are often labelled as 'productivity growth', 'increased efficiency', 'better quality', 'improvement' or 'innovation'. Innovation can be defined in many ways, and most definitions consist of two distinct elements: innovation should be based on a new idea and it should be usable. The most cited academic reference to define innovations is 'as new combinations of production factors such as the production of new goods, introduction of new processes, opening of new markets, access to new sources of raw materials and intermediates, and re-organisation of an industry' (Schumpeter, 1934).

'Innovation' is a term traditionally used in the private sector. This means that the usability or applicability of an innovation is measured in terms of economic growth or profitability in the market. This indicates that an innovation is more than an invention; it should be implemented and provide profit. In the long run, if a firm launches new innovations that do not make a profit, the firm will cease to exist (Fitjar, 2014).

On the other hand, public sector organizations have traditionally used concepts other than innovation when describing development and change, for example renewal, reformation or modernization (NOU, 2011), but *innovation* has now gained acceptance (NOU, 2011; St.meld. nr. 7, 2008–2009). One reason for this may be the focus of innovation on implementation, and that innovations deal with changes in practice (Sørensen and Torfing, 2012). Fitjar (2014) points to some of the problems of implementing the concept of innovation in the public sector: 1) economic benefits cannot be measured as in a market; 2) innovations that are not viable will not necessarily be terminated; and 3) a lack of measurable gains prolongs them for the same reason. Municipal care has got its own White Paper on innovation (NOU, 2011). In this, the term 'added value' is used to measure the outcome of innovation, although measuring or estimating added value in care work is difficult. In the project presented in this chapter, added value was discussed in depth, which we will come back to later.

The White Paper on innovative and sustainable development in Norway states:

> In the care sector, the importance of obtaining a sufficient number of employees is often addressed. This is a challenge that will become more important. The capacity of an individual carer is limited. However, through research and innovation, the capacity can increase. The care sector is characterized by a low level of education and little research. New methods, tools and care technology can contribute to both individuals in need of care receiving better services, and care workers having the pleasure of being in the job longer – and providing more and better care. (St.meld. nr. 7, 2008–2009, p. 131)

The current project contributes to the challenges cited above, as organizing the work better will provide more care with less difficulty, which can be defined as an *incremental organizational innovation*.

## INNOVATION AND GENDER: RESEARCH PERSPECTIVES

Among 106 994 articles from the Scopus database with 'innovation' in the title, only 2445 mentioned the word 'gender' in the text (Alsos et al., 2013). This is an indication of how research on innovation is gender blind. In the aforementioned article in a special issue on gender and innovation, Alsos et al. (2013) emphasize how the word 'innovation' is a masculine, male concept that requires research, which also accommodates innovation and renewal of women's work. They suggest that gender-sensitive innovation research should embrace one of three perspectives on gender: 1) *gender differences and similarities in innovation*, so-called 'gender as variable', which provides a quantitative approach to gender in innovations; 2) *gendered constructions of innovation* linked to the definition of innovation; or 3) *gendering processes of innovation* as 'doing gender'. The second perspective regards the construction of the innovation concept, which affects the definition of innovation. In our case, in the health care sector, how should the word be defined to embrace a renewal in work in which the result is not a product, but a service that does not measure added value in use, money or market share? The empirical basis for the article is a renewal of the rota system in nursing and care work in the public sector with primarily women employees. We discuss how we gendered the process, and whether – or eventually how – our results met the chosen definition. In this chapter, it is therefore the second perspective of Alsos et al. (2013) in particular that will be illuminated, the construction of the concept of innovation in the context of traditional women's work. In addition, we shed some light on women's experience in using or doing the concept of innovation. What new, innovative work shift arrangements could be developed in such a context, and how was the concept of innovation applied in these processes as a tool for promoting change? This formed the basis for the choice of research design.

## RESEARCH DESIGN

The main project was organized as a network project (Amble et al., 2005), in which the six sub-projects were linked together. Two of them are reported on in this chapter. The work on the sub-projects took place, respectively, within the limits and requirements of each participating institution. As a work form, the project was designed to arrange discussions and cooperation with the staff at the participating workplaces in employee-driven processes. Through regular network meetings, an exchange of knowledge, plans, progress and experiences between the involved projects was communicated. The main project included a total of five networking gatherings, and between the network meetings the local participants met and reported on the results and discussed further progress. Moreover, the project had three phases: a mapping phase, an implementation phase and an evaluation phase (Amble et al., 2014).

**Action Research as Interactive Research**

The project had an action research design. According to Greenwood and Levin (2007, p. 1), action research is a set of cooperative and democratically oriented strategies that generate knowledge and design actions; it includes cooperation between trained experts and local stakeholders.

One criticism of this variant of action research is that it often has too much of an emphasis on action and too little of an emphasis on the documentation of research of academic standards. As stated by Svensson (2002), it has become more common that action research attempts to distinguish a specific research design that emphasizes scientific knowledge production. This is done by introducing the term 'interactive research'. The concept of interactive research adds a greater emphasis on the *joint learning process* between the research field and the researchers, so that new knowledge will both be relevant and meet the necessary academic standards (Svensson and Nielsen, 2006). In Scandinavia, interactive research is distinctly different from action research because of its stronger connection to research in the public sector (Tydén, 2006).

We would like to emphasize how this research design supported the research question. In interactive research, much of the project activity is tied to a dialogue and discussion between the participants. In this way, the rhetorical use of the concept of innovation became relevant, as did how the concept of innovation was applied in these processes – whether something was innovative or not and how the concept became a tool for promoting change and turned out to be a meta-perspective on the interactive process.

## RESULTS: NEW, LONGER AND WIDER

The results from the project were on the level of both substance and process. The project produced concrete results for the participants, hence creating new knowledge for employees and employers in the actual context. Nevertheless, these results are based on some choices made during the process, choices that in themselves were the results of discussions, first the definition of the innovation concept and second the definition of added value. These are the meta-results that became guiding principles in the discussions at each participating workplace.

**A Definition of Innovation**

In our project, the idea was that work organized better could provide more work with the input of less energy and difficulty. Along with such thinking the Rota System as Innovation project anticipated an innovation concept that combines the American Kanter's (2000) definition, namely that 'innovation is the development and exploitation of new ideas', with the Danish Kristensen's (2008) welfare innovation as 'new and familiar knowledge brought into use in new contexts'. Taken together, these two make it possible to combine the situation in a local context with something new in relation to this. It means something that has been attempted elsewhere, though not in the current municipality or institution, which may be innovative, that is, the regional being a reference or context to whether something is innovative or not (Blake and Hanson, 2005). The definition has followed the project as a common thread, and has been repeated in the various discussions as a litmus test of the ideas discussed during the process.

**Perspective on Added Value**

The added value of our innovations caused a great deal of discussion and it was decided – though not by consensus – to use an overall strategy in which the added value of the innovation would be the fastest way to achieving a full-time work culture. This enabled a shift in focus from the individual employees' 'wanted workload' to a holistic focus on systems based on full-time positions, building a work culture in which the norm is full-time. The added value of this innovation is measurable in the number of employees per patient, a better coherence of services, and employees working more with less strain because the work is better organized. The opposite strategy, 'reducing numbers of unwanted part-time positions', usually starts with increasing all employees to a 40 per cent part-time position, which is the limit for pensionable income (Amble, 2008). With this 'bottom-up strategy', employees will increase their work hours until they have the work hours or income best suited for them. Even so, such a solution will neither prioritize the employer's needs to build holistic rota systems and thus use the carers more effectively, nor contribute to a culture in which the full-time worker is constructed as the norm. Instead, 'individually personalized shifts' become the norm. Experience from previous projects has shown that this individual tailoring strategy has its downside, not only in relation to the employer's interest in maximizing utilization of labour, but also for the service quality. It also has a downside for the carers, since they become the target of isolation

(Amble, 2013; Moland, 2013). In this project, the added value of the innovation was linked to capacity building, which helped to solve the future demand for human resources in care.

Our guiding principle for the thinking in the project became three-fold: something new, something usable, and getting closer to a full-time culture! We will come back to this in the discussion, but first we will look at the substantial innovations.

### Innovation 1: Working in Long Shifts

One of the four municipal sub-projects included two adjacent departments with 18 patients in a nursing home. After many long discussions between employees, unions, managers and project managers, a new rota system was developed. This new system included organizing the weekend by teams doing long shifts, working 13.5- and 14-hour shifts on Saturday and Sunday. In working long shifts, the employees increased their positions to full-time. This is a way of organizing shift work that requires a dispensation from the Work Environment Act. The stakeholders at a workplace can agree on shifts up to 12 hours, while for longer shifts they need permission from the regional union's representatives. The ward developing the shift system involved heavy care, as it has two sections for dementia patients. To the best of our knowledge, this was the first ward of its type in Norway, utilizing a rota system with teams organized in long shifts (Ingstad and Amble, 2015). On average, the team works every fourth weekend, working between 34 and 35 hours on the three shifts linked to the weekend, with two long shifts and one regular one on either Friday or Monday. The long shifts are actually a day shift and an evening duty added together. By working in this manner, each long shift team eliminates a shift change and the need for a second shift during the weekend, thus reducing the need for employees during the days in the weekend by half and giving more time to the patients.

The research showed that the wards gained in tranquillity, which created a better environment for the patients. The use of medicine declined, the food budget went up, the staff had more time for cooking, the patients got extra homemade food, and everyone was happy. A key success factor was the employee-driven planning process before the experiment started. In this process, the concept of *innovation* had been a vision guiding the discussions, often asking whether the different solutions discussed were innovative enough. All the staff, including the manager, were 'against' a long shift or did not believe that it was possible in a dementia ward. In Norway, it is normal to work 7.5-hour shifts, and the mental barrier for working longer than 8–9 hours in this service was high. In retrospect, it is easy to see that the sub-project manager was essential in bringing the planning process to an experiment in practice. She kept the project on track when progress was slow, as she met resistance not only from the participating employees, but also more widely. For example, the new rota shift plan was ready in December 2012, but the first attempt to implement it did not take place until April 2013; this was due to the application for dispensation and other factors. During this waiting period, the staff changed from being sceptical to being impatient, and they were 'geared up' to get started. They wanted to make it happen, despite the fact that the rest of the staff in the institution's other wards were negative. During this process, the staff started to feel proud of their new rota system. They became the owners of both the process and the solution; by having ownership, they made it possible to acknowledge the rhetorical use of the concept of *innovation* as a mechanism that had opened the solution from relatively small individual changes to ending in a real, novel shift in work systems.

The employers saw how the participants in the experiment, the women employees with unwanted part-time work, obtained better work conditions. Some of the employees had previously worked almost every possible weekend (more than 26 in a year by one account) in search of extra income. The municipality confirmed the perception of increased peace and prosperity and an improved quality of service for the patients on the wards, with the staff even saying:

> Now we can relax a little, we know that when we are at work we can also plan our leisure time. Next year, I know that I have 42 out of 52 weekends free. Previously, it was difficult to plan my spare time since I always had to be ready to take a shift if they asked. Now, both work time and leisure time are predictable, and I have a secure income. This is the best thing about the project.

### Innovation 2: Creating a Resource Team

Employees who work cross-sectionally in a hospital ward can be organized in different ways. In one model, employees can be called in whenever extra staff are needed, and they have to cover all units or work on all wards and have no specified work schedule. In another model, the employees have a full-time position, and are working on a schedule covering defined wards within the hospital. The models have different names, such as 'substitute pool', 'resource team' or 'staffing unit'. Baumann (2005) looked at the differences between a traditional substitute pool and a resource team. The difference between these two models is the number of units that a carer can work in. In a traditional substitute pool, the carer is considered a generalist who can work with different types of patients, whereas in a resource team the nurse is regarded a specialist and expertise is emphasized, and the nurse can only work on a limited number of wards. Baumann's (2005) study shows that the use of a resource team provides an efficient distribution of employees, while providing safety and better qualifications for the personnel. In our example, it was this method of organization, a staff unit organized as a resource team, that was selected to be tried out.

The reason for establishing a staffing unit was primarily to reduce involuntary part-time positions. The hospital conducted a survey showing they had a large number of employees involved in unwanted part-time work. They also found that the employees were not interested in increasing their workload if they had to work on multiple wards or work more shifts on weekends. The hospital had neither the financial resources nor a sufficient number of staff to be able to meet these requests. Instead, the hospital decided to design a staffing unit with full-time positions that covered the needs of most of the wards in the hospital. However, the plan was that each employee only had to alternate between five (later four) wards. The hospital advertised the positions – with these conditions – both internally and externally. Those who were employed agreed to take shifts on five wards, and as part of this solution the employees were to receive systematic training on the wards. There were 37 applicants for the positions, which was perceived as being surprisingly many. Interviews were conducted for all the applicants, and 14 people were employed.

The staffing unit, that is, the innovation, was evaluated after three months. The ward managers using the staffing unit were happy with the arrangement, and felt that the nurses from the resource unit were competent and had mastered their tasks. The employees rated their skills lower than the ward managers did, but altogether the experiences were consistently good. In the autumn of 2013, the project was expanded to 20 employees, and a coordinator with a 30 per cent position was hired. The coordinator was to prepare individual competency plans for the employees in the unit. Training was further organized based on the reported needs of the employees, and the unit had its own union representative. As of August 2014, the unit had expanded to 30, and the staff unit was extended to cover a further 14 wards at another location under the same organization. The sub-project period was completed in the spring of 2014, and the unit was permanently established as part of regular operations (Jahnsen, 2014).

**Innovation 3: A Tool to Promote Wider Change**

In this experiment, the steering committee of the main project had many discussions on what – if anything – was innovative about the different, proposed solutions. The definition of the word 'innovation' was therefore used to analyse the efforts – both before and after the actions – and maintain a focus on what distinguished this experiment and organizational choices from what was usual in the work of reducing unwanted part-time positions. There were three circumstances that we discussed and agreed upon as being essential. First, the project should leave the focus on employees who worked unwanted part-time shifts, turning the spotlight on creating a virtual organizational unit based on full-time work, and therefore creating a unit with a full-time culture from day one. This was a change in perspective which we perceived as innovative. Second, an organizational unit with sustainable conditions should be designed and the vacant positions advertised accordingly. Theoretically, this might not have encouraged the employment of those who had involuntary part-time positions, but rather employees who wanted full-time permanent positions and enjoyed working in multiple locations. Third, the 'virtual organization', for example the coordinator, union representative and skills development staff, should be in line with other physical departments of the hospital and acquire corresponding resources. This was also considered to be innovative. In addition, the use of the word 'innovation' met an internal 'need', by highlighting the awareness of how this development work was novel and innovative, which subsequently gave confidence and arguments to the local leaders of the sub-projects.

## DISCUSSION

This chapter presents an action research project in health care organizations with the aim of developing new, innovative work shift arrangements. The Rota System as Innovation project pinpoints that the concept of innovation could be a tool in itself to promote change in such a dialogue-based design. The two cases we have presented underscore the concrete but also more abstract results, and how the concept of innovation as a tool for change made it possible to get around barriers that traditionally would demand solutions other than those we actually chose.

The municipality example tells how the dementia wards used team-based long shifts covering several departments on the weekends. The new rota system combines regular shifts during weekdays and long shifts on weekends, which is also new. The combination – team and rota employees, who alternate between normal and long shifts in what is considered to be heavy care – is a completely new kind of work organization, in which the team effects are clearly appreciated. This is in accordance with newer research on long shifts (Ingstad and Amble, 2015). The traditionally heavy weekend has turned out to be good for employees, providing better quality for patients and relatives, as they meet permanent staff on all shifts at the weekend. Because of this organizational solution, the employees receive full-time positions. This solution is not general, but builds upon the fact that the vacant weekend positions on the ward were on employees' already-working weekend, so no collision with Sunday work, regulated by the law, occurred.

What we considered to be innovative in the hospital project was the organization of a virtual unit, with its own coordinator and union representative and the ability to maintain professionalism through the development of vocational training packages. Professionalism is about competence, and we found that skills development is the key to shifts based on full-time positions when they are cross-sectional. Expertise gives professional security and increases the staff's flexibility. It is innovative to reverse the processes of motivating involuntary part-time employees to be more flexible than they anticipate being, to design a sustainable organizational unit on paper and to openly advertise all positions. This turns the perception of employees in the unit from being substitutes to being resources on the ward.

The word 'innovation' was used in the discussions, particularly when discussing the choices of solutions in the sub-projects. It gave a focus, awareness and experience to how to build a full-time culture that would eventually remove the unwanted part in a long-term perspective. In retrospect, it is clear how the focus on innovation and how we defined it opened up the possible space for solutions, from individual to system, from cause to possibility.

During the various discussions, there was a repeated exposure of both negativity in relation to the word 'innovation' itself, as it was perceived not to belong in health care, and disappointment at how 'small' were the changes created by the word 'innovation'. In the final evaluation, a union representative conveys the attitude: 'If what we have done in this project is innovation, we can just throw out the whole word.'

At the same time, we as the experts who have worked on this issue for several years, and in many projects focusing on 'reducing unwanted part-time positions', see that the use of the word 'innovation' actually contributed to an entirely new perspective on this development work. We understand the negativity as impatience and sorrow when you realize you can't fix the problem with one project. This indicates how demanding it can be to accept the incremental side of an innovation. At the same time, and in line with Alsos et al.'s (2013) second perspective, we took time to discuss and choose a 'feminized' – adapted to the service – definition of the innovation term, 'a new or old idea used in a new situation', with the overall perspective of added value as building a full-time culture. But we also met resistance to such a soft, incremental definition. Some of the women themselves had masculine ideas of innovation, thereby expecting a larger change than achieved, often not valuing the new knowledge created, but missing the concrete manifestation of more radical change.

We find that the word 'innovation' is provocative for many women, yet we believe that the pros outweigh the cons of using it. The most striking experience is how the usage of the word opened up the field for solutions that would not have been possible if for example the name of the project had been 'Efforts against unwanted part-time work'. The role of the principal author as the researcher in the project has often been to 'reduce' the concept of innovation, focusing our definition on an incremental vision of steps toward a bigger goal: good work as a full-time culture!

The term 'innovation' gave other solutions than those we anticipated and in terms of connecting the added value of the innovation to full-time work culture, that is, a change of focus from part to whole, from short- to long-term. In the project group, we described this as a feeling of liberation, a 180-degree change from 'working to remove barriers' to 'finding possibilities'. To sum up, the concept of innovation seems to have created not only new – in the actual context – and creative solutions, but also solutions whose implementation makes it possible to reach longer and wider: solutions that point towards a more holistic organization of the typically women's work necessary to meet the estimated peak in care!

## NOTES

\*    The research was conducted as an action research project in close cooperation with the research participants.
1.    Full-time work includes positions of 80–100 per cent.
2.    OECD's adult PISA, testing basic skills in the population.

## REFERENCES

Aasen, T.M., K. Møller and A.F. Eriksson (2013), *Nordiske strategier for medarbeiderdrevet innovasjon*, Rapport fra arbeidsseminar om medarbeiderdrevet innovasjon (MDI) i Norden.

Abrahamsen, B. (2002), *Heltid eller deltid? Kvinners arbeidstid i kvinnedominerte og mannsdominerte yrker*, ISF Report 2002: 6, Oslo: Institutt for samfunnsforskning.

Abrahamsen, B. and A. Kalleberg (1986), *Arbeidstid og arbeidsmiljø. En artikkel om arbeidstid, arbeidstidsordninger og arbeidsmiljø*, ISF Report 1986: 3, Oslo: Institutt for samfunnsforskning.

Alsos, G.A., U. Hytti and E. Ljunggren (2013), 'Gender and innovation: State of the art and a research agenda', *International Journal of Gender and Entrepreneurship*, **5** (3), 236–256.

Amble, N. (2008), 'Ikke fullt og helt, men stykkevis og delt – om det uønskede deltidsarbeidets vesen', *Søkelys på arbeidslivet*, **3**, 367–380.

Amble, N. (2013), 'Autonomy and control when working with humans – a reflection on sociotechnical concepts', *Nordic Journal of Working Life Studies*, **3** (4), 45–62.

Amble, N. (2014), 'Å lære å lære – om læring i praksis', in S.I. Vabo and M. Vabø (eds), *Velferdens organisering*, Oslo: Universitetsforlaget, pp. 47–63.

Amble, N., K. Holstad and B.A. Sørensen (2005), *Tenke – ville – gjøre: Virkemidler mot uønsket deltid*, Oslo: Kommuneforlaget.

Amble, N., P. Axelsen, M.D. Hamre and L.K. Snerthammer (2014), 'Turnus som innovasjon', Sluttrapport, NAV/VOX.

Baumann, A. (2005), 'Nursing Resource Teams can recruit and retain nurses: New strategy could create full-time jobs in nursing', McMaster University, accessed 22 November 2013 at http://fhs.mcmaster.ca/main/news/news_archives/nursingteams.htm.

Bjørkeng, B. (2013), *Ferdigheter i voksenbefolkningen. Resultater fra den internasjonale undersøkelsen om lese- og tallforståelse (PIAAC)*, Rapporter 42/2013, Oslo: Statistisk sentralbyrå.

Blake, K.M. and S. Hanson (2005), 'Rethinking innovation: Context and gender', *Environment and Planning A*, **37** (4), 681–701.

Eikeland, O. (2012a), 'Action research and organisational learning: A Norwegian approach to doing action research in complex organizations', *Educational Action Research*, **20** (2), 267–290.

Eikeland, O. (2012b), 'Symbiotic learning systems: Reorganizing and integrating learning efforts and responsibilities between higher educational institutions (HEIs) and work places', *Journal of Knowledge Economy*, accessed at http.//dx.doi.org/10.1007/s13132-012-0103-x.

Ellingsæter, A.L. (2007), 'Postindustriell arbeidstid – nyere realiteter, nye begreper?', *Søkelys på arbeidslivet*, **24** (1), 15–23.

Enehaug, H. (2014), 'Læring i omstillingens tid – et teoretisk innspill om arbeidsmiljø og organisasjonslæring', *Tidsskrift for Arbejdsliv*, **14** (4), 68–84.

Fasting, M. (2013), 'God organisering vil gi god omsorg', *Søkelys på arbeidslivet*, **30** (1–2), 137–150.

Fevang, E., K. Røed, O. Raaum and T. Zhang (2004), *Undersysselsatte i Norge: Hvem, hvorfor oghvor lenge?*, Report 7, Oslo: Frischsenteret.

Fitjar, R.D. (2014), 'Innovasjon for utvikling i offentlig og privat sektor – noen prinsipielle betraktninger', Paper, Neon-dagene, UiS Stavanger, 26–27 November.

Gjefsen, H.M., T. Gunnes and N.M. Stølen (2014), *Framskrivinger av befolkning og arbeidsstyrke etter utdanning med alternative forutsetninger for innvandring*, Report 31, Oslo: Statistisk sentralbyrå.

Greenwood, D.J. and M. Levin (2007), *Introduction to Action Research*, 2nd edn, Thousand Oaks, CA: Sage.

Gustavsen, B., T. Qvale, B.A. Sørensen, M. Midtbø and P.H. Engelstad (2010), *Innovasjonssamarbeid mellom bedrifter og forskning – den norske modellen*, Oslo: Gyldendal Arbeidsliv.

Hartikainen, A., T. Anttila, T. Oinas and J. Nätti (2010), 'Is Finland different? Quality of work among Finnish and European employees', *Research on Finnish Society*, **3**, 29–41.

Hvid, H. (2009), 'To be in control – vejen til godt arbejdsmiljø, læring og innovation?', *Tidsskrift for Arbejdsliv*, **11** (1), 11–30.

Hvid, H. and A. Kamp (2012), 'The future beyond elderly care – beyond New Public Management?', in A. Kamp and H. Hvid (eds), *Elderly Care in Transition: Management, Meaning and Identity at Work – A Scandinavian Perspective*, Copenhagen: Copenhagen Business School Press, pp. 229–243.

Ingstad, K. (2011), 'Hele og delte sykepleiere. En kvalitativ studie av sykepleierenes arbeidsvilkår og arbeidstid i sykehjem', Ph.D. thesis, Norges tekniske-naturvitenskapelige universitet, Trondheim, Norway.

Ingstad, K. and N. Amble (2015), 'En ny ro med langturnus: Less job stress with 12-hours shifts', *Vård i Norden/Nordic Journal of Nursing Research*, accessed 18 June 2015 at http://njn.sagepub.com/content/early/recent.

Jahnsen, B. (2014), 'Bemanningsenhet som en ressurs i sykehus. En kvalitativ studie', Master's thesis, Nordic School of Public Health, Gothenburg, Sweden.

Kamp, A. and H. Hvid (2012), 'Introduction: Elderly care in transition', in A. Kamp and H. Hvid (eds), *Elderly Care in Transition: Management, Meaning and Identity at Work – A Scandinavian Perspective*, Copenhagen: Copenhagen Business School Press, pp. 13–28.

Kanter, R.M. (2000), 'When a thousand flowers bloom: Structural, collective and social conditions for innovation in organizations', *Research in Organizational Behavior*, **10**, 169–211.

Karasek, R. and T. Theorell (1990), *Healthy Work: Stress, Productivity and the Reconstruction of Working Life*, New York: Basic Books.

Kira, M. (2006), 'Bæredygtig arbejdsorganisationsutdvikling', *Tidsskrift for Arbejdsliv*, **8** (2), 9–23.

Kirkevold, O. and K. Engedal (2008), 'Quality of care in Norwegian nursing homes – deficiencies and their correlates', *Scandinavian Journal of Caring Science*, **22** (4), 560–567.

Kristensen, C.J. (2008), 'Organisatorisk forankring af velfærdsinnovation – en analyse med inddragelse af to cases fra aktiveringsområdet', *Tidsskrift for Arbejdsliv*, **10** (3), 73–87.

Lehto, A.M. and H. Sutela (2009), *Three Decades of Working Conditions: Findings of Finnish Quality of Work Life Surveys 1977–2008*, Helsinki: Statistics Finland.

Magnussen, M.L. (2013), 'Likestillingsfremskritt på Agder 2000–2010', in I.H. Stousland and H. Witsø (eds), *Likestilling 2013: Kunnskap og innovasjon på Agder*, Kristiansand, Norway: Portal akademiske forlag, pp. 29–41.

Magnussen, M.L. and C. Svarstad (2013), 'Kvinner i prosess- og olje-/gassindustri på Agder', in H. Stousland and H. Witsø (eds), *Likestilling 2013: Kunnskap og innovasjon på Agder*, Kristiansand, Norway: Portal akademiske forlag, pp. 93–113.

Moland, L.E. (2013), *Heltid – deltid – en kunnskapsstatus*, Report 2013:27, Oslo: Fafo.

Moland, L.E. and K. Bråthen (2012), *Hvordan kan kommunene tilby flere heltidsstillinger?*, Report 2012:14, Oslo: Fafo.

Nicolaisen, H. (2013), 'Løsninger på deltidsutfordringen – ingen "quick fix"', *Søkelys på arbeidslivet*, **30** (1–2), 151–157.

Nielsen, L.D. and K.A. Nielsen (2006), 'Er fleksibiliteten bæredygtig?', *Tidsskrift for Arbejdsliv*, **8** (2), 38–54.

NOU (Norges offentlige utredninger) (2008), *Skift og turnus – gradvis kompensasjon for ubekvem arbeidstid*, No. 2008: 17, Arbeids- og inkluderingsdepartementet.

NOU (Norges offentlige utredninger) (2011), *Innovasjon i omsorg*, No. 2011: 11, Helse- og omsorgsdepartementet.

NOU (Norges offentlige utredninger) (2012), *Politikk for likestilling*, No. 2012: 15, Barne-, likestillings- og inkluderingsdepartementet.

Oinas, T., T. Anttila, A. Mustosmäki and J. Nätti (2012), 'The Nordic difference: Job quality in Europe 1995–2010', *Nordic Journal of Working Life Studies*, **2** (4), 135–152.

Olsen, J.S., N. Amble and M.L. Magnussen (2013), 'Kvinners deltid og likestilling på Agder. I likestilling 2013', *Kunnskap og innovasjon på Agder*, in H. Stousland and H. Witsø (eds), Oslo: Portal akademiske forlag, pp. 73–93.

PAI/KS (2015), 'Diagram B – Samlet, kjønn, heltid- og deltid', accessed 1 March 2015 at http://ks.no/tema/Arbeidsgiver/lpas/Fravar/Sykefravarstall-for-kommuner-og-fylkes kommuner/.

Røvik, K.A. (2010), 'Managementtrender', *Praktisk økonomi og finans*, **27** (3), 61–72.

Schumpeter, J.A. (1934), *The Theory of Economic Development: An Inquiry into Profits, Capital, Credit, Interest, and the Business Cycle*, Cambridge, MA: Harvard University Press.

Sørensen, E. and J. Torfing (2012), 'Introduction: Collaborative innovation in the public sector', *Innovation Journal: The Public Sector Innovation Journal*, **17** (1), 1–14.

St.meld. nr. 7 (2008–2009), *Et nyskapende og bærekraftig Norge*, Tilråding fra Nærings- og handelsdepartementet av 5 desember 2008, godkjent i statsråd samme dag (Regjeringen Stoltenberg II).

Svensson, L. (2002), 'Bakgrund och utgångspunkter', in L. Svensson, G. Brulin, P.-E. Ellström and Ö. Widegren (eds), *Interaktiv forskning – för utveckling av teori och praktikk. Arbetsliv i omvandling*, No. 2002:7, Stockholm: Arbetslivsinstitutet.

Svensson, L. and K.A. Nielsen (2006), 'A framework for the book', in K. Aagaard Nielsen and L. Svensson (eds), *Action and Interactive Research: Beyond Practice and Theory*, Maastricht, Netherlands: Shaker Publishing, pp. 13–45.

Testad, I. (2010), 'Agitation and use of restraint in nursing home resident with dementia', Ph.D. dissertation, University of Bergen, Norway.

Trist, E. (1981), *The Evolution of Socio-technical Systems: A Conceptual Framework and an Action Research Program*, Occasional Paper No. 2, June, Toronto: Ontario Ministry of Labour/Ontario Quality of Working Life Centre.

Tydén, T. (2006), 'The organization of action research in Nordic countries', in K.A. Nielsen and L. Svensson (eds), *Action Research and Interactive Research*, Maastricht, Netherlands: Shaker Publishing, pp. 143–191.

Vabø, M. (2006), 'Nordiske velferdsstater i forandring. Perspektiver på omsorgspersonell i fire nordiske land', Paper for Arbeidslivskonferansen, 6 November.

Vabø, M. (2007), 'Organisering for velferd. Hjemmetjenesten i et styringsideologisk brytningstid', Ph.D. thesis, NOVA Report 22, University of Oslo (UiO), Det samfunns- vitenskapelige fakultet.

Vabo, S.I. and M. Vabø (eds) (2014), *Velferdens organisering*, Oslo: Universitetsforlaget.

# 9. Organizational innovation for gender equality in forestry and mining

*Malin Lindberg, Eira Andersson, Lisa Andersson and Maria Johansson*

## INTRODUCTION

This chapter explores organizational innovations designed to promote gender equality in men-dominated natural resource-based industries, focusing on the Swedish forestry and mining industries. During the past decade, several companies in men-dominated industries in Sweden have made efforts to change the gendered structures of their organizations and processes. Using forestry and mining as two empirical cases, this chapter analyses the extent to which these efforts can be understood as organizational innovations and how the degree of newness of these efforts affects the likelihood of their effecting structural changes in the gendered patterns of these industries. Such an analysis helps advance both theory and practice on the gendered aspects of innovation and organization by increasing our understanding of the relationship between socially innovative measures and structural changes in social relationships in organizations and society. Consequently, the analysis also helps to fill in the general knowledge gap in how types of innovation other than technological product innovation are developed and implemented. That is valuable both for the advancement of innovation research and for the corporate employees, politicians and civil servants managing organizational and societal processes of change, particularly – but not exclusively – in the area of gender equality.

This chapter identifies, describes and analyses the gender-equality efforts of one major Swedish forestry company and one major Swedish mining company over the past ten years. The two research questions guiding the study are: 1) What innovative traits can be discerned in the gender-equality measures carried out by the companies studied? 2) How can these innovative traits be analysed in the light of existing research on organizational innovation?

## ORGANIZATIONAL INNOVATION

This section outlines the existing research on organizational innovation that will be used to analyse the extent to which gender-equality efforts in the Swedish forestry and mining industries can be understood as organizational innovations and how the degree of newness of these efforts affects the likelihood of their effecting structural changes in the gendered patterns in these industries.

During the last decade, the field of innovation research has undergone significant expansion. Research in the field has focused primarily on innovation in the form of technological product and process development in basic, manufacturing and high-tech industries. The same focus has characterized the public promotion of innovation by means of policy programmes, business counselling, venture capital, incubators and so on. Innovations in other forms (e.g. organizational, service, social or market innovations), industries (e.g. service industries) and sectors (e.g. the public and non-profit sectors) have been paid significantly less attention (Fagerberg, 2005; Lindberg, 2012; Nählinder, 2005, 2010; Pettersson, 2007). Since the function of innovation is to introduce novelty into the economy, however, it is important to incorporate all forms of innovation, in all industries and sectors, into the scientific body of knowledge in order to properly understand how the economy is renewed by the introduction of new goods and services (see Fagerberg, 2005).

In the last few years this need has been addressed by an increasing number of researchers who have theoretical knowledge on organizational innovation, service innovation, social innovation and so on (Döös and Wilhelmson, 2009; European Commission, 2013; Hansson et al., 2014; Lam, 2005; Miles, 2005). Some argue that the various forms of innovation operate in crosscutting, complex, multilevel and spontaneous ways, for example that innovation in services leads to renewal, not only in the service industries but in all industries, including natural resource-based industries such as forestry and mining (see Fløysand and Jakobsen, 2011; Miles, 2005). On a general level, organizational innovation refers to the development and implementation of ideas or behaviours that are new to the organization (Lam, 2005). This type of innovation has been suggested to comprise different aspects of organizational renewal, for example as part of process innovation if divided into the categories of 'technological process innovations', referring to new types of machinery, and 'organizational process innovations', referring to new ways to organize work (Fagerberg, 2005).

Another type of organizational innovation is 'workplace innovation', referring to the democratic involvement of personnel and customers in organizational renewal as part of a process of organizational learning and knowledge creation, increasing the organization's capacity for change and adaptation (Alasoini, 2011). A widened perspective on organizational innovation includes arrangements involving multiple firms as well, such as innovative networks and cluster constellations, as well as reorganizations of entire industries (Fagerberg, 2005). The following classification of the scientific literature on organizational innovation into three different streams has been suggested by Lam (2005): 1) the relationship between organizational structural forms and innovativeness; 2) innovation as a process of organizational learning and knowledge creation; and 3) organizational capacity for change and adaptation.

Newness in innovation has been addressed by several researchers in an effort to pinpoint exactly how the implemented ideas differ from earlier ones. The introduction of a particular innovation in a context for the very first time might be esteemed as a high level of newness. But to introduce the same innovation in another context might also be esteemed as new in the sense that the imitation could lead to incremental innovation, since the transfer to a new context often requires considerable adaptation and organizational change in order to achieve the desired effects (Fagerberg, 2005). Newness in innovation refers then to something that is entirely new to the world or new to that particular context. In relation to innovations aiming to change gendered organizational structures, the newness might encompass the identification of hitherto unmet needs for gender equality among individuals, organizations or society, and the development of new solutions that diminish segregating and hierarchical gender patterns in a transformative manner (see Lindberg and Berglund, this volume, Chapter 11; Squires, 2005).

In the last decade, an increasing number of researchers have focused on gendered innovation, documenting and analysing the prevalence and transformation of gendered structures and understandings in policy, practice and research on innovation (Alsos et al., 2013; Andersson, S. et al., 2012; Danilda and Granat Thorslund, 2011; Lindberg and Schiffbänker, 2013; Pettersson and Lindberg, 2013; Ranga and Etzkowitz, 2010; Schiebinger, 2008). It has been shown that innovation has been associated mainly with men and with certain masculinities, through a focus on technological, industrial product, or process innovation in men-dominated industries such as basic, manufacturing and high-tech industries. Women and women-dominated organizations, active mainly in other industries such as service and creative industries in which innovation often takes the form of organizational, service or social innovations, have thus remained unacknowledged in most innovation policy, practice and research (Blake and Hanson, 2005; Fagerberg, 2005; Lindberg, 2012; Nählinder, 2005, 2010; Pettersson, 2007).

Applying a gender perspective to innovation has the potential to further our understanding of how innovation contributes to societal development, by broadening 'the scope of contexts, economic sectors and actors that they consider as potential sites and creators of innovation' (Blake and Hanson, 2005, p. 697). It is also in line with the general economic trend of declining manufacturing and rising services, motivating a replacement of the view that 'the economy is a whole comprised of a pre-established number of parts or sectors' with the view that the economy is 'an open-ended discursive construct made up of multiple constituents' (Cameron and Gibson-Graham, 2003, p. 152). Gender mainstreaming – that is, the integration of a gender perspective in all levels and areas of an organization or policy area – has been highlighted as an innovation per se with the potential to create more gender-equal structures in organizations and society (Schmidt, 2005; Squires, 2005). In line with these arguments, this chapter aspires to broaden the scope of contexts acknowledged as potential sites of innovation by analysing organizational innovation designed to increase gender equality in two men-dominated industries.

## RESEARCH DESIGN

The empirical data informing this study focus on one major forestry company and one major mining company in Sweden. The data were gathered in two separate R&D projects managed by Luleå University of Technology: From Macho to Modern: Gender Equality in Forestry Workplaces, financed by Vinnova;[1] and Nordic Mining and the Search for Women, 2014–2016, financed by NordMin.[2] Owing to increased global competition for qualified workers, business profits and natural resources, the studied companies view increased gender equality as an urgent matter in their organizational development. They still have a long way to go, though, before reaching more gender-balanced numbers, since both have a great majority of men in their current workforces, and there are still strong associations between forestry/mining and men/masculinities. The urgency has spurred the companies to implement a wide array of gender-equality measures to attain more gender-equal workforces and recruitment processes, making them suitable as study objects in organizational innovation with a potential to change gendered organizational structures.

A multiple case-study research design, inspired by Yin (2009), was used in the study. Each company constitutes one case, and within each case a number of examples of identified measures to promote increased gender equality form the basis of analysis and comparison. By comparing such sets of examples from each case, similarities and differences in the degree of newness and the variations in the likelihood of their evoking structural changes can be distinguished and analysed in relation to their organizational settings. Characteristic of multiple case-study designs is that a small number of cases that may share some features or character-istics are studied and compared. This approach is particularly fruitful when exploring a complex topic that is difficult to analyse with a large number of cases, as in the case of organizational innovation to further gender equality. The richness of the studied phenomenon requires a triangulating convergence of multiple sources of data in order to handle the vast number of possibly relevant variables. This study achieves that by combining document studies, participatory observations and inter-views held at the two companies.

## EXAMPLES FROM FORESTRY AND MINING

This section presents the empirical examples – the gender-equality efforts of one major forestry company and one major mining company in Sweden during the past ten years – focusing on their innovative traits.

### The Forestry Company

In the modern history of Western countries, industrial forestry has often been characterized by men-dominated workplaces based on the construc-tion of a specific, rural masculine identity amongst the forestry workers (e.g. Follo, 2002; Kuhn et al., 2002; Reed, 2008; Thomas and Mohai, 1995). Studies of job advertisements and media representation in Sweden and Norway have shown that the ideal forestry worker remains con-structed as a hard-working, nature-mastering man even today. The symbolic perception of forestry as linked to a traditional 'macho' masculinity engaged in practical, heavy forestry work in rural areas has been augmented with another more 'modern' masculinity, however one that is linked to business management in forestry offices in urban areas. However, this newer type of forestry-oriented masculinity also derives its power by reference to previous experience of practical forestry work (Brandth and Haugen, 2000, 2005; Lidestav and Sjölander, 1997).

Today, while the forestry sector is still heavily men-dominated, women are entering the sector in increasing numbers. The technological and organizational transformations of forestry during the past few decades have changed working conditions and skill requirements in the sector, potentially paving the way for men and women to enter the sector on equal terms (Follo, 2002; Kuhn et al., 2002; Reed, 2008; Thomas and Mohai, 1995). There is clearly still gender segregation in positions and occupations *within* the sector, with women primarily in white-collar positions and men dominating the blue-collar positions closer to the forest. Rather than the gendered structures being altered in forestry, 'spaces of exception' that it is possible for women to break into have been created, enabling earlier associations of forestry with men and masculinity to prevail, even as more women enter the sector (Johansson et al., 2014).

The Swedish forestry company studied here has highlighted the importance of gender equality in the industry as a whole and in its organization in particular for around ten years. As early as 2003, the company launched a network for women as forestry workers, in which all employed women with forestry-related duties were invited to participate, with the aim of empowering its members through information, contacts and exchange of experiences, and attracting more women among the forestry graduates to the company. The network has annual meetings at which lectures are combined with workshops and discussions on various topics, leading to a continuous exchange of experience and knowledge between the participants.

Recently, the company's senior management established an overall objective – of 30 per cent employed women and 70 per cent employed men – to be reached by 2020. The objective is broken down and followed up on several levels in the company, in the same way as are the company's profitability targets. This means that managers have considerable responsibility for ensuring that their part of the company reaches the gender-equality goal. This and other gender-equality issues are followed up through an employee survey every second year. The survey covers topics such as working conditions, occupational health, work satisfaction, work/life balance and career opportunities, among other things. The company's management has also recently adopted a set of 'core values' that are intended to guide all of the activities of the company. Gender equality is part of these core values. In order to spread awareness of these core values, a game was developed. The idea is that playing the game will give employees an opportunity to discuss and reflect on a number of dilemmas that they may face in their day-to-day work. Many of the issues discussed in the game concern how people treat each other from an equality and diversity perspective.

In order to attract and keep women in the company, the recruitment processes have been reviewed and changed so that all vacancies are announced internally before being published externally, and all women applicants are interviewed. In all parts of the recruitment process, from advertising to interview, the presence of women in the company is highlighted – in texts, pictures and representatives. The company has also implemented measures to help both men and women employees combine work and family life. This includes a financial contribution from the employer to supplement the parental leave allowance established in the collective agreements. The geographically dispersed activities of the organization imply considerable travelling for many employees. Therefore, the company has adopted a set of principles that allow employees to participate in meetings via teleconferencing and never have to schedule meetings too early in the morning or late in the evening, in order to facilitate dropping off and picking up of children at day-care. To help employees on parental leave to maintain their ties with the office, managers are responsible for keeping employees in the loop.

In order to develop their gender-equality efforts further, the forestry company studied cooperated with gender researchers at the regional university in the R&D project From Macho to Modern: Gender Equality in Forestry Workplaces, financed by Sweden's national innovation agency Vinnova in 2013–2015 (one of the projects in which the data for this study were collected). The aims of the project were to: 1) document and highlight the experiences and results of gender-equality measures in the participating forestry companies; 2) explore how gender theories can be used to better understand mechanisms restoring or challenging existing gendered patterns in forestry; and 3) develop innovative methods to promote gender equality in forestry. The development of innovative methods of promoting gender equality in forestry took place in creative workshops exploring and challenging gendered patterns in forestry generally and in the participating companies specifically. The creative workshops were arranged in two different forms: one in which a broad range of forestry actors from the private, public, academic and non-profit sectors participated, and one in which design teams consisting of representatives of different parts of the companies participated together with the gender researchers involved in the project.

In the workshops, the participants discussed various gendered aspects of forestry, such as management, workplace culture, masculinity, recruitment, internal and external communication, education, ownership, clusters and networks. Based on the results of the discussions, creative processes were organized in which the participants developed new ideas for gender-equality measures in the industry and companies. The processes were led by a specialized consultant, and the gender researchers' role was to induce existing knowledge on gendered patterns in organizations generally and forestry organizations specifically. One of the results of the creative workshops was an innovative model for forestry companies' external communication of their internal organizational progress in achieving gender equality in entirely new arenas, in entirely new forms and with entirely new messages. This would enable forestry companies to reach out to a broader spectrum of potential employees and highlight aspects of forestry work other than those dominating the traditional perception of the industry.

## The Mining Company

Research studies have identified mining as another natural resource-based industry in which men clearly dominate the workforce. Even if the number of women entering the sector has increased somewhat in the past few years, there is clear gender segregation in mining companies, with women working mainly in the administrative, financial and sales departments, leaving the heavy men-dominance in underground mining work intact (e.g. Abrahamsson et al., 2014; Andersson et al., 2013).

Like the forestry industry, the mining industry has undergone technological and organizational transformations during the past few decades, potentially paving the way for more gender-equal organizations. The associations between mining, men and certain masculinities remain, though, partly as a result of organizational and workplace cultures idealizing a certain type of 'macho' mining masculinity connected to the old manual, heavy and dangerous mining work (Abrahamsson and Johansson, 2006; Andersson, 2012). Research studies show that these remaining gender structures hamper efficiency, learning, security and technological development in workplaces in the mining sector. Some men view new technologies such as automation, computerization and robotization as a 'feminization' of their work (Abrahamsson and Somerville, 2007; Andersson, 2012; Olofsson, 2010).

The studied mining company has highlighted the importance of gender equality in the industry as a whole and in its organization in particular for around ten years. To ensure profitability and efficiency, the company strategically pursues organizational development to develop lean, innovative and learning work organizations with multi-competent workers collaborating in several areas and fields along the production line.

Advanced technology plays a crucial part in these efforts (e.g. visualization, simulation, decision support and computerized global social networks). New types of co-workers, both blue-collar and white-collar, will need to be recruited in the future, requiring new technical education and training that will enable them to develop new attitudes and behaviours, particularly when it comes to gender equality. This need for expanded recruitment patterns is reflected in the increased willingness of many Swedish mining companies to be perceived as modern and attractive employers for both men and women.

During the last few years, the studied mining company has implemented several gender-equality measures, both within the company itself and in collaboration with public authorities. These include networks for women employees, gender-awareness training, recruitment efforts to increase the number of women, financial support to a high-school programme in mining with the aim of attracting 50 per cent girls, and strategic communication of women's presence in text and graphics as an important part of the new modern mining industry.

A few years ago, the company financed and participated in an R&D project at the regional university, Occupational Safety, Attitudes and Gender in the Mining Industry, in order to transform its masculine workplace culture to a more gender-equal and safe culture. The project acknowledged and challenged traditional macho masculinity ideals, identities and practices among miners that had been perceived as impeding necessary development in the industry. These involved, for example, resistance to following the company's official safety procedures or the implementation of new technology in the company, owing to a perception of these as 'feminine' or 'unmanly'. During the project, several groups of employees (both men and women) participated in creative workshops and developed a handbook for gender-aware workplace cultures, with a particular focus on safety issues. In the workshops, the participants studied their own workplaces from a gender perspective and discussed mining workers' professional roles as well as mining masculinities in times of organizational and technological change. Examples of topics surfacing in the discussions were the prevalence of peer pressure, excessive risk-taking, loneliness and the unfair treatment of women.

## ANALYSIS

This section analyses the extent to which the gender-equality initiatives carried out by the mining and forestry companies can be understood as organizational innovations and how the degree of newness of these initiatives affects the likelihood of their leading to structural changes in the gendered patterns of these industries.

For the purpose of our analysis, the identified measures have been classified as either 'traditional measures' or 'innovative measures', based on their degree of newness. Those classified as 'traditional measures' are the ones that have been used before in several other organizational contexts, with limited contextual adaptation and organizational changes. Those classified as 'innovative measures' are the ones that are either entirely new to the world or new to the studied organizational contexts with considerable contextual adaptation and organizational changes (see Fagerberg, 2005; Lam, 2005). All identified measures are classified in Table 9.1.

*Table 9.1   Classification of gender-equality measures in the companies*

|  | Traditional measures | Innovative measures |
|---|---|---|
| The forestry company | Gender-equality goals Employee survey Core-value game Recruitment procedures Work/life balance Network for women | Creative workshops (including design teams) Cooperation with gender researchers Engaging in challenging masculinities |
| The mining company | Gender-equality goals Gender-awareness training Recruitment procedures Communication strategies High-school programme Network for women Handbook | Creative workshops Cooperation with gender researchers Engaging in challenging masculinities (with a safety focus) |

The measures classified as innovative will here be scrutinized in detail concerning their innovative traits in the light of existing research on organizational innovation. By sorting different theoretical aspects of organizational innovation into Lam's (2005) three streams, the organizational innovativeness of the gender-equality measures identified in forestry and mining will be assessed. Since both innovation and forestry/mining are permeated by masculine norms, the analysis of innovative traits will be intertwined with an analysis of the likelihood of the said measures leading to structural changes in the gendered patterns of these industries (see Lindberg and Berglund, this volume, Chapter 11).

We have sorted Fagerberg's (2005) 'organizational process innovations', referring to new ways to organize work, as well as the part of

Alasoini's (2011) 'workplace innovation' concerning the democratic involvement of personnel and customers in organizational renewal into the first stream, *the relationship between organizational structural forms and innovativeness*. We consider this kind of innovative trait to be mainly reflected in the companies' use of creative workshops. This view is based on seeing the workshops as new ways to organize the companies' responses to gender-equality issues – ways that involve a broad spectrum of employees as well as external actors. In the mining company, groups of employed men and women participated in creative workshops in which they conducted joint studies of their own workplaces from a gender perspective and discussed their professional roles and symbolic masculinities. In the forestry company, employees from different parts of the company participated in a design team in which they identified and analysed gender-related challenges in the company and creatively developed suggestions of how to meet these challenges. The forestry company also took part in creative workshops with a broad range of forestry actors from the private, public, academic and non-profit sectors, exchanging ideas on effective gender-equality interventions in forestry organizations.

The first type of innovative trait can be seen in the creative workshops, in the democratic involvement of the employees in organizational renewal, since in both cases the participants were seated so as to promote the sharing of experiences and knowledge development between employees from different parts of the companies. The formation of employee groups to find solutions to gender-equality issues is not entirely new, but the specific aim and design of the creative workshops, and their use in men-dominated natural resource-based industries as a tool by which to achieve theoretical development and practical change are relatively new – to the world – and entirely new to the companies studied. Concerning their innovativeness from a gender perspective, using the creative workshops as a way to promote gender equality in the companies can be considered as based to a great extent on the identification of hitherto unmet needs for gender equality among organizations and society, since the uneven gender distribution in these industries has been identified, by the companies and by public authorities, as a great problem as regards the future supply of qualified workers. The likelihood of this measure leading to structural change is harder to establish, since in its creative design it reveals an unclear potential to diminish segregation and hierarchical gender patterns combined with a clearer potential to do this in a transformative manner.

We have sorted the part of Alasoini's (2011) 'workplace innovation' considering organizational learning and knowledge into the second stream, *innovation as a process of organizational learning and know-ledge creation.* We consider this kind of innovative trait to be reflected mainly in the forestry and mining companies' cooperation with gender researchers, and in their shared focus on challenging masculinities, which in the mining company's case was closely intertwined with its focus on safety issues. This view is based upon seeing the companies' cooperation with gender researchers as a new way to develop theoretical knowledge and practical tools for gender equality in forestry and mining, in dialogue between researchers and employees. In these practical instances, then, theory and practice are intertwined, using existing gender research to inform the gender-equality measures in the companies, and using the employees' input in the design and implementation of these measures to contribute to academic knowledge. Even if there is a long tradition of interaction between gender researchers and various societal actors, part-nerships between gender researchers and actors from men-dominated natural resource-based industries in the interests of theoretical and practical advancement are still rare and entirely new to the studied companies, with considerable adaptation of similar attempts elsewhere. Concerning its innovativeness from a gender perspective, these com-panies' cooperation with gender researchers in an effort to promote gender equality can be considered to be based to a great extent on the identification of hitherto unmet needs for gender equality among organ-izations and society, since systematized knowledge of how to change gendered structures has been sought by both the companies and public authorities. The likelihood that this measure will lead to structural change is harder to establish, since it exposes an unclear potential to diminish segregating and hierarchical gender patterns alongside a clearer potential to do this in a transformative manner when intertwining theoretical knowledge and practical experiences in joint development of theories and tools.

The dimension of organizational learning and knowledge can also be discerned in the companies' shared focus on challenging masculinities, since this constitutes a shift from one-sidedly focusing on the under-represented group, namely women, for example by designing measures to attract them to forestry and mining to a greater extent, to focusing on the masculine norms permeating the companies and industries, for example by designing measures to change workplace cultures such as miners' attitudes towards safety issues. In both companies, traditional ideals, identities and practices of a macho type of masculinity were highlighted as hampering the positive effects of gender-equality measures. Peer pressure, excessive risk-taking, loneliness and unfair treatment of women were perceived as reasons for failing to comply with the mining company's official safety procedures or resisting the implementation of new technology in the company. In the forestry company, discussions were held and measures were devised to change both the traditional perception of forestry work as physically hard, lonely and remote, and the emerging modern, urban, business-focused masculinity in forestry. Since existing research shows that both innovation and forestry/mining are permeated by masculine norms, perceptions and identities, this focus on identifying and challenging masculinities might be considered innovative – specifically, in the organizational context of the studied companies, and generally, in men-dominated natural resource-based industries. Concerning its innovativeness from a gender perspective, the focus on challenging masculinities as a measure to promote gender equality in the companies can to some extent be considered as based on the identification of hitherto unmet needs for gender equality among individuals and organizations, since the macho-type masculinities permeating these industries have been highlighted as a great obstacle to psychological, organizational and technological renewal both in individual employees and in the companies overall. The likelihood of this measure leading to structural change can be considered quite high, as it indicates, in its identification of masculine norms, a clear potential to diminish segregation and hierarchical gender patterns, and reveals, in its focus on the normative majority instead of the deviant minority, an equally clear potential to do this in a transformative manner.

We have sorted the part of Alasoini's (2011) 'workplace innovation' concerning increase of the organizational capacity for change and adaptation into the third stream, *organizational capacity for change and adaptation*. We consider this kind of innovative trait to be reflected in the creative workshops held by both companies, as well as in the companies' focus on challenging masculinities. This view is based on the creative workshops being seen as sites of innovative organizational change in times of industrial renewal. Old cultures and perceptions of work in these industries need to be updated owing to the technological and organizational transformations that have occurred over the past few decades, potentially paving the way for more gender-equal organizations. Engaging employees with differing views on the companies in the creative workshops makes it possible to identify and exploit potential trajectories leading to changed gender patterns.

As argued above, these workshops can be considered as primarily innovative from an organizational perspective and partially innovative from a gender perspective. This view is also based on the idea that challenging masculinities increases organizational capacity for change in times of technological and organizational renewal, when old habits and perceptions of suitable work tasks and safety attitudes for men and women are to be challenged and updated to new social norms. Also as argued above, engaging in challenging masculinities can be considered innovative from both an organizational and a gender perspective.

A fourth innovative trait not covered by Lam's classification is Fagerberg's (2005) notion of organizational innovation as new arrangements involving multiple firms in innovative networks and cluster constellations, as well as reorganization of entire industries. We consider this kind of innovative trait to be reflected in the companies' cooperation with gender researchers as well as in their determination to challenge masculinities. Cooperation between industry and academia as a network constellation is not new per se; however, cooperation between gender researchers and actors in men-dominated natural resource-based industries on the joint development of new knowledge and tools is new, especially in the organizational contexts of the companies studied. As argued above, the cooperation with gender researchers can be considered as primarily innovative from an organizational perspective and partially innovative from a gender perspective.

The challenging of masculinities could be considered a reorganization of the entire forestry and mining industries, since an eradication of masculine norms and perceptions in these contexts would imply considerable transformation of most workplace cultures, work tasks and recruitment patterns in the industries. If realized to its full extent, it could indeed be classified as an entirely new organizational innovation. As argued above, engaging in challenging masculinities can be considered innovative from both an organizational and a gender perspective, harmonizing with Schmidt's (2005) view of gender mainstreaming – in terms of the integration of a gender perspective on all levels and in all areas of an organization – as an innovation per se.

## CONCLUSIONS

Using forestry and mining as empirical cases, this chapter has analysed the extent to which these efforts can be understood as organizational innovations and how their degree of newness affects the likelihood of their leading to structural changes in the gendered patterns of these industries. In order to achieve its aim, the chapter identified, described and analysed gender-equality efforts made by one major Swedish forestry company and one major Swedish mining company. The identified innovative measures in the promotion of gender equality are: creative workshops (including design teams in the forestry company); cooperation with gender researchers; and engaging in challenging masculinities (focusing on safety issues in the mining company). The innovative traits of these measures consist of four streams: the relationship between organizational structural forms and innovativeness; innovation as a process of organizational learning and knowledge creation; organizational capacity for change and adaptation; and new arrangements involving multiple firms in innovative networks and cluster constellations, and the reorganization of entire industries.

The innovativeness of each of the three measures – creative workshops, cooperation with gender researchers, and challenging masculinities – was found to be high. The extent of the innovativeness, however, varied, with all of them reaching a high level of contextual innovativeness but only parts of them doing so in relation to the whole world. Concerning their innovativeness from a gender perspective, all of the measures can be considered as based on the identification of hitherto unmet needs for gender equality among individuals, organizations and to some extent society at large. The likelihood of the measures resulting in transformative structural change varies more considerably, with the challenging of masculinities showing the highest potential to do so, and then only if thoroughly realized.

These conclusions regarding the transformative potential of organizational innovation in the forestry and mining companies' gender-equality measures help advance both theory and practice in the gendered aspects of organizational innovation by increasing our understanding of the relationship between socially innovative measures and structural change in social relations in organizations and society. This advancement is achieved by broadening the scope of contexts acknowledged as potential sites of innovation, by analysing organizational innovation designed to promote increased gender equality in two men-dominated natural resource-based industries. In this way, our conclusions help to fill the general knowledge gap as regards how types of innovation other than technological product innovation are developed and implemented. This is valuable both for the advancement of the scientific field of innovation research and for those managers, politicians and civil servants managing organizational and societal processes of change, particularly – but not exclusively – in the area of gender equality.

## NOTES

1.   Vinnova, the Swedish Governmental Agency for Innovation Systems, is Sweden's national innovation agency.

2. NordMin is a Nordic network of expertise for a sustainable mining and mineral industry funded by the Nordic Council of Ministers.

# REFERENCES

Abrahamsson, L. and J. Johansson (2006), 'From grounded skills to sky qualifications – a study of workers creating and recreating qualifications, identity and gender when meeting changing technology in an underground iron ore mine in Sweden', *Journal of Industrial Relations*, **48** (5), 657–676.

Abrahamsson, L. and M. Somerville (2007), 'Changing storylines and masculine bodies in Australian coal mining organisations', *Norma*, **2** (1), 52–69.

Abrahamsson, L., E. Segerstedt, M. Nygren, J. Johansson, B. Johansson, I. Edman and A. Åkerlund (2014), *Mining and Sustainable Development: Gender, Diversity and Work Conditions in Mining*, Luleå, Sweden: Luleå University of Technology.

Alasoini, T. (2011), 'Workplace development as part of broad-based innovation policy: Exploiting and exploring three types of knowledge', *Nordic Journal of Working Life Studies*, **1** (1), 23–43.

Alsos, G.A., E. Ljunggren and U. Hytti (2013), 'Gender and innovation: State of the art and a research agenda', *International Journal of Gender and Entrepreneurship*, **5** (3), 236–256.

Andersson, E. (2012), 'Malmens manliga mysterium – en interaktiv studie om kön och tradition i modernt gruvarbete' [The masculine mystery of minerals – a participatory study of gender and tradition in modern mining work], Doctoral thesis, Luleå, Sweden: Luleå University of Technology.

Andersson, E., Y. Fältholm, L. Abrahamsson and M. Lindberg (2013), *Breaking Ore and Gender Patterns: A Gender-aware and Socially Sustainable Research and Innovation Agenda for the Swedish Mining Industry (GenderSTRIM)*, Luleå, Sweden: Luleå University of Technology.

Andersson, S., K. Berglund, J. Thorslund, E. Gunnarsson and E. Sundin (eds) (2012), *Promoting Innovation: Policies, Practices and Procedures*, Stockholm: Vinnova.

Blake, M.K. and S. Hanson (2005), 'Rethinking innovation: Context and gender', *Environment and Planning A*, **37** (4), 681–701.

Brandth, B. and M.S. Haugen (2000), 'From lumberjack to business manager: Masculinity in the Norwegian forestry press', *Journal of Rural Studies*, **16** (3), 343–355.

Brandth, B. and M.S. Haugen (2005), 'Text, body, and tools – changing mediations of rural masculinity', *Men and Masculinities*, **8** (2), 148–163.

Cameron, J. and J.K. Gibson-Graham (2003), 'Feminising the economy: Metaphors, strategies, politics', *Gender, Place and Culture*, **10** (2), 145–157.

Danilda, I. and J. Granat Thorslund (2011), *Innovation and Gender*, Stockholm: Vinnova.

Döös, M. and L. Wilhelmson (eds) (2009), *Organising Work for Innovation and Growth: Experiences and Efforts in Ten Companies*, Stockholm: Vinnova.

European Commission (2013), *Social Innovation Research in the European Union*, Brussels: European Union.

Fagerberg, J. (2005), 'Innovation – a guide to the literature', in J. Fagerberg, D.C. Mowery and R.R. Nelson (eds), *The Oxford Handbook of Innovation*, Oxford, UK: Oxford University Press, pp. 1–27.

Fløysand, A. and S.E. Jakobsen (2011), 'The complexity of innovation: A relational turn', *Progress in Human Geography*, **35** (3), 328–344.

Follo, G. (2002), 'A hero's journey: Young women among males in forestry education', *Journal of Rural Studies*, **18** (3), 293–306.

Hansson, J., F. Björk, D. Lundborg and L.E. Olofsson (eds) (2014), *An Ecosystem for Social Innovation in Sweden: A Strategic Research and Innovation Agenda*, Lund, Sweden: Lund University.

Johansson, K., M. Johansson, E. Andersson and G. Lidestav (2014), '"Affirmative action is the most unequal there is" – men forestry workers meaning making of gender and gender equality', Paper presented at the Nordic conference on research on men and masculinities, 4–6 June, University of Iceland, Reykjavik.

Kuhn, M.R., H.A. Bragg and D.J. Blahna (2002), 'Involvement of women and minorities in the urban forestry profession', *Journal of Arboriculture*, **28** (1), 27–34.

Lam, A. (2005), 'Organizational innovation', in J. Fagerberg, D.C. Mowery and R.R. Nelson (eds), *The Oxford Handbook of Innovation*, Oxford, UK: Oxford University Press, pp. 115–147.

Lidestav, G. and A.E. Sjölander (2007), 'Gender and forestry: A critical discourse analysis of forestry professions in Sweden', *Scandinavian Journal of Forest Research*, **22** (4), 351–362.

Lindberg, M. (2012), 'A striking pattern – co-construction of innovation, men and masculinity in Sweden's innovation policy', in S. Andersson, K. Berglund, J. Thorslund, E. Gunnarsson and E. Sundin (eds), *Promoting Innovation: Policies, Practices and Procedures*, Stockholm: Vinnova, pp. 47–67.

Lindberg, M. and H. Schiffbänker (2013), Entry on 'Gender and innovation', in E.G. Carayannis (ed.), *Encyclopedia of Creativity, Invention, Innovation and Entrepreneurship*, New York: Springer.

Miles, I. (2005), 'Innovation in services', in J. Fagerberg, D.C. Mowery and R.R. Nelson (eds), *The Oxford Handbook of Innovation*, Oxford, UK: Oxford University Press, pp. 433–456.

Nählinder, J. (2005), 'Innovation and employment in services: The case of knowledge intensive business services in Sweden', Doctoral thesis, Linköping University, Sweden.

Nählinder, J. (2010), 'Where are all the female innovators? Nurses as innovators in a public sector innovation project', *Journal of Technology Management and Innovation*, **5** (1), 13–29.

Olofsson, J. (2010), 'Taking place – augmenting space: Spatial diffusion in times of technological change', Doctoral thesis, Luleå University of Technology, Sweden.

Pettersson, K. (2007), *Men and Male as the Norm? A Gender Perspective on Innovation Policies in Denmark, Finland and Sweden*, Stockholm: Nordregio.

Pettersson, K. and M. Lindberg (2013), 'Paradoxical spaces of feminist resistance: Mapping the margin to the masculinist innovation discourse', *International Journal of Gender and Entrepreneurship*, **5** (3), 323–341.

Ranga, M. and H. Etzkowitz (2010), 'Athena in the world of techne: The gender dimension of technology, innovation and entrepreneurship', *Journal of Technology Management and Innovation*, **5** (1), 1–12.

Reed, M.G. (2008), 'Reproducing the gender order in Canadian forestry: The role of statistical representation', *Scandinavian Journal of Forestry Research*, **23** (1), 78–91.

Schiebinger, L. (ed.) (2008), *Gendered Innovations in Science and Engineering*, Stanford, CA: Stanford University Press.

Schmidt, V. (2005), *Gender Mainstreaming – an Innovation in Europe? The Institutionalisation of Gender Mainstreaming in the European Commission*, Leverkusen, Germany: Barbara Budrich Publishers.

Squires, J. (2005), 'Is mainstreaming transformative? Theorizing mainstream in the context of diversity and deliberation', *Social Politics*, **12** (3), 366–388.

Thomas, J. and P. Mohai (1995), 'Racial, gender and professional diversification in the Forest Service from 1983 to 1992', *Policy Studies Journal*, **23** (2), 296–309.

Yin, R.K. (2009), *Case Study Research: Design and Methods*, London: Sage.

# PART IV

# GENDER IN INNOVATION POLICY

# 10. Governing gendered understandings of innovation: a discourse analysis of a national innovation policy programme

*Trine Kvidal-Røvik and Birgitte Ljunggren*

## INTRODUCTION

Innovation is regarded as a central aspect in creating national competitive advantage, and key to technological development within industries and sectors (Malerba, 2002). Innovation processes are seen to enhance economic growth and thereby create prosperous nations and regions (Alsos et al., 2013; Fagerberg et al., 2005; Lindberg, 2010; Ljunggren and Alsos, 2010; Lundvall, 1992; Verspagen, 2005). Many nations thus encourage and support innovation initiatives, for instance through national and regional policy programmes. In light of the central position innovation processes have for national and regional development, the innovation arena is of vast importance when it comes to power and influence in society.

Innovation processes are not neutral. Power relations are always at play, related to for instance decisions about allocation of regional or national resources to innovation projects. In terms of power, gender scholars have pointed to a systematic marginalization of women in the innovation arena, even in so-called 'gender equal' Scandinavia (Pettersson, 2007). Scholars link the imbalance to understandings of gender embedded in innovation systems and processes (Busholt and Kugele, 2009; Pettersson, 2007). Furthermore, researchers claim that dominant perspectives on innovation enable a conceptualization of these systems and processes as gender-neutral and also allow gender to be seen as irrelevant when it comes to participation in innovation (Kvidal and Ljunggren, 2014).

Innovation policy programmes can play a central role in terms of involvement and influence on the innovation arena, through the practices, projects and initiatives to which a policy leads. In addition, innovation policy discourses construct dominant understandings of what innovation is, how it is to be done and who has the required competence to be a central actor in innovation processes.

In this chapter, we are particularly interested in this discursive relevance of innovation policy programmes. Here we explore the Norwegian Programme for Regional R&D and Innovation (VRI), which since 2007 has been the Research Council of Norway's main support mechanism for research and innovation throughout Norway's regions. We are interested in VRI based on its role in contributing to dominant gendered understandings of innovation, and consequently in distributing power and influence in the innovation arena.

We approach the topic with a perspective inspired by governmentality and discourse theories. From these perspectives, policy programmes, like VRI, can be seen as having a central role in facilitating and encouraging particular ways of being, which (re)produce a particular ordered society under prevailing political rationalities. That is, in a Norwegian context, the VRI programme plays a role in defining the social field of innovation and in creating dominant understandings of who is more or less suitable as an innovator or has more or less potential to become a valuable contributor to innovation processes.

Using discourse analysis, particularly the concept of articulation, we examine dominant understandings of innovation in VRI policy texts with a gender perspective. This approach enables us to analyse the 'taken-for-grantedness' of innovation and gendered governing of innovation, and to discuss the indirect governing of gender and innovation taking place. The basis for our analysis consists of programme plans, strategies and selected government-level White Papers published from 2007 to 2014. By examining innovation concept articulations in these policy texts and analysing the gendered consequences of these understandings, we contribute with knowledge on the relation of innovation, gender and power.

## THEORETICAL UNDERPINNINGS

### Governmentality

Governmentality is a concept presented by Michel Foucault (1991) to address the workings of power in modern rule. A clue to the meaning of governmentality lies in the word itself, namely the government of mentality. Mentality describes a person's or population's mindset and a way of relating to and making sense of the (social) world. Governmentality is a form of power that seeks to shape conduct at a distance. This is referred to as 'conduct of conduct' (Dean, 1999; Rose, 1999). It describes the indirect ways the state or other agents govern through attempts to shape the action of the population towards certain ends (e.g. innovation) by acting on understandings, will, mentality, knowledge, morality or sense of self (Dean, 1999).

Governmentality has to do with working on the repertoires of meaning, knowledge and morality available to people. Lemke (2001, p. 191) explains that, on the one hand, it has to do with specific forms of *representation*, defining 'a discursive field in which expressing power is "rationalized"'. This can occur by 'the delineation of concepts, the specification of objects and borders, the provision of arguments and justifications' and thus enables a problem to be addressed by means of certain strategies (Lemke, 2001, p. 191).

On the other hand, says Lemke (2001), the concept of governmentality has to do with the structuring of specific forms of *intervention*, as a political rationality is not pure, neutral knowledge, but rather constitutes the intellectual processing of the reality, which political technologies can then tackle. Such interventions can be seen as the technologies applied in ruling at a distance and as 'bearers' of ruling discourses. Policies are one of several government technologies applied to rule the population 'at a distance'.

Governmentality as a form of power attempts to shape conduct by instituting and influencing particular sets of spaces and subjects and illuminates 'how the governable subject is discursively constituted and produced through particular strategies, programmes and techniques' (McKee, 2009, p. 467). Following this framework, understandings found in innovation policy texts are interesting, as they, via their articulation, constitute the 'truth' about the phenomena to which they refer, in our case innovation. This constitutive effect makes visible the productive power of discourses, making them interesting to analyse as part of government.

A governmentality perspective, then, moves away from an instrumentalist view of policy, which regards policy as a top-down tool to regulate a population through rewards and sanctions (Shore and Wright, 1997). Instead, in policies, particular ways of being are facilitated and encouraged, which (re)produce a particular ordered society under prevailing political rationalities (Rose, 1999). Meanings constructed in policy are thus seen as constitutive discourses aimed at structuring the space of action for the population.

Knowledge is central in governing. That is, to be governed, objects of government have to be knowable and defined, and have their boundaries set (Prince et al., 2006). It is for example hard to govern towards more innovation without an understanding of what innovation is, how it comes about and why one should encourage innovation. It is also hard to govern towards innovation if the ones governed do not share these understandings. As Dean (1999) states, 'we govern others and ourselves according to what we take to be true about who we are, what aspects of our existence should be worked upon, how, with what means and to what ends' (p. 18). These understandings are again embedded in the programmes used for governing. In a governmentality perspective, policies – manifested as policy texts – are seen as powerful discursive articulations, as they constitute social entities and social subjects. They become 'a repertoire of meaning' available for the individual.

It is important to keep in mind academic debates about more general and profound governing discourses, called state rationalities, which form the backdrop of national policy programmes. State rationalities are the overarching dominating discourses forming the general government at large. Present-day state rationality is described as advanced liberalism, dominated by a neo-liberal state rationality (others are neoconservatism) (Dean, 1999; Rose, 1996, 1999). The new state task constructed within this frame is to reform individuals and institutions, making them more competitive and effective, to increase competitiveness and performance compared to other nations or regions (Dean, 1999). A central aspect of a neo-liberal governmentality is to promote and enhance the organisational and subjective conditions for the self-governed entrepreneur. In the process, the individual is made responsible for the prosperity of the state in other ways than before (Nadesan, 2008). Consequently, there appears to be a correspondence between individual freedom and the nation's prosperity (Rose, 1999). The entrepreneur is the ideal subject called upon. Innovation is regarded as essential to promote the competitiveness of nations or states (Malerba, 2002) and finds resonance in these arguments.

**Discourse Theory**

When trying to get a better understanding of how policies articulate social entities and social subjects in line with a governmentality perspective, discourse theory represents a valuable contribution. Discourse can be seen as a system of representation that fuses language and practice, and 'the state of knowledge' on a certain topic at any one time (Foucault, 1996). A discourse fixes a web of meanings within a particular domain. Discourses thus do not reflect or represent social entities and relations, but construct or constitute them.

Knowledge and power are based in the ways in which social orders are arranged (Foucault, 1996). The constitution of a discourse involves a reduction of possibilities, and thus an exercise of power. Discourse also regulates what can be said under certain social and cultural conditions, regulating who can speak, when and where. In this sense, discourses do more than just tell us how to think about an object; they offer positions that individuals (can) take up in relation to their object, known as subject positions (Braun and Clark, 2013).

When discourses are hegemonic, the social practices they structure appear so natural that members of a society fail to see that they are the result of political hegemonic practices. Discourses then reach the level of 'common sense'. Their origins and intrinsic contingency are forgotten (Laclau and Mouffe, 1985).

Within the broad discourse analytical field,[1] we align ourselves with perspectives put forth by scholars like Laclau and Mouffe (1985, 1990). Their analytical concept of articulation is of particular use to us. Articulations are forms of social constructions within a specific context. They are connections of different elements that make a unity under certain conditions and contexts, bound by power of custom and opinion (Hall, 1980; Slack, 1996). Articulations are for instance based in descriptions of the phenomena, underlying logics, intertextual references, associations and attributions (Kvidal and Ljunggren, 2014). Discourses are the structured totality resulting from this articulatory practice. For example, within a dominating innovation discourse, the concept of innovation is 'articulated on the basis of ideas concerning a new product or service and the use of new technology. Perceived success criteria, which also play into the articulation, are such things as patent numbers and economic profit' (Kvidal and Ljunggren, 2014, p. 41).

The connections articulations are made up of are not set, and it is always a possibility to rearticulate, even when something seems natural or common. This means that the innovation concept *could* be articulated differently – 'for example, related to organisational structures or procedures and with success criteria such as improved work environment, gender balance, or quality of life' (Kvidal and Ljunggren, 2014, p. 41).

Rearticulating a concept is a question of challenging existing power structures and part of ongoing discursive struggles.[2] For example, if innovation is articulated differently from the above-described dominating innovation discourse, it could imply 'a shift in who would be considered experts on the issue of innovation and who should be targeted in innovation policy programmes' (Kvidal and Ljunggren, 2014, p. 41).

**A Gender Perspective**

In this chapter, we are interested in the 'taken-for-granted' articulations of innovation as created in VRI from a gender perspective. A gender perspective, however, does not have one set meaning,[3] but in line with the theoretical perspectives outlined above, we align ourselves with a social constructivist approach, where opening up the possibility for change by looking at things differently is central.

By making visible how the innovation concept is constructed in ways that have gendered consequences in terms of power and influence, we hope to enable new thoughts on innovation and inspire continued discussions on the topics of innovation, gender and power. Here we build on previous research, in related areas, which takes a discursive approach to address gender inequality (e.g. Ahl, 2004; Fenwick, 2004; Halford, 2003; Katila and Meriläinen, 1999; Kelan, 2007; Kvidal and Ljunggren, 2014; Lindberg, 2008; Moore et al., 2008).

## CASE DESCRIPTION AND DATA MATERIALS

The VRI programme web page describes VRI as a 'Research Council of Norway initiative, targeted toward *research and innovation* at the regional level in Norway' (VRI, 2014, para 2). Furthermore, key components of VRI presented on the web page are research activity, professional and financial support, exchange of experience and learning. VRI has a time-frame of ten years (2007–2017) and offers professional and financial support to long-term, research-based development processes in the regions. The programme is divided into three periods. The current VRI period – VRI 3 – runs from 2014 to 2017 and has a budget of NOK188 million. VRI implemented a gender-balance plan in 2008 (Kvidal and Ljunggren, 2014).

### Analysed Texts

To get at the articulation of innovation in VRI, we analysed programme plans, strategies and relevant government-level White Papers (those referenced in programme plans and in texts related to the establishment of VRI) from the beginning of the policy programme in 2007 and through to 2014. An overview of the analysed texts can be found in Table 10.1.

*Table 10.1   Analysed document titles, year of publication and publisher*

| Document title | Year | Author/publisher |
| --- | --- | --- |
| *VRI Programplan 2007–2010* [VRI Programme Plan 2007–2010] | 2007 | Research Council of Norway |
| *Veiledning. Virkemidler og aktiviteter i VRI-programmet (Virkemidler for regional FoU og innovasjon). Med produktark 1. febuar 2007* [Guidance for applying VRI 2007–2010 with product sheet] | 2007 | Research Council of Norway |
| *Handlingsplan for meir eintreprenørskap blant kvinner* [Action plan for more entrepreneurship among women] | 2007 | Barne- og likestillingsdepartementet, Kommunal- og regionaldepartementet, Nærings- og handelsdepartementet, Arbeids- og inkluderingsdepartementet, Fiskeri- og kystdepartementet, Kunnskapsdepartementet and Landbruks- og matdepartementet[1] |
| *Strategi for kjønnsbalanse I VRI* [Strategy for Gender Balance in VRI] | 2008 | Research Council of Norway |
| *VRI Programplan 2010–2014* [VRI Programme Plan 2010–2014] | 2010 | Research Council of Norway |
| White Paper No. 39 (2012–2013): *Mangfold av vinnere. Næringspolitikken mot 2020* [Diversity of winners: Industry policy towards 2020] | 2012 | Ministry of Trade and Industry |
| White Paper No. 18 (2012–2013): *Lange linjer-kunnskap gir muligheter* [Long-term Perspectives: Knowledge Provides Opportunity] | 2012 | Ministry of Education and Research |
| *Gender Balance and Gender Perspectives in Research and Innovation: The Research Council's Policy 2013–2017* | 2013 | Research Council of Norway |
| *VRI Programme Plan 2014–2017* | 2014 | Research Council of Norway |

*Note:*   [1] The structure and naming of these offices have changed somewhat since the original document was published. The table refers to the departments as they were referenced in the original publication.

We specifically analysed documents for innovation articulations from a gender perspective, but also analysed the innovation documents for understandings of gender.

While there is no recipe for analysing articulations, we developed our operationalization inspired by Kvidal and Ljunggren (2014) and considered aspects such as *descriptions, attributions, intertextual references* and *underlying logics*.

In terms of *descriptions*, we analysed how innovation (implicitly and explicitly) is described, defined, operationalized and 'measured' in the document. For example, we asked how the documents say innovation is measured or what is going to be improved with more innovation. In analysing *attributions*, we looked for which factors were mentioned in the texts in terms of affecting innovations. For example, we asked: 'What is said to be important in order to promote innovation?' and 'What tools are highlighted as beneficial in order to promote innovation?'

*Intertextual references* refer to finding which other texts are put to use to give the analysed documents credibility. Examples can be: references to other documents; sources of information and research; use of statistics, graphs, pictures and illustrations; reference to research; and highlighted participants.

Finally, in terms of *underlying logics*, we searched the analysed texts for logics (arguments, paradigms and perspectives) anchoring the innovation concept in other concepts or discourses. For example, we looked for which industries were selected as prioritized areas, and the arguments for why these areas were chosen.

## INNOVATION ARTICULATIONS IN VRI

In this section we present our key findings based on our articulation analyses for descriptions, attributions, references and underlying logics related to innovation in the documents.

### Innovation as Collaborative Systemic Process

We can see that innovation as a concept is addressed both explicitly and implicitly in the analysed VRI documents, although specific definitions of the concept are generally not provided. There are however descriptions of how innovation comes about.

A first point in relation to such descriptions is that a systemic understanding of innovation processes (versus for example a more linear perspective) is clearly part of the VRI innovation discourse.[4] An example can be seen in the first programme plan, which states: 'VRI is based on a system perspective, where innovating is seen as a collective and interactive process' (Research Council of Norway, 2007, p. 2).[5] There are also frequent references made to research done on regional innovation systems, and VRI is presented as a way to support, strengthen and develop the regional innovation systems in Norway. In short, VRI as a policy programme is based on the idea of regional and collaborative *systems* for innovation.

The triple helix system approach[6] to innovation is brought up in several different places in the VRI documents. In line with this view of innovation, the parts in the system which the VRI programme aims at mobilizing are R&D institutions, enterprises and public sector institutions.

Collaboration is another central concept in the VRI discourse. For instance, the 2007 programme plan states that VRI takes a collective system perspective 'because businesses get impulses and competence from many actors, and it is an interactive process because it entails mutual learning among actors' (Research Council of Norway, 2007, p. 2). It is the collaboration among the parts that will ensure innovation, it is said. That is, when relevant actors (defined to be on a meso level) collaborate and learn from each other, this is something seen as enabling innovation processes. For example, the VRI web page explains that the VRI programme activates and aligns a large 'machinery' of actors, relations, and production of knowledge in order to reach the defined goal of enhancing innovation (VRI, 2014).

Research findings are used in the VRI texts to back up claims about the importance of collaboration. The programme plan reads: 'At the same time, research shows that companies which are able to combine experiential knowledge and research-based knowledge have the highest level of innovation' (Research Council of Norway, 2014, p. 7). This underscores regional collaboration between trade and industry, R&D institutions and the government authorities as an important aspect of VRI. Potentially uneven power relations in the systems and collaborative efforts are not mentioned in the texts.

The emphasis put on systems and collaboration seems consistent throughout the documents we have analysed, and we see no difference in terms of the weight put on these concepts in the documents published between 2007 and 2014. This indicates that this specific aspect of the understanding of innovation is not changing much in the discourse, nor being challenged in the texts, thus enabling a perpetuation and legitimization of the status quo in terms of this systemic perspective on innovation.

## A Changing Understanding of (the Object of) Innovation

While focus on systems and collaboration is constant in the texts, there is some tension related to what is to be the object of innovation, and the question of what should be improved by means of innovation. In several places in the texts, products and services are mentioned as objects of innovation. For example, the second programme plan states that 'competencies, technologies and attitudes are crucial for the actors' success in developing for example a new product or a new service' (Research Council of Norway, 2010, p. 2). Yet, in reading the 2008 VRI gender-balance strategy, a critique is posed against a 'too narrow' focus on product innovation in VRI. The call for a broadening of the object of innovation challenges understandings of innovation.

This movement in the object of innovation, and where it takes place, shows a movement in the understanding of innovation. The dominant understanding of a new product, service or technology, measured via patent numbers or economic profit, is challenged, and with it the articulation of innovation might be seen as slightly changed.

As an elongation of the service theme, in the second programme plan from 2010 public sector innovation is discussed for the first time as a VRI-relevant arena for innovation. It is said that, in terms of VRI's objectives and target groups, 'the public sector can become a focus for VRI' (Research Council of Norway, 2010, p. 4). In the last programme plan from 2014, the public sector is emphasized more and included as a target group, as the text reads: 'Activities under the VRI programme seek to promote innovation in public and private sectors in all parts of the country, which is one of the main tasks of the Research Council (section 2 of the statutes)' (Research Council of Norway, 2014, p. 5). It is specifically the public health and care sectors which are described as interesting. The understanding is that some of the means used in VRI might also be used in public sector innovation processes.

Another aspect that might be seen as challenging the dominant understanding of innovation has to do with gender in a more explicit sense. The 2008 VRI gender-balance strategy points to a biased focus on technological innovations and product innovations in fields where women are in the minority. This can be seen as challenging the understanding of innovation as gender-neutral. It thus might also be seen as changing the understanding of innovation.

The shifting object of innovation seems to go in the direction of involving more women-dominated workplaces, thus potentially rearranging who are considered relevant actors in innovation processes. Furthermore, in the second programme plan, from 2010, the object of innovation is expanded from product and service to also include organizations, as the plan explains that 'competencies, technologies and attitudes are crucial for the actors' success in developing for example a new product or a new service *or in organizing the labour process better*' (Research Council of Norway, 2010, p. 3, our emphasis).

## Knowledge and Innovation

An explicit objective in the VRI programme is defined as developing knowledge about innovation and support collaboration and innovation processes. Throughout the VRI documents, then, it is not surprising that there is an emphasis on knowledge, in terms of both transfer and learning, as well as general arguments for the importance of knowledge for success with innovation.

The VRI documents present knowledge as an important propellant for innovation and specifically research-based knowledge. Research and knowledge is especially emphasized in the programme plan document from 2014. The texts often describe this as a vital contribution to the innovation process. Thus, research-based knowledge is called for, preferably in combination with individual and collective experience-based knowledge. What type of research-based knowledge, or experience-based knowledge, will be of particular relevance is not specified.

From a gender perspective, this is worth reflecting on, as the type of research and experiences called upon impacts who gets called to contribute in innovation processes. As Norway's work life is gender segregated (Alsos et al., 2011), it is of importance if it is men's or women's knowledge fields that are defined as relevant in the VRI discourse.

The analysed documents also show an interesting tension in relation to competence and diversity. The first plan document, from 2007, states that businesses' ability to find and use other actors' competence, and their 'absorptive capacity' (Research Council of Norway, 2007, p. 2), is important for the businesses' innovation ability. The last plan, from 2014, states that it is important to innovation ability to find and use competence that other actors have and that it therefore is necessary to include different types of actors in the processes. Furthermore, tight local networks are described as presenting a risk of 'lock-in', preventing contributions of new ideas and competence (Research Council of Norway, 2007, p. 2). In other words, openness toward others and the ability to absorb new ideas and new competencies are seen as positive. Implicitly, this openness prevents being 'locked in' to old ways of doing things. This implies focusing more on relations and a valuation of difference, although it is not specified what this difference entails.

In sum, a central finding is that innovation is articulated as a collaborative and interactive process of developing new products or services that will lead to new, increased financial gain for businesses and other actors. Innovation rests on a system perspective that interpellates people as discursive resources in order to provide the knowledge required in order to ensure the desired collaborative processes of developing something new and profitable. That is, in order to become innovative, businesses must have access to different human resources, which then collaborate to create something new, contributing to profit making. Profitable businesses make the nation of Norway sustainable and competitive internationally.

**The Ideal VRI Actor and the Issue of Diversity**

Subject positions available in a discourse reveal who is interpellated as more or less central and normal in the discourse at hand, and tell us about the expectations facing those stepping into these subject positions.

In the VRI discourse, several interesting elements are connected to taking part in successful innovation processes. That is, the VRI innovation discourse calls for certain 'subjects' with necessary capabilities demanded in order to be ideal contributing actors. In short, the ideal actor should be willing to cooperate, share knowledge, and have a positive attitude toward new ideas and new knowledge (absorptive capacity), as well as an openness to difference.

We find a particularly strong weight put on 'different approaches' as strengthening innovation processes (Research Council of Norway, 2014, p. 12), yet what this 'difference' entails is not further defined. An interpretation of 'different approaches' can be different discourses that might bring the innovators out of familiar patterns of thinking, hence direct them into new practices. Inherent in such an understanding is the incentive to 'think outside the box', and leave 'normal' and habitual thinking by adding something different and perhaps unconventional. A premise for succeeding is nevertheless being an inclusive and attentive actor for this 'otherness'. These kinds of fuels might be interpreted as 'discursive fuel', since they are about ways of understanding and mental schemes for practice.

To drive innovation processes, different mental schemes – 'approaches' – are in demand. Yet this way of understanding the innovative process presupposes the existence of something 'normal' or conventional or a 'standard approach' that has to be changed in order to become open to something different in order to become innovative. Openness and inclusiveness become wanted characteristics of the normal actor. The ideal (normal) innovation actor (subject) in VRI is supported by the implicit perspective of open innovation found in the texts. Here, open innovation might be interpreted as a process fuelled by some important elements in order to become well-functioning or even in order to take place.

Interestingly, there is a change over time in the VRI texts in terms of who is understood as the ideal and normal subject in VRI. The VRI documents from the early programme period define and operationalize this as the firm or a business. The programme plan of 2007 states that that 'competence, technology and attitudes in individual businesses determine if *businesses* succeed in developing for instance a new product or a new service' (Research Council of Norway, 2007, p. 2, our emphasis). The unit that is supposed to become innovative and gain the ability to renew itself and then develop a competitive advantage is the firm. The firm is framed as neutral; that is, it does not lend itself to seeing actors in the innovation system as gendered.

Over time, we see less of this operationalization of the actor as a firm, and instead the 'actor' is left unspecified, thus broadening the potential participants called upon. The new definition opens for micro-level actors (individuals as women and men) as well as public sector organizations. In the programme plan from of 2014 it is said that 'Expertise, technology and attitudes play and essential role in whether the *actors* will succeed in developing a new product or new service or organising work processes in a better way' (Research Council of Norway, 2014, p. 7, our emphasis).

Importantly, the connections among the firm, the institution, the region and the nation all relate to the meso and macro levels. These connections are recognizable and meaningful in the frame of advanced liberal governing rationality (a neo-liberal governing rationality), where the micro and meso levels are positioned as responsible for the economic and sustainable aspects of the system in general. In such a frame, VRI is a technology for mobilizing and enabling the actors to play this part and answer to the expectation of being useful for the totality.

## Supporting Higher Goals: Reasons for Innovation

Overall, the policy documents put forth two dominating reasons for improving innovation capacity. One has to do with *being competitive* in a global marketplace, and the other has to do with *securing the welfare* of the population. While both these two 'basic' reasons for innovation are visible in the texts, and they are often presented as interconnected, our analyses show that, in the VRI discourse, the competitive reason takes the position of an underlying premise for the welfare reason.

The first reason for competitiveness in a global sense presents the ability to innovate as vital for making the nation's economy (and Norway) more competitive in a global market. An example of how this comes about can be found in the first programme plan from 2007, which states that: 'VRI should contribute to increased value creation in the regional businesses through R&D projects, which both develop existing and open up completely new business areas' (Research Council of Norway, 2007, p. 3). Another example can be found in a White Paper published in 2012, which claims that 'the global competition demands innovation, and innovation demands competence' (Ministry of Education and Research, 2012, p. 60).

Another facet of the competitiveness reason is the nation's ability to foster innovative regions. This mobilizing of available competitive advantages is reflected in phrases such as: 'In Norway and the rest of Europe, development and innovation are increasingly regarded as a key factor in the creation of vigorous regions' (Research Council of Norway, 2007, p. 1).

Regional development becomes essential to this competitiveness when it produces and uses its competitive advantages to fuel innovation processes. As one programme plan states, 'To capitalize on Norway's national and regional advantages, VRI will contribute to increased value creation in the regional businesses through R&D projects which both develop existing and open up completely new business areas' (Research Council of Norway, 2007, p. 1).

The competitive advantages are resources attached to the work force and local settings. Innovation processes, thus, are fed not only by 'discursive fuel', but also by using other resources such as natural resources (for instance nature and culture available in a specific area) and an educated work force (which includes women).

The second reason for promotion of innovation in the VRI discourse, has to do with securing people's welfare. A global competitive economy (in which being innovative is a competitive advantage) is described as vital to the mere sustainability of the future welfare of the population, for example in phrases from a 2012 White Paper, such as 'A prerequisite to exploiting the value creation potential is that the whole country's resources are put to use. Good use of available resources is the departure point for succeeding in obtaining a highly sustainable welfare society over time' (Ministry of Trade and Industry, 2012, p. 53). In another instance, it is said that, 'in the long run, production growth means a great deal for our living standard' (Ministry of Trade and Industry, 2012, p. 54). The link is then made between innovation and keeping a desirable living standard. Everybody in the country, then, will benefit from businesses' innovation activities. The same document refers to the economist Paul Krugman, and puts forward a quote from him, stating that productivity, and a country's ability to improve its standard of living over time, 'depends almost entirely on its ability to raise its output per worker' (Ministry of Trade and Industry, 2012, p. 54). Following this, it is explained that 'production growth will be obtained via many forms of innovation and technological progress, better leadership and "smarter" production methods' (Ministry of Trade and Industry, 2012, p. 54). Consequently, innovation, the use of the nation's national resources, economic growth and the population's continued welfare and standard of living are presented as connected. This connects to ongoing debates about the economic sustainability of the welfare state (Pierson, 1999).

In sum, innovation is articulated as important for making Norway and Norwegian regions more competitive globally, and for the sustainability of the Norwegian population's welfare. The neo-liberal governmentality frames the understanding of innovation in VRI, fixing it as a tool to enhance competitive abilities and social-economic sustainability. In order to reach this goal, subjects are called upon, in so far as they are capable or have a potential to be capable, to contribute to innovation processes, whether this be knowledge, different approaches or collaborative competences. This political rationality makes it hard to discuss other reasons to innovate. Contingently, one could imagine other underlying logics for supporting innovation, such as promoting environmental sustainability, social inclusion (not only through the labour market) or an ethic of care (Sevenhuijsen, 1998).

## Articulating Gender in VRI

When trying to get at the articulations of innovation from a gender perspective, it is useful to discuss how gender is constructed in the innovation policy texts. While the innovation concept is dealt with extensively, both explicitly and implicitly, the gender concept is relatively invisible in the policy documents. As a theme, however, gender becomes more and more visible in the documents over time. For example, while gender is not mentioned at all in the 2007 programme plan, it is explicitly mentioned nine times in the programme plan from 2014.

In the first programme plan, from 2007, the issue of gender is only implicitly addressed. In fact, it only comes up when women and young people are talked about as something to consider when applying for project funding. Later the *Strategy for Gender Balance in VRI* was launched, in 2008, responding to demands from higher levels in public administration regarding gender mainstreaming. The strategy states that

'The VRI regions have been given the task of developing action plans for what they will do to obtain a gender-balanced participation' (Research Council of Norway, 2008, p. 1). Hence, the understanding of gender as relevant for VRI is not generated from within the programme,[7] but is 'given as a task' or demanded 'from above'.

### Gender = Women

The dominating articulation of gender in the documents is in line with an essentialist gender approach, where gender qualities are linked to bio-logical gender and not as something constructed (Connell, 2006). It is thus a binary understanding of gender as either women or men that circulates in the documents. One key example is the whole argument presented in the 2008 gender strategy document, where the issue to be dealt with is described as the lack of women taking part in innovation processes (or research). The metaphor, as the title of the document underscores, is the need for a gender *balance*; but the explicitly formu-lated problem throughout the text is that there are too few women. While this actually means that there are too many men, this is not spelled out.

The focus thus remains on the (lack of) women. Men and women are relevant as different countable categories. This understanding is found in higher-level documents like the Research Council's gender policy, which states that '*Gender balance* implies that both genders participate in research on an equal footing. The overall target is for an equal number of women and men to be active in all areas and at all levels' (Research Council of Norway, 2013, p. 2). This exemplifies a gender-as-variable understanding. This understanding arguably makes gender easy to meas-ure (as a person is either a man or a woman), but it is also an approach which highlights the differences between the sexes (Connell, 2006).

The 'numeric' approach to gender is embedded in the instruments presented for improving awareness of the issue of gender balance in the VRI gender policy. The majority of the instruments aim at increasing the number of women in the VRI projects, and there is no discussion on lowering the amount of men. In addition, who should define what are the relevant parts to be gendered is not discussed.

The binary understanding of gender is reproduced in other places as well, for example in the *Strategy for Gender Balance in VRI* (Research Council of Norway, 2008), which says that regional VRI initiatives shall be managed by steering committees consisting of key VRI actor and target group representatives. The strategy explains that, with an existing male-dominated top management, it 'proves difficult to reach the goal of 40% women. It is however, possible to influence this positively by making people conscious, creative and willing' (Research Council of Norway, 2008, p. 3). Again we can see an understanding of gender as variable put forth. Also, the described objective of 40 per cent speaks to women, not men. It is stated that 40 per cent women is the *goal*, and thus it can only be assumed that the current number is lower than this, and that 40 per cent represents an improved number for women. In theory, it could be stated that the goal was 60 per cent men, but as in the example above, the focus remains on the (lack of) women. The attention is directed to the notion that women have to get 'in' to improve the statistics, while the flipside of this argument – namely that men have to get 'out' – is left out.

The binary way of defining gender is the building block of the argumentation for raising the number of women in innovation processes. Arguments for 'adding women' are for the most part outspoken in the 'higher-level' documents and are about portraying women as resources. In the documents, the focus on numbers and ratio between women and men is described as a phase in development toward a more profound altering of the systems, where a gender dimension will be integrated as a perspective in all relevant parts of research programmes. Skewed numbers can be altered by working on cultural attitudes:

> The Research Council is of the opinion that improving the gender balance must be regarded as a maturing process. The first step is to develop measurements for counting. Later it will become more correct to turn focus towards more substantial, professional issues and work towards the integration of the gender dimension in all relevant parts of the programme. (Research Council of Norway, 2008, p. 1)

Men are not articulated as the problem – it is never stated that they are too many, that they are dominating or that they are in surplus. They remain the stable and invisible majority – the norm(al). Unless the total number of people involved in the innovation arena is to grow considerably, a call for gender balance could in fact be explained as a call for some men to exit and some women to enter.

In sum, the concept of gender as variable dominates the VRI texts. This understanding of gender as one of two clearly definable categories highlights the differences between the biological sexes and makes gender something that can be counted. Importantly, this gender as variable is linked to women. That is, when gender is brought up, it is often in relation to a lack of women. Gender and women are regarded as the same thing. Women – or the lack thereof – represent the problem, and women also represent the solution.

### Women as Resource

In VRI, innovation is understood as an open process, dependent on 'difference' as a fuel. In this dependence on difference, innovation merges with gender in VRI. We have already seen that gender is understood as women in the texts. So, when an argument is made for including a gender perspective, interpreting this as a woman perspective seems obvious, as in the following quote: 'Gender as a *perspective* implies that biological and social gender is reflected in research *content*. A growing number of studies show that diversity, including gender balance and gender perspectives, helps to enhance the scientific quality and social relevance of research' (Research Council of Norway, 2013, p. 2).

Consequently, women are understood in VRI as contributing to innovation by representing difference or diversity. Hence, women positioned as something different are regarded as a resource for a process in need of new ideas and perspectives. 'Women as a resource' is an underlying logic in VRI, since introducing women is a solution presented to enhance innovation. This underlying logic is articulated in the last programme plan: 'Efforts related to gender balance under the VRI programme have their basis in the need for a broad-based expertise and scientific perspectives, which in turn may contribute to creativity and higher quality.' (Research Council of Norway, 2014, p. 8). Women in that manner represent a discursive capital useful to fuel the innovation process and hinder 'lock-in'. Being a woman is a resource in itself, and this is supported by the underlying assumption that being a woman represents diversity.

We see this understanding reproduced in documents referring to each other chronologically, including the VRI gender-balance strategy (Research Council of Norway, 2008), the Research Council's gender-balance strategy (Research Council of Norway, 2013) and the latest programme plan (Research Council of Norway, 2014). Another example of this underlying logic is presented in the Research Council's strategy for gender balance:

> Innovation processes are dependent upon a rich assortment of ideas and perspectives to meet various needs. Both in ERA and Horizon 2020 it has been pointed out that gender perspectives are not a sufficiently integral part of research and innovation. This applies in Norway as well. Integrating gender perspectives into innovation activities will pave the way for new opportunities and better results. (Research Council of Norway, 2013, p. 8)

The understanding of women as resources in the innovation process presupposes a binary way of looking at gender underscoring the difference between men and women.

The women as resource of difference logic is also present in an economic argument for increasing the number of women in innovation processes. Excluding women is regarded as a societal squandering of resources available in the nation (not only for the innovation process). The nation's citizens are regarded as necessary human capital to use and develop in order to secure social development. Women are in this perspective regarded as an equally important resource to men. Not using the resource women represent is a waste and undermines society's development and welfare on a macro level in society. As the action plan states, 'The Government wants to promote social development where we use the resources of both men and women. Norway is a small nation that cannot afford to use only parts of the human capital' (Barne- og likestillingsdepartementet et al., 2007, p. 5). Similarly, gender equality policy is a described as a 'competitive advantage. A nation that offers everybody an opportunity to succeed will also succeed in industrial and commercial development, innovation and value creation' (Ministry of Trade and Industry, 2012, p. 7).

The women-as-resource argument, articulated in the VRI policy, makes sense in an advanced governing rationality where the individuals are relevant in so far as they can contribute to securing the totality. Related to the innovation process, being a female and seemingly different is regarded as a sufficient resource. There is also a striking resonance here with Nicolas Rose's argument of a correspondence between the self-interest of the economic subject and the patriotic duty of the citizen in advanced liberalism. Freedom is redefined as the capacity for self-realization through individual activity in the market (Rose, 1999, p. 145).

In sum, gender balance becomes a means to ensure variety in the knowledge that is brought to the table; it reproduces an understanding of men and women as different. Gender is seen as relevant by representing it as a resource for innovation. Gender balance is framed as something that will contribute to variety and difference. Implicitly, having both men and women involved will ensure diversity in knowledge in comparison to having only men involved. This is an essentialist conceptualization of gender, as women and men are conceived of as representing different types of knowledge.

As there is a majority of men in the processes to begin with, the goal is repeatedly to get more women involved, as this ensures that 'difference' is brought into the process. One could imagine that, if the point was to ensure variety in types of knowledge, the idea would be to involve people with different educational backgrounds or different occupations. In this sense, the 'genderedness' of this governmentality is striking. Subjects are not called upon in a gender-neutral way in the policy.

Our findings are similar to what Ahl (2004) pointed out in terms of how gender is constructed in entrepreneurship research discourse. She shows how the construction of entrepreneurship (re)creates the assumption of men and women being 'different by nature' in such powerful ways that it 'excludes a discussion of similarities between men and women' and actually 'precludes a discussion of the meaningfulness of investigating gender differences and it prevents a questioning of the usefulness and consequences of gendered norms for humans of either sex' (p. 167).

## A Small Crack in the Ice: Gender as Perspective

The dominating articulation of gender in the VRI policy documents is an essentialist one framed by the underlying neo-liberal, resource-oriented logic. There is, however, another, less visible articulation of gender, of a more reflective and critical kind. We find it in the Research Council's gender strategy, but it is particularly outspoken and explicitly related to innovation in the 2008 *Strategy for Gender Balance in VRI*. Here, 'gender as perspective' questions traditional approaches to innovation and the present focus on technological industries. There is a critique of the previous focus in VRI on technology innovation rather than service innovation. One can read that:

> The concept of innovation can be challenged: the rather confined definition of innovation that traditionally has been used (for example with the number of patents as counting instrument) is a weakness with the concept of innovation. The concept is based on a small number of industries where service industries and public sector are excluded. By studying innovation as a gendered phenomenon, one would achieve a better understanding of what it really implies. (Research Council of Norway, 2008, p. 7)

Furthermore, in the last VRI programme plan (Research Council of Norway, 2014) it is stated:

> The VRI programme puts special emphasis in strengthening the participation of women in innovation processes and strives for gender-balanced participation in the programme at all levels and in all key processes. This means that all participants within the VRI programme must be aware of the choices made at all levels for the project and the significance of these for women and men and for the understanding of innovation. (p. 15)

It argues that innovation has previously been understood too narrowly ('confined'), which produces a blind spot regarding what is understood and acknowledged as innovation and who is seen as an innovator. This perspective also opens for questioning the way decisions in VRI affect women and men differently. Gender as perspective allows women to participate in innovation processes for reasons other than using one's resources or being a resource. It enables us to discuss participation and inclusion in innovation processes connected to a democratic underlying logic: 'Loss of talent and biased recruitment is both a democratic challenge and an obstacle to achieving the ambitious objectives set for Norwegian research' (Research Council of Norway, 2013, p. 2).

Even though the argumentation still rests on an essentialist understanding of gender, it allows for critical questions. It makes us see and discuss gendered structures in terms of change and continuity as well as posing a critique of the balancing ('numeric') perspective for being insufficient. But, most interestingly, it attempts to challenge and reframe the innovation concept, to frame it within a logic other than that of neo-liberal political rationality.

## DISCUSSION

In this chapter, positioned in a theoretical landscape of governmentality and discourse theory, we have examined gender and innovation articulations in VRI, wanting to shed light on the indirect governance of innovation in the Norwegian context. Focus has been on the discursive understandings produced in VRI policies, as such understandings are seen as ways through which power works.

Innovation is articulated as a systemic and collaborative process that will lead to new, increased financial gain for businesses and other actors. It is important for making Norway and Norwegian regions more competitive globally, and for the sustainability of the Norwegian population's welfare. Subjects are called upon in so far as they are capable, or have the potential to be capable, of contributing to innovation processes, whether this is through providing knowledge, collaborative competences or difference. This political rationality makes it hard to discuss other reasons to innovate. Consequently, one could imagine other underlying logics for supporting innovation, such as promoting environmental sustainability, social inclusion (other than through the labour market) or an ethic of care (Sevenhuijsen, 1998).

A variable understanding of gender dominates the discourse, highlighting the differences between the biological sexes and making gender something that can easily be counted and reported. When gender is brought up, it often refers to a lack of women. In this sense, the 'genderedness' of this governmentality is striking. Subjects are not called upon in a gender-neutral way in the policy. Gender balance becomes a means to ensure variety, thus reproducing an understanding of men and women as different. That is, this is an essentialist conceptualization of gender, as women and men are conceived of as representing different types of knowledge. One could imagine that, if the point was to ensure variety in types of knowledge, one could involve people with different educational backgrounds or different occupations.

Through this policy women are constituted as different, and it is through this difference that they are legitimized as participants in innovation. VRI reproduces essentialist gender assumptions, positioning women as different, perhaps not really belonging in the innovation discourse.

There is, as we have seen, a 'crack in the ice' which opens up to allow other ways of thinking about gender; it opens up for questioning the cultural, gendered structures. However, innovation to promote business or societal competitiveness or sustainability is not openly discussed related to gender as perspective. There are some dispositions for such reflections when innovations and gender are framed by a democratic discourse, albeit weak. The ways innovation is articulated in VRI and understood in relation to gender are marked by an advanced liberal governmentality making social subjects relevant only as resources to strengthen some kind of totality.

We find that the dominating articulation of innovation in VRI creates a premise for the possible understanding of gender in VRI. That is, the dominating innovation articulation demands an articulation of gender as a potential resource. The articulation of innovation (framed by a neo-liberal governmentality) found in the VRI policy represents a type of cognitive or theoretical path-dependency that brings policy into a 'lock-in' that reproduces the same gendered understanding that previous research has pointed out. It shuts off other perspectives on why it might be good to innovate and the premises for inclusion which would allow gender to be rearticulated in the discourse – or, the other way around, allow a gender perspective to rearticulate innovation.

## ACKNOWLEDGEMENTS

This research has been conducted as part of the GENINNO project, made possible by funding from the Research Council of Norway.

# NOTES

1. For an overview of different approaches within discourse analysis, see Jørgensen and Phillips (2010).
2. This refers to how a broad array of discourses, each structuring reality in a different way, compete to define 'truth' within a particular aspect of the social world (Laclau and Mouffe, 1985, 1990).
3. It is beyond the limits of this chapter to provide an overview of gender perspectives, but for a relevant overview and discussion of gender perspectives in the related field of entrepreneurship see for instance Ahl (2004), in particular chapter 1.
4. Early innovation models were dominated by a linear perspective and drew a line from basic research through applied research to innovation (Kline and Rosenberg, 1986). It has mostly been rejected in favour of approaches related to collective learning and innovation systems (e.g. Asheim, 1994; Lazonick, 2005). The main idea of such system approaches is that innovations are interactive and collective learning processes. Relationships between actors in different systems, and concepts such as clusters and networks are areas of interest (Porter, 2000). For an overview of systems perspective, see Edquist (2005).
5. All Norwegian document quotes have been translated from Norwegian to English by the authors.
6. Simply stated, the triple helix model refers to university–industry–government relationships and is a model first suggested by Etzkowitz and Leydesdorff (1997).
7. This is not to say that the interest in a gender focus was not present within the VRI programme itself, but rather that the demands 'from above' were central in making gender an explicit theme in VRI.

# REFERENCES

Ahl, H. (2004), *The Scientific Reproduction of Gender Inequality: A Discourse Analysis of Research Texts on Women's Entrepreneurship*, Malmö, Sweden: Liber Malmö.

Alsos, G.A., R. Steen-Jensen and E. Ljunggren (2011), 'Gender and entrepreneurship: Revealing constructions and underlying processes – the case of Norway', in C.G. Brush, E.J. Gatewood, A. de Bruin and C. Henry (eds), *Women's Entrepreneurship and Growth Influences: An International Perspective*, Cheltenham, UK and Northampton, MA, USA: Edward Elgar, pp. 40–56.

Alsos, G.A., E. Ljunggren and U. Hytti (2013), 'Gender and innovation: State of the art and a research agenda', *International Journal of Gender and Entrepreneurship*, **5** (3), 236–256.

Asheim, B.T. (1994), *Regionale innovasjonssystem: Teknologipolitikk som regionalpolitikk*, STEP Report 18/1994, Oslo: STEP Group.

Barne- og likestillingsdepartementet, Kommunal- og regionaldepartementet, Nærings- og handelsdepartementet, Arbeids- og inkluderingsdepartementet, Fiskeri- og kystdepartementet, Kunnskapsdepartementet and Landbruks- og matdepartementet (2007), *Handlingsplan for meir eintreprenørskap blant kvinner* [Action plan for more entrepreneurship among women], Oslo: Departementa.

Braun, V. and V.V. Clark (2013), *Successful Qualitative Research*, London: Sage.

Busholt, U. and K. Kugele (2009), 'The gender innovation and research productivity gap in Europe', *International Journal of Innovation and Sustainable Development*, **4** (2/3), 109–122.

Connell, R.R. (2006), *Gender*, Cambridge, UK: Polity Press.

Dean, M. (1999), *Governmentality: Power and Rule in Modern Society*, London: Sage.
Edquist, C. (2005), 'Systems of innovation: Perspectives and challenges', in J. Fagerberg, D.C. Mowery and R.R. Nelson (eds), *The Oxford Handbook of Innovation*, Oxford, UK: Oxford University Press, pp. 181–208.
Etzkowitz, H. and L. Leydesdorff (1997), *Universities and the Global Knowledge Economy: A Triple Helix of University–Industry–Government Relations*, London: Pinter.
Fagerberg, J., D.C. Mowery and R.R. Nelson (2005), *The Oxford Handbook of Innovation*, Oxford, UK: Oxford University Press.
Fenwick, T. (2004), 'What happens to the girls? Gender, work and learning in Canada's "new economy"', *Gender and Education*, **16**, 170–185.
Foucault, M. (1991), 'Governmentality', in G. Burchell, C. Gordon and P. Miller (eds), *The Foucault Effect: Studies of Governmentality – with Two Lectures by and an Interview with Michel Foucault*, Chicago, IL: University of Chicago Press, pp. 87–104.
Foucault, M. (1996), *Tingenes orden*, Oslo: Aventura.
Halford, S. (2003), 'Gender and organizational restructuring in the National Health Service: Performances, identity and politics', *Antipode*, **35** (2), 287–308.
Hall, S. (1980), 'Race, articulation and societies structured in dominance', *Sociological Theories: Race and Colonialism*, Paris: Unesco, pp. 305–345.
Jørgensen, M.W. and L. Phillips (2010), *Diskursanalyse som teori og metode*, Roskilde, Denmark: Roskilde universitetsforlag.
Katila, S. and S. Meriläinen (1999), 'A serious researcher or just another nice girl? Doing gender in a male dominated scientific community', *Gender, Work and Organization*, **6**, 163–173.
Kelan, E.K. (2007), 'I don't know why – accounting for the scarcity of women in ICT work', *Women's Studies International Forum*, **30**, 499–511.
Kline, S.J. and N. Rosenberg (1986), 'An overview of innovation', in R. Landau and N. Rosenberg (eds), *The Positive Sum Game*, Washington, DC: National Academy Press, pp. 275–306.
Kvidal, T. and E. Ljunggren (2014), 'Introducing gender in a policy programme: A multi-level analysis of an innovation policy programme', *Environment and Planning C: Government and Policy*, **31**, 39–53.
Laclau, E. and C. Mouffe (1985), *Hegemony and Socialist Strategy: Towards a Radical Democratic Politics*, London: Verso.
Laclau, E. and C. Mouffe (1990), 'Post-Marxism without apologies', in E. Laclau, *New Reflections on the Revolution of Our Time*, London: Verso, pp. 97–132.
Lazonick, W. (2005), 'The innovative firm', in J. Fagerberg, D.C. Mowery and R.R. Nelson (eds), *The Oxford Handbook of Innovation*, Oxford, UK: Oxford University Press, pp. 29–55.
Lemke, T. (2001), '"The birth of bio-politics": Michel Foucault's lecture at the Collège de France on neo-liberal governmentality', *Economy and Society*, **30** (2), 190–207.
Lindberg, M. (2008), 'Ett slående mönster: Hur Sveriges innovationspolitik formar genus och vice versa', *Genus i Norrsken*, **1** (2), 3–12.
Lindberg, M. (2010), 'Samverkansnätverk för innovation. En interaktiv och genusvetenskaplig utmaning av innovationspolitik och innovationsforskning', Ph.D. dissertation, Luleå Technological University, Sweden.
Ljunggren, E. and G.A. Alsos (2010), 'Gender and innovation: Conceptualizations of concepts', in *Gender and Innovation: Learning from Regional VRI-projects*, NF Report 2/2010, Bodø, Norway: Nordland Research Institute, pp. 20–40.
Lundvall B.-Å. (1992), *National Systems of Innovation*, London: Pinter.
Malerba, F. (2002), 'Sectoral systems of innovation and production', *Research Policy*, **31** (2), 247–264.
McKee, K. (2009), 'Post-Foucauldian governmentality: What does it offer social policy analysis?', *Critical Social Policy*, **29** (3), 465–486.

Ministry of Education and Research (2012), *Lange linjer – kunnskap gir muligheter* [Long-term Perspectives: Knowledge Provides Opportunity], White Paper No. 18 (2012–2013), Oslo: Norwegian Government Administration Services.

Ministry of Trade and Industry (2012), *Mangfold av vinnere. Næringspolitikken mot 2020* [Diversity of winners: Industry policy towards 2020], White Paper No. 39 (2012–2013), Bergen, Norway: Fagbokforlaget.

Moore, K., M. Griffiths, H. Richardson and A. Adam (2008), 'Gendered futures? Women, the ICT workplace and stories of the future', *Gender, Work and Organization*, **15**, 523–542.

Nadesan, M.H. (2008), *Governmentality, Biopower, and Everyday Life*, New York: Routledge.

Pettersson, K. (2007), *Men and Male as the Norm? A Gender Perspective on Innovation Policies in Denmark, Finland and Sweden*, Nordic Research Programme 2005–2008, Report 4, Stockholm: Nordregio.

Pierson, C. (1999), *Beyond the Welfare State? The New Political Economy of Welfare*, Cambridge, UK: Polity Press.

Porter, M.E. (2000), 'Locations, clusters, and company strategy', in G.L. Clark, M.P. Feldman and M.S. Gartler (eds), *The Oxford Handbook of Economic Geography*, Oxford, UK: Oxford University Press, pp. 253–274.

Prince, R., R. Kearns and D. Craig (2006), 'Governmentality, discourse and space in the New Zealand health care system, 1991–2003', *Health and Place*, **12** (3), 253–266.

Research Council of Norway (2007), *VRI Programplan 2007–2010* [VRI Programme Plan 2007–2010], Oslo: Research Council of Norway.

Research Council of Norway (2008), *Strategi for kjønnsbalanse i VRI* [Strategy for Gender Balance in VRI], Oslo: Research Council of Norway.

Research Council of Norway (2010), *VRI Programplan 2010–2014* [VRI Programme Plan 2010–2014], Oslo: Research Council of Norway.

Research Council of Norway (2013), *Gender Balance and Gender Perspectives in Research and Innovation: The Research Council's Policy 2013–2017*, Oslo: Research Council of Norway.

Research Council of Norway (2014), *VRI Programme Plan 2014–2017*, Oslo: Research Council of Norway.

Rose, N. (1996), 'Governing "advanced" liberal democracies', in A. Barry, T. Osborne and N. Rose (eds), *Foucault and Political Reason: Liberalism, Neo-liberalism and Rationalities of Government*, London: UCL Press, pp. 37–64.

Rose, N. (1999), *Powers of Freedom: Reframing Political Thought*, Cambridge, UK: Cambridge University Press.

Sevenhuijsen, S. (1998), *Citizenship and the Ethics of Care*, London: Routledge.

Shore, C. and S. Wright (1997), *Anthropology of Policy: Critical Perspectives on Governance and Power*, London: Routledge.

Slack, J.D. (1996), 'The theory and method of articulation in cultural studies in Stuart Hall', in D. Morley and K.H. Chen (eds), *Critical Dialogues in Cultural Studies*, London: Routledge, pp. 113–130.

Verspagen, B. (2005), 'Innovation and economic growth', in J. Fagerberg, D.C. Mowery and R.R. Nelson (eds), *The Oxford Handbook of Innovation*, Oxford, UK: Oxford University Press, pp. 487–513.

VRI (2014), Programme description, accessed 2 August 2014 at http://www.forskningsradet.no/prognett-vri/Programme_Description/1224529235302.

# 11. 'Gendered social innovation': a new research stream for gender-inclusive innovation policy, research and practice
*Malin Lindberg and Knut-Erland Berglund*

## INTRODUCTION

Earlier research exposes that gender has an impact on innovation regardless of whether it is explicitly acknowledged or not. And, since gendered innovation is still a dawning research field, there is a perceived need for more conceptual studies to better understand various gendered aspects of innovation (Alsos et al., 2013; Andersson et al., 2012; Danilda and Granat Thorslund, 2011; Lindberg and Schiffbänker, 2013; Ranga and Etzkowitz, 2010). This chapter addresses that need by investigating the extent to which the main conclusions drawn in the scientific field of social innovation might enrich the scientific field of gendered innovation and vice versa, owing to their similarities and differences in scope and depth, in a way that furthers our understanding and promotes gender-inclusive innovation policy, research and practice. This enriching potential has been unlocked in the past decade by the simultaneous growth of social innovation and gendered innovation as research fields, each of which specifies inclusive means and ends of innovation from its own particular point of view.

This chapter discusses the extent to which the fields of social innovation and gendered innovation might enrich each other, by: 1) highlighting a more inclusive range of actors, industries and innovations; and 2) contributing to the transformation of social structures in society. The answers to these questions serve as a springboard for a discussion of how social innovation and gendered innovation might help advance each other as research fields in a way that would help to inform the design of more gender-inclusive innovation policy, research and practice.

The chapter begins with an account of the research design of the study. Existing research on gendered innovation and research on social innovation are then outlined in order to be compared with regard to scope and depth in the analysis section. Finally, implications for policy, research and practice are discussed and the establishment of the joint research stream of 'gendered social innovation' is proposed.

## RESEARCH DESIGN

The research design consists of a conceptual study of the scope and depth of the scientific fields of social innovation and gendered innovation, in order to explore how the identified similarities and differences could provide mutual reinforcement of the social aspects of the processes and results of innovation. The conceptual study is based on a selection of the most significant publications in the two emerging research fields. The selection criteria were: representativeness of the field (i.e. dealing with aspects discussed in several publications); encompassing approach (e.g. anthologies and overviews); and crucial discussions (on aspects that are especially important for the character and development of the field). The publications were identified by scanning the reference lists of the most well-known publications in both areas (e.g. Andersson et al., 2012; European Commission, 2013). In the field of social innovation, the selection involved eight publications, of which only two are published in the form of scientific articles – the other six being scientific reports – probably since the field is still in its infancy. In the field of gendered innovation, the selection involved 12 publications, of which five are published in the form of scientific articles, five are anthologies or anthology chapters, one is a scientific report and one is a doctoral thesis, implying that this field has developed a bit further than has the field of social innovation.

The study was performed as part of the research project Gendered Social Innovation, carried out by Luleå University of Technology in 2013–2015 with funding from the national research and innovation agency Vinnova. The project is intended to increase the capacity of the Swedish innovation and business-support system in accordance with the government's gender-equality policy objectives to ensure that men and women are equally empowered to influence society and their own lives, especially in terms of democratic and economic gender equality. The problem identified in earlier studies is that Sweden's innovation and business-support system is permeated by masculine norms and has therefore mainly been able to support the realization of business and innovative ideas in the form of technical product and service innovations among men in men-dominated industries (see Lindberg, 2012; Pettersson, 2007). This is similar to the conclusions in the existing literature on social innovation, namely that there is a lack of proper knowledge and support for the development of social innovations (see European Commission, 2010c; Hansson et al., 2014; Howaldt and Schwarz, 2010).

## RESEARCH ON GENDERED INNOVATION

Over the past two decades, innovation has become an increasingly common subject of political action and scientific studies in Europe and worldwide. This interest emanates from the widespread understanding that the development and dissemination of innovations transform economies, making them more dynamic and knowledge-based. This vision permeates the OECD's innovation strategy as well as the new European Union strategy Europe 2020 and its flagship initiative Innovation Union. Simultaneously, the need for more gender-inclusive innovation policy, research and practice has been articulated by gender scientists and gender-equality officials. This need is evidenced by the fact that most Western policies and research studies on innovation have prioritized a narrow range of actors, areas and innovations in a distinct, gendered pattern marginalizing women's innovation (Alsos et al., 2013; Andersson et al., 2012; Blake and Hanson, 2005; Danilda and Granat Thorslund, 2011; Lindberg and Schiffbänker, 2013; Pettersson and Lindberg, 2013; Ranga and Etzkowitz, 2010; Schiebinger, 2008).

Gendered innovation has grown into a viable research field during the last decade, with researchers in the Nordic countries as pioneers, accompanied by a few colleagues in, notably, Austria, the UK and the USA. Gender has been addressed as a relevant aspect of innovation in a number of research fields, for example feminist science and technology studies, political science, history of science, business economics, human geography and industrial design. Different aspects of innovation have been addressed in these studies, such as policies, counselling, networks, processes, management and organizational culture (Alsos et al., 2013; Andersson et al., 2012; Lindberg and Schiffbänker, 2013).

Some encompassing conclusions can be distinguished in the existing research studies on gendered innovation: 1) innovation policy and research primarily acknowledge innovation among men as entrepreneurs and innovators, men-dominated networks and industries, and technological product innovations; 2) innovation policy and practice are hampered by gendered stereotypes, as well as underestimation of the innovation potential among women as innovators and entrepreneurs, among industries employing mostly women, and among service, social and organizational innovations; and 3) innovation policy in the EU and Sweden increasingly uses 'smart specialization'[1] as a strategy for regional growth, implying prioritization of a few areas of (existing or potential) regional excellence and competences, which often implies prioritization of men-dominated industries and settings at the expense of those involving mainly women (Danilda and Granat Thorslund, 2011; Lindberg and Schiffbänker, 2013).

These gendered patterns in innovation research, policy and practice could, according to some researchers, be challenged by acknowledging that innovative activities also occur 'in economic sectors and by actors that are typically ignored or undervalued by current research and by policy' (Blake and Hanson, 2005, p. 681). Integrating other areas such as services and the creative industries – in both the private and the public sectors – could widen our understanding of innovation and acknowledge the contribution of women-dominated industries and settings (Lindberg, 2012; Nählinder, 2005, 2010; Pettersson, 2007; Ranga and Etzkowitz, 2010). Broadening the spectrum of actors, industries and innovations relevant to innovation policy, research and practice to include women and men equally could be regarded as a 'democratization of innovation', referring to the involvement of a broader range of voices and needs regarding the development of new knowledge, products and services, as well as 'democratic innovation', referring to new institutions specifically designed to increase and deepen citizens' participation in the political decision-making process (see von Hippel, 2006; Smith, 2009). This kind of democratization of innovation can be regarded as part of the general trend of opening up innovation to society, motivated by the transition from a primarily industrial to a more knowledge-focused society (see Howaldt and Schwarz, 2010; Lindberg, 2014).

## RESEARCH ON SOCIAL INNOVATION

Interest in social innovation (i.e. the development of new products and services that are social in their means and ends) among researchers, policy makers and practitioners worldwide has increased significantly during the last decade (Mulgan et al., 2007). One reason is the perception of social innovation as one of the main tools by which to handle societal challenges such as poverty, unemployment, ageing populations and climate change (European Commission, 2013). The new growth and innovation strategy of the EU includes an outspoken commitment to promote social innovation (European Commission, 2010a, 2010b). The importance of social innovation for growth and welfare is also underlined in Sweden's national innovation strategy (Ministry of Enterprise, Energy and Communications, 2012).

The realization of social innovations on a grand scale is perceived as being hampered, though, by a lack of relevant knowledge and support, in terms of counselling, training, networks and funding, tailored for social innovation (European Commission, 2010c; Hansson et al., 2014). Most support systems for innovation are primarily adapted to technological product innovations, which can be regarded as infeasible with the increasing importance of knowledge-based service production in Western economies (Howaldt and Schwarz, 2010). The study presented in this chapter contributes knowledge about the character and mechanisms of gendered social innovation that can inform the design of more inclusive innovation policy, research and practice.

The origin of 'social innovation' as a scientific concept can be traced back to the early 1900s but was thereafter used only sporadically in scientific contexts until it was reintroduced to research and policy agendas in the 1990s as a way to understand and handle economic restructuring, financial crises and unemployment. Since then, social innovation has grown as a research field in parts of Europe and North America, even though there are still many aspects and empirical data to be analysed before the field can be regarded as fully established. In most countries, research on social innovation is still very scarce (social entrepreneurship, which can be considered an overlapping but not identical field of research, is however well researched). The existing scientific studies on social innovation internationally are primarily produced by researchers in Germany, the UK and Canada, representing a number of disciplines, ranging from economics, business studies, technology and innovation studies to social anthropology, sociology and political science. Some attempts to summarize and synthesize the field, contributing with mappings, categorizations and frameworks, have been made (e.g. Cajaiba-Santana, 2013; Dawson and Daniel, 2010; European Commission, 2013; Howaldt and Schwarz, 2010; Mulgan et al., 2007; Rüede and Lurtz, 2012; Young Foundation, 2012).

In existing research studies, social innovation is generally defined as the process of developing new goods and services that are social in their means and ends. More specifically, social innovation has been discerned on four levels: new goods and services; new methods; new organizations; and new structures. On an even more detailed level, seven main categories of social innovation have been identified: 1) doing something good in or for society; 2) changing social practices and/or structures; 3) contributing to urban and community development; 4) reorganizing work processes; 5) imbuing technological innovations with cultural meaning and relevance; 6) making changes in the area of social work; and 7) innovating by means of digital connectivity (European Commission,

2013; Howaldt and Schwarz, 2010; Mulgan et al., 2007; Rüede and Lurtz, 2012; Young Foundation, 2012). Only one of the identified publications, Hansson et al. (2014), has briefly addressed gendered aspects of social innovation, despite gender being a prominent social perspective in innovation, as demonstrated in the field of gendered innovation. The study presented in this chapter contributes to filling this knowledge gap by exploring the potential for social innovation and gendered innovation to enrich each other in a way that would support the designing of more gender-inclusive innovation policy, research and practice.

## MUTUAL REINFORCEMENT OF SOCIAL INNOVATION AND GENDERED INNOVATION

In this section, the two research fields, social innovation and gendered innovation, are brought together in an analysis of the extent to which their differing scope and depth might further our understanding and narrow the gender gap in innovation theory, policy and practice.

Challenging social norms and generating new social structures and relationships are at the heart of both social innovation and gendered innovation. The research field of gendered innovation illustrates that gendered norms permeate innovation rhetoric and practice in policy, research and practice, and that gender inclusiveness might enhance and broaden innovation as a theoretical concept as well as a practical phenomenon. The research field of social innovation illustrates that innovation might take various forms, far beyond technological product innovations, and that a wide range of actors and areas – from all societal sectors – might participate in the development of innovations. Consequently, both social innovation and gendered innovation promote a 'democratization of innovation', by involving a broader range of voices and needs regarding the development of new knowledge, products and services (see von Hippel, 2006). They do this from different angles, though, which will be used here as an argument for why they could mutually reinforce each other as research fields. Four main differences between the fields have been identified, namely their approach to the social content of innovation, their approach to the inclusiveness of innovation, their definitions of 'democratic innovation', and their scope and depth concerning social ends. As explained in detail below, social innovation helps the field of gendered innovation to: 1) specify the social content of innovation by distinguishing the process from the results; 2) challenge the social norms that delimit innovation to technical product innovations in industrial and high-tech settings; and 3) appreciate the socially transformative potential in the establishment of new institutions while transforming existing ones. Likewise, gendered innovation helps the field of social innovation to: 1) specify the gendered aspects of the social content of innovation; 2) specify the gendered aspects of social norms and spectra of innovation; and 3) identify and analyse the potential to increase gender inclusiveness within existing structures.

The first difference between the fields concerns their specific approaches to the *social content* of innovation displayed in each field. The approach of the social innovation field is displayed in its general definition of social innovation as a process of developing new goods and services that are social in their means and ends. This definition highlights the social content of innovation processes by distinguishing between inclusiveness in the *process* (i.e. means) of developing innovation and inclusiveness in the *results* (i.e. ends) of innovation processes. This focus on the social content specified as the distinction between process and result could help further the research field of gendered innovation as well. There, the social content could be specified as gender awareness and gender inclusiveness in processes of innovation policy development, research and practice being complemented by gender equality – defined by the Swedish government as the equal distribution of power among women and men to shape society and their own lives (www.government. se/government-policy/gender-equality, accessed 26 July 2015) – as a social result. It would then be made more evident that gendered innovation could inspire the inclusion of more women in innovation policy, research and practice (being a hitherto marginalized group in the development of new goods and services) and the development of new products and services that increase gender awareness and/or gender equality in a specific area. Social innovation thus helps the field of gendered innovation to specify the *social content* of innovation and to make an explicit distinction between inclusiveness in the *process* of developing innovation and in the *results* of innovation processes. Gendered innovation, in turn, helps the field of social innovation to specify the gendered aspects of the social content of innovations as gender awareness and gender inclusiveness.

The second difference concerns their specific approaches to *inclusiveness* in innovation. This reflects the definition of 'democratization of innovation' (see von Hippel, 2006) as the involvement of a broader range of voices and needs in the development of new knowledge, products and services. The concept and phenomenon of social innovation fundamentally challenges the narrow focus on technical product and service innovations in manufacturing, basic and high-tech industries that has characterized innovation research, policies and processes. Social innovation displays a significantly wider range of actors, industries, sectors and innovations as relevant in efforts to map, analyse and promote innovation. The wider spectrum encompasses service and creative industries, all three sectors of society (public, private and non-profit), and social, organizational and service innovations. In the field of gendered innovation, this could imply acknowledgement and inclusion of women's entrepreneurship and innovation, women-dominated innovation networks, women's contributions to the private, public, academic and civil sectors, the public and private service industries employing mainly women, and the various forms of innovations developed by women. Social innovation thus helps the field of gendered innovation to challenge the *social norms that delimit innovation* to technical product innovations in industrial and high-tech settings, by acknowledging and including *a wider spectrum* of actors, industries, sectors and innovations as relevant to innovation policy, research and practice. Gendered innovation, in turn, helps the field of social innovation to specify the gendered aspects of these social norms and spectra as marginalizing women and the industries and sectors where they mainly work.

The third difference reflects the definition of *democratic innovation*, which refers to new institutions specifically designed to increase and deepen citizens' participation in the political decision-making process (see Smith, 2009). While the field of gendered innovation has explored the possibilities of developing new institutions in terms of gender mainstreaming in policies, networks, organizations and processes, the field of social innovation has explored the same possibilities on the levels of social change by new structures, new organizations, new methods, and new goods and services. The institutions foreseen in gendered innovation are by its gender-mainstreaming approach more likely to increase and deepen citizen participation within existing structures, while the ones foreseen in social innovations constitute new structures separate from the existing ones. Entirely new institutions might reach beyond existing gendered structures of innovation in a way that truly challenges and changes the masculine norms in innovation policy, research and practice (see Pettersson and Lindberg, 2013). Social innovation thus helps the field of gendered innovation to appreciate the socially transformative potential in the establishment of *new institutions* alongside the transformation of the existing ones. Gendered innovation, in turn, helps the field of social innovation to identify and analyse the potential to increase gender inclusiveness within existing structures.

The fourth difference between the fields concerns the new *social ends* distinguished in the general definition of social innovation. The seven categories of social innovation specify such specific ends as: 1) doing something good in or for society; 2) changing social practices and/or structures; 3) contributing to urban and community development; 4) reorganizing work processes; 5) imbuing technological innovations with cultural meaning and relevance; 6) making changes in the area of social work; and 7) innovating by means of digital connectivity (Rüede and Lurtz, 2012). Paired with the gendered aspects of social innovativeness highlighted in the field of gendered innovation, these categories could serve to specify the social ends of gender-inclusive innovation policy, research and practice. We here demonstrate this in relation to five of the seven categories. The first category – doing something good in or for society – might be specified as, for example, attaining equal power for women and men in society by innovative means. The second category – changing social practices and/or structures – might be specified as challenging and changing how 'smart specialization' is used as a strategy for regional growth, widening its narrow prioritization of a few areas of regional excellence and competences to beyond men-dominated industries and settings. The third category – contributing to urban and community development – might be specified as widening the scope of actors, industries and innovations considered relevant to societal and economic development by acknowledging women as entrepreneurs and innovators, women-dominated innovation networks, industries employing mainly women, and service, social and organizational innovations. The fifth category – imbuing technological innovations with cultural meaning and relevance – might be specified as acknowledging gendered stereotypes in technological innovations and challenging them by highlighting and promoting the development of new goods, services and methods that are not designed with dualistic notions of gender in mind. Consequently, the fields of social innovation and gendered innovation help each other to specify *distinct social ends* of gender-inclusive innovation.

## CONCLUSIONS

This chapter has aimed to investigate the extent to which the main conclusions drawn in the scientific fields of social innovation and gendered innovation could enrich each other, owing to their similarities and differences in scope and depth, in a way that would further our understanding and promote gender-inclusive innovation policy, research and practice. In the analysis, four potentials of mutual reinforcement have been identified:

1. highlighting the gendered social potential in the establishment of *new institutions* alongside the transformation of the existing ones;
2. highlighting the gendered social potential in making an explicit distinction between inclusiveness in the *process* of developing innovation and in the *results* of innovation processes;
3. highlighting the gendered social potential in acknowledging and including a *wider spectrum* of actors, industries, sectors and innovations as relevant to innovation policy, research and practice;
4. highlighting the gendered social potential in specifying distinct *social ends* of gender-inclusive innovation.

These four potentials illustrate how social innovation and gendered innovation together might highlight a more gender-inclusive range of actors, industries, sectors and innovations in innovation policy, research and practice, as well as contribute to the transformation of gendered social structures of innovation. These potentials stem from social innovation being gendered in a different way from that in the dominant understandings of innovation as mainly concerning men as entrepreneurs and innovators, men-dominated networks and industries, and technological product innovations.

**Establishing the Field of 'Gendered Social Innovation'**

The conclusions presented above serve as a springboard for discussing how the fields of social innovation and gendered innovation could be merged into a new stream of research, developing knowledge that helps inform the design of gender-inclusive innovation policy, research and practice.

Since existing research on social innovation in Europe and globally has rarely explored the exclusionary patterns related to gender, there is an opportunity for pioneering efforts taking their starting point in present knowledge on both social innovation and gendered innovation. Based on our analysis of the similarities and differences in scope and depth of these research fields, identifying four potentials of mutual reinforcement, we propose the establishment of 'gendered social innovation' as a new stream of research. This new stream could provide essential knowledge on how the development of innovations takes place among a significantly broader spectrum of actors, areas and forms than is acknowledged in present innovation research and policy. It might thus help form a more empirically sound scientific knowledge base regarding the sources, characteristics and effects of innovation for societal and economic development. It might also inform the design of more gender-inclusive innovation policies and practices, promoting the development of innovation in various contexts. Policy frameworks, support structures and innovation parks could then become better adapted to suit the specific character and needs of women as innovators, industries and sectors employing mainly women, and service, social and organizational innovations. This would contribute to fulfilling the EU's desire to effectively promote social innovation in order to deal with societal challenges such as poverty, unemployment, ageing populations and climate change (see European Commission 2010a, 2010b). In this way, research could contribute to more actors, areas and innovations than are currently participating in the shaping of future society.

## NOTE

1.  Smart specialization is the new strategy and working method of the European Union to promote the efficient and effective use of public investment in research. Its goal is to boost regional innovation in order to achieve economic growth and prosperity, by enabling regions to focus on their strengths, instead of spreading investment too thinly across several frontier technology fields with the risk of limiting the impact in any one area (European Commission, 2015).

## REFERENCES

Alsos, G.A., E. Ljunggren and U. Hytti (2013), 'Gender and innovation: State of the art and a research agenda', *International Journal of Gender and Entrepreneurship*, **5** (3), 236–256.

Andersson, S., K. Berglund, J. Thorslund, E. Gunnarsson and E. Sundin (eds) (2012), *Promoting Innovation: Policies, Practices and Procedures*, Stockholm: Vinnova.

Blake, M.K. and S. Hanson (2005), 'Rethinking innovation: Context and gender', *Environment and Planning A*, **37** (4), 681–701.

Cajaiba-Santana, G. (2013), 'Social innovation: Moving the field forward – a conceptual framework', *Technological Forecasting and Social Change*, **82**, 42–51.

Danilda, I. and J. Granat Thorslund (2011), *Innovation and Gender*, Stockholm: Vinnova.

Dawson, P. and L. Daniel (2010), 'Understanding social innovation: A provisional framework', *International Journal of Technology Management*, **51** (1), 9–21.

European Commission (2010a), *Europe 2020: A European Strategy for Smart, Sustainable and Inclusive Growth*, Brussels: European Union.

European Commission (2010b), *Europe 2020 Flagship Initiative: Innovation Union*, Brussels: European Union.

European Commission (2010c), *This Is European Social Innovation*, Brussels: European Union.

European Commission (2013), *Social Innovation Research in the European Union*, Brussels: European Union.

European Commission (2015), 'Research and innovation: Regional dimensions of innovation', accessed 14 August 2015 at http://ec.europa.eu/research/regions/index_en.cfm ?pg=smart_specialisation.

Hansson, J., F. Björk, D. Lundborg and L.E. Olofsson (eds) (2014), *An Ecosystem for Social Innovation in Sweden: A Strategic Research and Innovation Agenda*, Lund, Sweden: Lund University.

Hippel, E. von (2006), *Democratizing Innovation*, Cambridge, MA: MIT Press.

Howaldt, J. and M. Schwarz (2010), *Social Innovation: Concepts, Research Fields and International Trends*, Dortmund, Germany: Sozialforschungsstelle Dortmund.

Lindberg, M. (2012), 'A striking pattern – co-construction of innovation, men and masculinity in Sweden's innovation policy', in S. Andersson, K. Berglund, J. Thorslund, E. Gunnarsson and E. Sundin (eds), *Promoting Innovation: Policies, Practices and Procedures*, Stockholm: Vinnova, pp. 47–67.

Lindberg, M. (2014), 'From exclusion to inclusion in public innovation support? Innovative practices in bottom-up networks', *Scandinavian Journal of Public Administration*, **18** (4), 91–107.

Lindberg, M. and H. Schiffbänker (2013), Entry on 'Gender and innovation', in E.G. Carayannis (ed.), *Encyclopedia of Creativity, Invention, Innovation and Entrepreneurship*, New York: Springer.

Ministry of Enterprise, Energy and Communications (2012), *Den nationella innovationsstrategin* [The national innovation strategy], Stockholm: Näringsdepartementet.

Mulgan, G., R. Ali and S. Tucker (2007), *Social Innovation: What It Is, Why It Matters and How It Can Be Accelerated*, Oxford, UK: University of Oxford, Said Business School.

Nählinder, J. (2005), 'Innovation and employment in services: The case of knowledge intensive business services in Sweden', Doctoral thesis, Linköping University, Sweden.

Nählinder, J. (2010), 'Where are all the female innovators? Nurses as innovators in a public sector innovation project', *Journal of Technology Management and Innovation*, **5** (1), 13–29.

Pettersson, K. (2007), *Men and Male as the Norm? A Gender Perspective on Innovation Policies in Denmark, Finland and Sweden*, Stockholm: Nordregio.

Pettersson, K. and M. Lindberg (2013), 'Paradoxical spaces of feminist resistance: Mapping the margin to the masculinist innovation discourse', *International Journal of Gender and Entrepreneurship*, **5** (3), 323–341.

Ranga, M. and H. Etzkowitz (2010), 'Athena in the world of techne: The gender dimension of technology, innovation and entrepreneurship', *Journal of Technology Management and Innovation*, **5** (1), 1–12.

Rüede, D. and K. Lurtz (2012), *Mapping the Various Meanings of Social Innovation: Towards a Differentiated Understanding of an Emerging Concept*, EBS Business School Research Paper No. 12-03, Oestrich-Winkel, Germany: EBS University.

Schiebinger, L. (ed.) (2008), *Gendered Innovations in Science and Engineering*, Stanford, CA: Stanford University Press.

Smith, G. (2009), *Democratic Innovations*, Cambridge, UK: Cambridge University Press.

Young Foundation (2012), *Social Innovation Overview – Part I: Defining Social Innovation*, A deliverable of the Theoretical, Empirical and Policy Foundations for Building Social Innovation in Europe (TEPSIE) project, Brussels: European Commission, DG Research.

# PART V

# GENDER IN DESIGN AND MATERIALITY

# 12. Innovating is not of the spirit world – depicting a female inventor's unique path with materiality-friendly gender concepts

*Seppo Poutanen and Anne Kovalainen**

## INTRODUCTION

It is fair to say that the current levels of knowledge and research concerning women's inventions and innovations are still relatively low. Another area of knowledge that is lacking is gendered understanding, that is, understanding related to the social, economic and cultural realities of innovation activities with anchorage in biological sexes. These outcomes are not due to a lack of women's innovations but rather arise as a result of the gender blindness of the research area in question. Studies that address gender in relation to innovations have shown that the numbers of women innovators and inventors are increasing, but still the question 'Why are there so few women innovators that we know about?' is worth addressing. Gender is however not just about women and men. It is equally relevant to ask 'How does the gendering of inventions and innovations take place?' These two questions can redirect the issue of gender and innovations towards the processes of innovations, and force a re-evaluation of previous analyses of gender and innovations.

The lack of women in the key fields of invention and innovation, that is, science and technology, has previously been systematically researched, but there is still much to learn (Alsos et al., 2013; Wyer et al., 2013; Wynarczyk and Marlow, 2010). The entrance of women into the science community, and the current minority in terms of positions held, has also led to research which resembles the 'history of great men', where women act as substitutes for men but the explanation for an individual's rise remains the same. As part of this explanation, the exceptionalities of women are emphasized (e.g. Fara, 2004; Jardins, 2010). Even when raising the profile of women to the forefront, one of the major problems associated with this type of analysis is that it maintains the male norm as the measure of excellence and success, and categorizes women as exceptions. Feminist histories of science and the philosophy of science have systematically developed critical analyses since the 1970s and 1980s (e.g. Fox Keller, 1985; Harding and Hintikka, 1983), and have used gender as the focal point of understanding science, technology and related fields.

Most contemporary innovations, if 'social innovations' are excluded, are based on science and its applications in adaptations both in basic and applied research and in technology. However, the fact is that relatively few contemporary studies focusing on the relationship between innovations and gender refer to the actual studies and classics of the field, where the relationships between gender and science have been explored. It is as if innovations and inventions are mainly understood in a contemporary and rather naively empiricist context that is unrelated to the broader questions of gendered science, technology and business. While the history of science, for example, unfolds the gendered nature of many inventions and innovations, the actual and concrete processes in question are still largely untold.

This chapter anchors its contributions to the theoretical novelty of the processualist approach. For essential historical background, that is, for the mentioned need to reconnect with the classics, this chapter first briefly describes the classical concept of tokenism (Kanter, 1977) and highlights its limitations. We then introduce our revised concept of tokenism named 'process tokenism' (Poutanen and Kovalainen, 2013). The chapter subsequently details the well-known concept of intersectionality, which, according to its key contemporary critique, outlines the important concept of co-mingled social forces but is hard to pin down with any exact meaning in empirical research (McCall, 2014; Walby et al., 2012).

We suggest in this chapter that 'intersectionality' works best when it is given a process tokenistic reading, that is, when the co-mingled social forces are shown through their complex cooperation in both a material and a concrete context as demonstrated in reasonably delimited *cases*. The processualist approach applied emphasizes the spatial and temporal dynamism of all social reality, and so the cooperation referred to is arguably best captured and explicated in narrative form. Accordingly, the majority of this chapter details the story of chemistry engineer Sarah and her gendered invention and innovation.

## CLASSIC TOKENISM THEORY AND ITS LIMITATIONS

Rosabeth Moss Kanter's classical theory on tokenism in organizations concerns a situation where a small subgroup, the 'token', represents a numerical minority of people who are perceived as different from those in other subgroups within an organization. While there may be several subgroups, not all are treated in a similar way. In Kanter's example of men and women of the corporation, the tokens were most often women, and the defining trait of the token position was a numerical minority. More generally, 'token' refers to any 'skewed' number or share among organizational groups, and, owing to their specific under-representation in the group, the minority is viewed as a symbol or a token (Kanter, 1977, p. 209).

Kanter's idea is that those with token positions in organizations are expected to face a variety of overt and covert problems in their workplaces. These problems range from issues such as isolation and limited opportunities to heightened visibility among colleagues. Kanter also suggests that stereotyping persons labelled as tokens as 'different' from the majority group can result in the perception of 'barriers' preventing their exerting influence on group decisions, for example.

The mechanisms related to tokenism within organizations are many. Tokenism can range from invisibility and overlooking the token person within organizational settings to heightened visibility in other contexts. Some of the problems related to tokenism merge with other subtle forms of discrimination, such as forgetting that the person is or has been a member of the team or group, diminishing her/his work tasks and capabilities, and so on. Of the different shapes and forms of tokenism, three types are proposed: assimilation, visibility and contrast (Kanter, 1977, p. 210).

A stereotypical role encapsulation is produced, maintained and pre-scribed in the 'assimilation' phase by the dominant members of the group. This encapsulation can result in missed opportunities for advance-ment, for example. In instances of 'heightened visibility' tokenism, the members of the dominant group emphasize the differences between themselves and the token member(s) in the workplace, group or organ-ization. The mechanisms that produce 'contrast' and divisions are related to internal divisions in the workplace, such as minority/majority posi-tions. Contrasting mainly results from the pressures to assimilate all individuals into set roles prescribed by the dominant members of the organization (Kanter, 1977, p. 210) and leads to isolation and polarization in workplace settings.

Tokenism in its different dimensions has most often been analysed in empirical studies conducted across 'gender-inappropriate' workplaces and in professions such as fire-fighting and the police (Gustafson, 2008). It has also been studied within a group of employees working in financial markets on Wall Street (Roth, 2004), and among scientists (Shachar, 2000). Central to the theme of this chapter is an observation that attempts to relate the mechanisms of tokenism to innovation and invention activities in organizations are practically non-existent in the research literature.

Kanter's tokenism theory has received significant attention, but has also garnered criticism because of its emphasis on 'headcounts'. It looks incorrigibly naive to assume that the simple equalization of the numbers of women and men in an organization leads to gender equality. The findings of the critical literature show that tokenism in itself is not a problem of headcounts, but rather one of attitudes and perceptions prevalent in society in general (e.g. Lewis and Simpson, 2012). The findings of further empirical study are best summarized by Yoder (1991, 1994), who argues that tokenism is a complex and subtle phenomenon and not a simple question of relative numerical representation.

## REVISING TOKENISM FOR ANALYSIS OF ORGANIZATIONAL INVENTION AND INNOVATION ACTIVITIES

The clear and persistent examples of gender differences and gendered segregation found both within the horizontal and at the hierarchical levels of different businesses and manufacturing industries, for example, are well documented (Caraway, 2007; Downs, 1995; Grimshaw, 2007; Rubery et al., 1999). The same differences also concern innovation and invention activities, whose unfolding is typically located within the science and technology fields (Kariv, 2013). However, the reproduction of the aforementioned macro-level segregation across micro-level innovation activities at modern plants and factories, for example, has arguably received significantly less attention in critical gender analyses.

Feminist research has shown that workplaces are infused with gendered practices and that these practices take active positioning in the ways the work is labelled as gendered (e.g. Acker, 1990, 1992; Calás and Smircich, 1992; Martin, 2003). The question of how the gendering takes place is still a crucial one (e.g. Risman, 2009). According to Risman, we need to pay attention to 'whether our research is documenting different kinds of gender, how doing gender may be changing or whether it is being undone' (Risman, 2009, p. 82).

Accordingly it is crucial to analyse the practices and processes related to the production of gender differences, and it is appropriate to identify the kinds of micro-level processes that take place during segregating practices. Some of these segregating mechanisms are well known through macro-level analyses (e.g. Bradley, 2007), but both new micro-level studies focusing on production and the reformulation of gendering in organizational practices need to be considered, as the dynamics of segregation at the micro-level are still poorly understood.

Research on gender and work in general has changed its focus over time to incorporate the differing forms, shapes and patterns of gender constructions, both discursively and corporeally. The idea of visible and non-visible gender, and the multiple ways of doing and undoing gender have subsequently become of interest with these changes (e.g. Deutsch, 2007). This shift implies several changes in the ways gender is theorized, and generally a move towards a more constructionist and even Butlerian approach to gender has taken place (Butler, 1993, 2004). In the broadly Butlerian sense, the individual becomes essentially defined through social, negotiated and performed gender, which takes different forms and attaches not only to human bodies and actions but also to *non-human actors*, as our empirical example in this chapter will demonstrate (e.g. Callon, 1986; Latour, 1988; Law, 2004).

How should we analyse the gendering that takes place in organizations, with their inventive and innovative activities specifically in focus, and where can we 'see' the gendering processes taking place? One suggested target for the analysis, that is, 'seeing the gendering process', is situations where the conventional essentialism of binary distinctions between people based on sex category is challenged, as suggested by Sprague (2005). However, the stereotypical creation and reinforcement of practices actually do the 'gendering in process'. Thus the processes in question are performed not only in deviating situations but, more importantly, in everyday situations. Clearly the ability to distance oneself from such situations in order to see them anew demands a kind of hermeneutic sensitivity from the agencies present in the contexts, as well as from researchers.

The first step in reformulating and revitalizing the theoretical concept of tokenism is to focus on the ways unequal gender positions are being both created and reinforced in organizations. Even if 'tokenism' as a theoretical tool seems to have lost much of its appeal in contemporary gender analyses of work, the concept of tokenism as a robust empirical phenomenon is thriving at both organizational and workplace levels. It is facilitated and assisted by various kinds of practices, as research convincingly shows (e.g. Romei and Ruggieri, 2014; Stroshine and Brandl, 2011; Turco, 2010). To further strengthen the analytic feasibility of 'tokenism', it is necessary to grasp actual occurrences of tokenism in intersection with other relevant factors, such as the hegemonic masculine engineering culture in certain workplaces, and specific organizational practices and power struggles, for example.

The practices in organizations derive from specific cultures that are intersected with other factors and displayed through implicit and explicit rules. Drawing from contemporary gender theoretical thinking, we suggest *process tokenism* as a revised concept that can better sensitize social research to the recognition of the process's actual pathways and transformations, where the invention and innovation activities of organizational life, among other things, are brought into their unique and transitory existence through various gendered practices and power relationships (Poutanen and Kovalainen, 2013). The new concept of process tokenism retains the basic Kanterian point of gender asymmetry and emphasizes the manifold agencies that go into engendering and shaping the particular innovation processes.

## INTERSECTIONALITY REFORMULATED IN AN ENSEMBLE THAT OPENS TO THE NON-HUMAN

Intersectionality as a theoretical idea basically emphasizes that gender is, among other things, an organizing principle of the social world that engenders asymmetrical power relationships and is inevitably entangled with other kinds of principles with analogous functions (e.g. Anthias, 2001; Verloo, 2006). As a conceptual perspective, intersectionalism is rooted in post-colonial analyses, and a multitude of systematic studies have focused on 'simultaneous and linked' social identities with the help of the intersectionality concept (e.g. Brewer, 1993; Lorber, 1994; Mohanty, 1991).

The idea of intersectionality challenges the notion of gender as the sole or most significant basis of any social or organizational discrimination process, for example. However, while the basic idea of the intersection of several 'forces' of social life is still considered valid, it has proved difficult to pin down just exactly how such forces cooperate in the empirical world (Choo and Ferree, 2010; Davis, 2008). To some extent, intersectionality has come to mean prescribed and assumed positions such as gender, race and class with generally fixed ideas relating to the contents and outcomes of such positions (McCall, 2014; Walker, 2003).

Gender, race and class presumably have some real effects in organizational life, but 'intersectionality' in its conventional meaning is not obviously apt to shed light on types of real and dynamic empirical cases that the revised concept of process tokenism is intended to grasp. Nevertheless, a mutually beneficial relationship between the two concepts can be built: 'intersectionality' breaks the isolation of tokenism as a purely gendered phenomenon, whereas 'process tokenism' frees inter-sectionality from rigid and ostensibly self-evident categorizations, instead relating to the unpredictable dynamism of concrete empirical cases.

Compared to the traditional Kanterian tokenism studies, further positive input from intersectionality theorization entails a shift of perspective from individual females and males to the processes of social construction, broadly understood, that bring about distinctive female and male actors in specific contexts of action. For research there are, of course, typically many relevant intermediate concepts depending on the context, and, in our empirical case study concerning a female inventor, 'hegemonic masculine engineering culture' is one such useful intermediate concept (e.g. Faulkner, 2007; Servon and Visser, 2011). From the story of Sarah, our inventor, it becomes rather obvious that a contextually bound version of the hegemonic masculine engineering culture[1] significantly shaped Sarah's path and development as an inventor.

The sensitizing and contextualizing of hegemonic masculine engineering culture concepts are key to understanding how different elements intersect with each other in analysed cases, and how for example gender is functioning as part of the whole. On the other hand, and by taking the lead from our female inventor's in-depth story, the process tokenism reading of intersectionality now radicalizes the aforementioned concept in the sense that no categorical restrictions are placed on the potential social forces that may intersect when producing the characteristics of any given case. Regarding the various ways that gender, race and class may be operationalized, they are in fact not necessarily the only or even the most significant contributors to a discerned case of intersectionalities at hand. Conceptually a door is opened for *non-human* forces to make an impact, for example.

The idea that the non-human 'furniture' of reality (stones, bacilli, animals, raw materials, technological devices, etc.) should be considered to be similar to humans in terms of being actors and producers of the social world may look odd, but the idea is well established in contemporary science and technology studies (STS), especially in actor–network theory (e.g. Callon, 1986; Latour, 1988; Law, 2004). In this analytical STS framework, such human attributes as self-consciousness, language or volition are not necessary qualities for something to be classified as an actor; it is enough that this something *can make a difference* in the studied course of events at hand.

The actor–network theory understanding of action brings two immediate benefits to the kind of invention and innovation activity analyses where 'tokenism' and 'intersectionality' are mutually reformulated as detailed above. The first thing to consider is the well-known phenomenon of an inventor being absorbed in her ideas, materials, practices and so on throughout an intensive working period. This absorption can be focused on to a suitably in-depth extent, when for example the raw material of the process is considered an active participant that guides and shapes the inventor and other contributors by means of its distinctive properties. In addition, the gendered and ethnic characteristics of a social episode, for example, are taken to be constructed from the bottom up. In other words and in contrast with conventional intersectionality theorizing, the actor–network approach does not regard terms like 'gender', 'race', 'ethnicity' or 'social class' as references to the types of independent, context-free social forces that can be brought in to *explain* the concrete course of an invention process. The exact content and feasibility of 'gender', 'ethnicity' and so on need to be defined, and this can only be achieved by minute analysis of actual social occurrences.

The adoption of certain insights from actor–network theory does not imply the implausible view that the social world is without organization or structure, or that it must be constantly constructed anew from scratch. The industrial plant where our female inventor worked carries spatially and temporally structured continuity, where formal organizational and leadership ideas, raw materials, chemical reactions, machines, humans, work practices and so on come together to bring new things into reality. A useful focusing device for the objective of this chapter is also the powerfully argued view of critical feminist research according to which organizations of the industrial plant kind tend to produce and sustain gendered inequalities (e.g. Acker, 1992, 2012; Gherardi and Poggio, 2001; Metcalfe and Woodhams, 2012; Scott, 1986). To put this view more precisely, one typical outcome from the workings of such an organization is seen to be the distribution of agency positions in a way that actors defined as 'male' come to enjoy the benefits of asymmetrical power relationships at the expense of actors defined as 'female'. The concept of hegemonic masculine engineering culture introduced earlier elaborates certain significant features of this constructed asymmetry.

## NARRATING THE INVENTOR/INNOVATOR'S STORY – RATIONALE FOR THE METHODOLOGICAL STRATEGY

The spatially and temporally dynamic process whose one result was a gendered invention is understood through the revised concepts of tokenism and intersectionality in our analysis. To gain a meaningful understanding of the whole process, we utilize a narrative approach on a single case study. More precisely, the basic empirical materials used in this chapter consist of the narrative interviews of a female inventor who worked in a manufacturing plant strongly characterized by hegemonic masculine engineering culture, and of document materials related to the inventor's creation. Narrative offers one very useful way of looking into the specific phenomenon of tokenism and the complexity of gendering processes at the workplace. Furthermore, narrative as a social scientific approach is understood to take an individual's experience as its subject matter and to illustratively infer from this experiential knowledge the broader social location inhabited and embodied by the individual (e.g. Eriksson and Kovalainen, 2008, pp. 210–226; Frank, 2012). In our specific case, the social location was a factory in the chemical industry, a plant which is part of a globally functioning corporation.

The female inventor worked at the aforementioned plant for several years, but our narrative focuses on the first two years of her career in the company, during which time she created a new production process for the raw material produced by the company. We call our inventor Sarah, and use her story as an intrinsic case study (e.g. Stake, 2005). In an intrinsic case study, a single case forms the focus of the research, in contrast to a study of multiple cases, where cases are used more instrumentally. The single case itself becomes interesting through the variety of questions it raises and through the theoretical themes and categorizations it allows us to elaborate upon, while pushing the boundaries of qualitative research (e.g. Plummer, 2005; Poutanen and Kovalainen, 2009). The idea that through analysing the particularities of an individual case we can study the general broadly refers to important and shared cultural understandings and the idea of 'unique adequacy' (e.g. Poutanen and Kovalainen, 2009, pp. 260–264; Psathas, 1995, pp. 139–155).

· A social scientific narrative interview method was used for 'teasing out' biographical information, and the interviews were conducted in an open, non-directed way. This type of interview is also called an 'episodic interview' with strong narrative character (Flick, 2002, pp. 104–110; Wagner and Wodak, 2006). The narrative both as a form of interviews and particularly as a form of analysis allows for complexity to be taken into account in research. Researchers empathize with the narrated story by trying to understand it, even during the interviews themselves, instead of intervening with straightforward questions with the intent of directing the course of the interview (Flick, 2002, p. 98).

Consequently, an analysis of the diverse perspectives the informant may have concerning particular events is made possible. As social researchers often emphasize, the strict authenticity of a narrative is not the key issue, because biographical interviews are constructed from the interviewee's social position and life situation at the moment of the interview, and thus coloured by and through them, as well as by the interviewing situation and the operative interpretative frameworks in it (e.g. Meyer, 2001; Sunderland, 2004, pp. 165–190).

On the other hand, the aim of narrative analysis is not to strive for 'biographical illusion', a concept used for an ostensibly coherent description of a life path (see for example Bourdieu, 1977). Instead, we trace disruptions in work-related issues, such as questions concerning career moves, the gendering of the invention process, and possibilities for what might be called feminine space in a male-dominated industrial plant. A kind of bricolage process of employing different methodological strategies in the unfolding context of the research can thus be present when a narrative approach is applied in research (Kincheloe and McLaren, 2005).

The empirical materials used in the narrative construction consist of several in-depth interviews and e-mail interviews with Sarah, the key person. Many e-mails were exchanged to clarify various details of the invention process, and e-mails were also utilized to explicate certain work-related incidences and, more generally, invention-, innovation-, organization- and company-related questions. For the background analysis, multiple types of documentary material were gathered from the raw material that was the essential element in both Sarah's invention process and its wider use beyond the chemical industry.

The in-depth interview materials were interpreted with thematic questions that focused closely on 'thick descriptions', in relation to which multiple interpretations of how social life is enacted and represented become possible (e.g. Atkinson and Delamont, 2005). The biographical materials utilized offer the additional possibility of examining self as a 'reflexive project' (see Beck and Beck-Gernsheim, 2002; Lash and Urry, 1994), and a chance to test the ability of the reshaped concepts of processualist tokenism and intersectionality in order to shed light on the phenomenon of gendered invention. These conceptual and theoretical questions come under scrutiny after parts of Sarah's story are first told in a rather straightforward manner.

## WELL-RESOURCED TOKEN CHEMISTRY ENGINEER BREAKS THROUGH SILENCING

During the time when chemistry engineer Sarah was employed in a large chemical corporation's R&D department as one of its research managers, she was among the first individuals possessing the highest academic degree, a Ph.D., to work in that specific factory, and among the very few women with this degree to work in the company as a whole. During the final stages of the recruitment process, Sarah was given the opportunity to choose the new products unit as her place of work, and was given a laboratory and a budget as resources with which to carry out her work. The plant factory of the multinational chemical corporation where she began to work had specialized in the business-to-business production of raw materials for the chemical industry, more specifically for branches where the raw material produced was used in products such as coatings, paints and colours. When Sarah entered her new position, the corporation was growing rapidly, buying new units and diversifying its production lines on a global scale. By the time Sarah began working at the plant, the corporation had grown into one of the world's largest producers of the raw material titanium dioxide.

Shortly after her recruitment as a research expert with managerial tasks, Sarah was granted a small research group of her own that consisted of technicians who also worked as Sarah's subordinates. Sarah started to acquire knowledge of the production process and was made aware of the experiments conducted at the unit prior to her arrival. She had discussions with other researchers in the department who were running their own laboratories and groups, and gained experience of how the firm's operations were carried out, as well as the way research work was arranged. In other words and conventionally put, Sarah was socialized into the working culture of the organization, and at the same time she began to contribute some changes to this culture with her own actions. Quite soon Sarah discovered that the research work at the plant was corroborative and repetitive rather than innovative. Accordingly, patenting in the laboratories was rare if not non-existent.

New and original innovations were not particularly encouraged across the firm, but gradual improvements to the main production processes were recognized, rewarded and, indeed, conceived by laboratory personnel. If needed, practicalities such as new tests for products and, more generally, any potential renewal operations on the production lines were always discussed at departmental meetings. No formal acceptance for small improvements was required in the meetings, but any substantial changes in the production process were supposed to be jointly accepted by any senior staff present. These presumptions might be called, following Gherardi and Poggio, the 'necessary conditions to be respected in the organization' (Gherardi and Poggio, 2001, p. 252), which concern all members, women and men alike. Departmental meetings thus constituted one such necessary condition in Sarah's organization.

Some months after her recruitment, Sarah failed to get herself heard on the meeting agenda at the first departmental meeting she attended. She had been introduced to most members of the department before the meeting when the personnel manager introduced her to the department. She had also met many of her research colleagues at the plant on other occasions. Sarah had been briefed concerning the plant's meeting culture by her subordinates, of whom two had worked in other departments prior to moving to Sarah's lab. Based on the knowledge she obtained about meetings, which focused on renewal issues raised by personnel, Sarah assumed that she would enter the meeting on equal terms. In other words, she expected she would be able to present and discuss issues about production process development in an open manner. Sarah's planned meeting intervention was actually going to be significant, as she intended to highlight a production process problem that had not been identified as such earlier, and subsequently deliver her own solution to the problem.

All other participants at the meeting were familiar with each other, having worked at the company for a long time, and informality and familiarity within the group was the prevailing atmosphere. No clear space was created for Sarah to participate or to give her presentation. As there was no formal agenda or opening address, there was also no explicit introduction of Sarah to the departmental meeting. She was nominally part of the group, yet she felt considerably ostracized and, before she noticed, people started to leave the room and the meeting was over. Nobody had given her the opportunity to introduce herself and her ideas.

Thus during the course of the informal chatting and discussion that took place through the meeting, there emerged no acceptable or legitimate space where Sarah could have raised her voice and intervened in the discussion, even though she had planned significant changes and improvements to one of the main production processes at the plant. After the meeting Sarah felt invisible – none of the chiefs or production managers had been made aware of her improvement plans. She realized that it was difficult to interrupt others during the meeting in order to take the floor, because she saw herself as being a newcomer and felt like an outsider. At the same time, Sarah had felt intimidated by the familiarity and buddy feeling of the meeting, where she was the only woman attending.

At some point after the departmental meeting had passed, Sarah decided to test-drive the production process she had altered without informing other production managers of her plans in advance. She did however discuss the intended improvements she had devised with her subordinates. The older laboratory workers had their doubts, but they were, after some discussion, willing to give the experimentation a try. As a result, Sarah managed to carry out test drives of the new process on one of the plant production lines. After talks with Sarah, and through her persistence, the production technicians agreed to try her new formula. The formula quickly proved to be a success during the very first tests, and subsequent test drives confirmed the already outstanding results.

Sarah had envisioned a re-engineering of the overall production process for titanium dioxide, an industrial raw material. Moreover, because numbers relating to this new process concerning product quality, production method and cost structure all proved to be positive, Sarah's invention started receiving considerable attention both from within the company and from its management. Sarah's views and insights were suddenly considered worthy of attention by her older male engineering colleagues in all subsequent departmental meetings.

Sarah's professional and productive creativity promptly translated into significant progress being made in her career. For example, she was among the very few individuals accepted for a specific entrepreneurial and leadership executive training course organized within the company, and she was able to hire three new members for her laboratory team. After only having worked for a short time at the corporation's new products unit, Sarah had managed to increase the productivity and efficiency of the titanium dioxide production process to a level that had not been accomplished by any other production unit in the world.

## TOKENISTIC INVENTIVE SUCCESS CAN BE HARD TO TAKE – TOWARD FRUITFUL CONCEPTUALIZATION OF THE INVENTION/INNOVATION PROCESS

The renewed and successful implementation of the titanium dioxide production process raised a lot of interest among Sarah's colleagues at the plant, as well as causing the company as a whole and competitors within the chemical industry to sit up and take notice. The company's business clients also became aware of the ground-breaking innovation's positive aspects. Hence the significance of Sarah's work for production capacities, the company's general productivity and, particularly, the position of the titanium dioxide production line within the company were quickly understood by all of the most important associates.

In a negative turn of events, however, Sarah soon came to the realization that many of her male colleagues were more or less directly expressing their desire to replace Sarah and seize the whole new products unit from underneath her. The company was experiencing a growth period at the time, and managerial competition over crucial innovations, new products and success in general had intensified. During this decisive phase in her professional career, Sarah had given birth to a baby, and her male colleagues began to raise questions such as why Sarah was working and not at home raising children. Another question raised was why she was not on prolonged care leave nursing the baby. Sarah was typically confronted with these queries in situations and places where no third parties were able to witness the heavily intimidating questions. Face-to-face discussions and lifts were popular locations for such questioning sessions.

According to Sarah's account of the situation, she did not feel harassed or intimidated at the time these questions were being asked, as they were usually delivered in an informal tone and she still felt these types of questions were appropriate among colleagues. It was only some time afterwards that Sarah began to consider the questions inappropriate, as they clearly framed her as a non-professional and a person of the 'wrong' sex to carry out work at the plant. From the analytical viewpoint applied in this chapter it can be noted, for a start, that a certain engendered and context-specific version of the hegemonic masculine engineering culture was realized in the most immanent way in these interactions between Sarah and her colleagues. Of course, Sarah was also a female token at the industrial plant in the basic Kanterian sense, and the queries made by her male colleagues seemed to attach to her heightened visibility and stereotypical role capsulation, for example, to use Kanter's specification of the tokenism's content (Kanter, 1977, p. 230).

Nevertheless, we argue for revision of Kanter's important contribution with the concept of process tokenism, which is meant to achieve a more dynamic grasp of the actual transformations where the invention activity of an organization, for example, arrives at some particular realization through manifold gendered practices and power relationships. Attention therefore should be diverted from the headcounts of males and females, and from the dubiously universal-looking 'mechanisms' of tokenism. In Sarah's case the beginning of the tokenism process can be located in her appointment to a notably important position in the company. Details of the selection process are not known to us, but the management's possible doubts concerning Sarah's sex did not keep it from hiring a person with the highest formal qualification and several other relevant merits.

Sarah surely can be considered to be a creative and inventive person, but necessary factors for the emergence of her particular invention included several key features of the old titanium dioxide, as well as certain qualities of the minerals that make up titanium dioxide's composition. The fact that *non-human agents* of this kind can contribute to an invention in a pivotal manner is simply bypassed in conventional human-centred discourse and theorizing. However, the concept of inter-sectionality is revised in our study to trace the manifold active minglings and cooperations of a human agent with her materials and her technological environment.

All of the potential agents or actors that participated in the formulation and later phases of Sarah's invention – or in Sarah's personal changes throughout the process for that matter – are impossible to elaborate upon in one book chapter. Owing to this limitation and our general research interests, we will only slightly further define Sarah's tokenistic turns of fortune as an 'intruder' in the local variant of hegemonic masculine engineering culture, the dynamic intersection of certain qualities of the purer titanium dioxide that Sarah's invention made possible, and an intriguing occurrence of *gendering* that was highlighted during the process.

## CREATIVE ALLIANCE-MAKING SECURES THE CHEMISTRY ENGINEER'S ACCOMPLISHMENTS

It can be easy to overlook the fact that Sarah's recruitment to the firm quite obviously entailed tokenistic elements that are not necessarily related to any specific gendered meaning or Kanterian framework. It was unusual to have a Ph.D. recipient among the engineers of the factory, and the job of leading a new products unit in an organization that, until then, had not been interested in delivering new products or innovations was highly unusual. Analytically thus different dimensions of 'uniqueness' can be separated in our case, although they became practically insepara-ble during the progression of the events experienced by Sarah. Accordingly, it is difficult to judge whether an inexperienced *male* leader of the new products unit with a Ph.D. would have been asked to explain his plans at a departmental meeting, or whether it was the case that the established team of engineers just had no interest in any new people or ideas, plain and simple.

Soon after the end of the departmental meeting in which Sarah was forced to play the role of a silent token (broadly understood), Sarah manifested qualities stereotypically associated with *men* by independ-ently and assertively taking the risky move of testing her invention on an experimental basis on one of the plant production lines. In order to initiate testing, however, Sarah needed to persuade a number of crucial *allies* to be on her side, that is, particular laboratory workers and production technicians, who, in spite of formally being Sarah's sub-ordinates, needed some convincing all the same. What is more and in light of the actor–network theory introduced earlier, the great success of the experiment meant that Sarah's team also managed to win to its side such difference-making *non-human* actors as the certain qualities of titanium dioxide's base minerals and the novel industrial chemical processes, for example.

Without compliance from the decisive non-human actors, Sarah would not have achieved the apparently gender-neutral success that followed in her career. On the other hand, during the latter stages of the process, in which Sarah's rival male managers evidently tried as a result of the earlier key events and trajectory of the company to put her in 'her place' as a female token, not only did Sarah undergo personal change into a more gender-aware person but the titanium dioxide process itself became equipped with new functions that are definable as *gendered*. The development's turning point occurred when Sarah defended both her discoveries and her leadership of the new products unit against the efforts of management figures to usurp her position. Equally important was the strategy she implemented to do so.

As was previously mentioned, the titanium dioxide produced with the new methods envisioned by Sarah was of a significantly purer quality than the factory's old product. Sarah began to explore the uses of the raw material in detail and found out that, because of the improvement in its quality, the factory's titanium dioxide would now generate the highest amounts of revenue if sold to the cosmetics industry. The biggest buyers of titanium dioxide had traditionally been the painting and coating industries, but the cosmetics industry was increasingly beginning to use the raw material and it was actively searching for titanium dioxide of the highest standard. Encouraged by her discovery, Sarah made contact with several commercial agents who worked within the highly auspicious industry, and they became, quite expectedly, very interested in this highest-quality raw material.

The cosmetics industry is a deeply gendered branch of business, as its products essentially design and generate the ideals of both female and male attractiveness and beauty in the contemporary world. The gendered meanings in question involve certain images of refinement and class, and from the analytic viewpoint applied in this chapter it can be seen that Sarah adjusted the titanium dioxide itself to match the pertinent gendered expectations present in her negotiations with the cosmetics industry. This she did by creating new quality packages of relatively small size, in which the best-quality titanium dioxide available would be delivered to customers in the cosmetics industry. The painting and coating industries of course also wanted to receive the improved raw material, but they would continue to receive their goods in huge standardized sacks with capacities totalling hundreds of kilos as before.

The first-rate titanium dioxide became even more attractive to the commercial agents of the cosmetics industry during the course of the negotiation process after Sarah had, through her package innovation, rendered the raw material itself an articulated element and actor in the cosmetic industry's manufacture of products that are heavily loaded with gendered ideals of beauty, attractiveness, handsomeness, refinement and so on. The actor–network theory thus considers titanium dioxide as an actor, because the substance creates an essential difference in the intersectional association of manifold agents. However, and more explicitly, the justification for calling this raw material a *gendered* actor requires it to join an actor–network of a special kind, for which the condition is, in our case, most clearly met, as a result of the detailed involvement of the cosmetic industry. Titanium dioxide's career after it is taken out of those fine packages and put into the production processes of the industry is also worth noting here. The substance's one task as an ingredient of many facial creams is to prevent ultraviolet radiation from harming and ageing the face's skin – phenomena that carry gendered meanings of many kinds in our culture.

Both Sarah's cost calculations, which served to demonstrate possible highly profitable revenue streams when doing business with the cosmetics industry, and her ensuing successful negotiations with its representatives were positively received by the upper management of her company. The role of Sarah's new products unit was also crucial to the general scheme, as the service of the cosmetics industry's product development needs was seen as the unit's central assignment in future. All these plans and prospects were eventually made public during a departmental meeting, and quite soon afterwards Sarah noticed an interesting turn of events. The same male colleagues who were earlier eager to push Sarah homewards and to seize her research group notably lost interest. In spite of the group's forecast prosperity and progress, the engineers in question did not want to be involved in the end.

In light of our analytical perspective, the gendered linkage that was created via the sale of improved titanium dioxide to the cosmetics industry had, when put in the interpretative framework of the local hegemonic masculine engineering culture, contaminated the whole new products unit in a way that might be called 'repugnantly feminine'. Male or 'real' engineers are assumed to make careers in coating and painting manufacture, for example, and such apparently ostensibly neutral fields of industry were revealed also to harbour gendered associations. The outcome of the described process for Sarah meant that she was left in peace with her unit and her new customers in the cosmetics industry, for the time being at least.[2]

## CONCLUSION – REVISING TOKENISM AND INTERSECTIONALITY FOR MORE MATERIALITY-CONSCIOUS GENDER THEORIZING IN INVENTION AND INNOVATION STUDIES

This chapter introduces reformulated conceptual tools to achieve a better understanding of the innovation, and especially invention, processes, which take place in steadfastly gendered organizations. Feminist research has convincingly articulated many gendered power asymmetries that penetrate organizational *structures, practices* and *cultures,* for example. At the same time, conceptualizations of the mentioned kind can be argued to be too rigid and general to grasp, owing to their fluidity and, at least to some extent, as unique phenomena such as new innovations and inventions that emerge in an organization. Inventions do not arise out of nothing, nor do they typically arise from gender-neutral social spheres. In fact they often carry the potential to disrupt and change seemingly established ways of doing things.

Both social and organizational structures, practices and cultures are produced, reproduced and changed in concrete social action. In order to get an interpretative grip of the relative uniqueness of an invention activity in its detailed and gendered organizational context, we have found it helpful to utilize and revise two well-known if not classic concepts from feminist research, namely 'tokenism' and 'intersectionality'. Our essential theoretical move is to make the two concepts work for each other in such a way that both become more apt at depicting relatively unique invention and innovation processes in all their complexity.

The key person of our narrative, Sarah, did not belong to a minority group of women at her workplace, but she was a 'true token', that is, the only female engineer and research manager at the industrial plant. Classic Kanterian ideas of tokenistic asymmetries and mechanisms apparently catch some features of Sarah's path (she was made to feel invisible, and was stuck with the mother's role), but it is equally important to note that she was recruited as a highly qualified professional to fill a powerful position, and not as some representative of her sex to boost the company's equality image. A relatively uncommon starting point for our narrated case was thus settled, and we apply the reshaped concept of *process tokenism* to summarize such further unforeseen turning points in Sarah's career as her becoming a 'risk-taking, assertive male', that is, her embodiment of stereotypically male attributes when pushing through test drives of the new production process. Probably the most intriguing example of how tokenistic elements can dynamically contribute to *innovation* was Sarah's manner of defending her position and research unit against her male colleagues' seizure attempts. She not only opened a new channel to the cosmetics industry but also creatively *gendered* the raw material this industry needed.

To better understand the invention and innovation process under scrutiny we reject the conventional social scientific view, according to which the material world simply constitutes a passive environment and resources for humans to do their 'social thing', that is, innovating, organizing and so on. Instead, and in accordance with key ideas from contemporary science and technology studies, and especially actor–network theory (e.g. Callon, 1986; Latour, 1988; Law, 2004), the material world is here considered to be active, in fact an unlimited set of actors that continuously co-construct reality with us in ways concerning which any principal or universal demarcation between 'the social' and 'the material' becomes impossible. Therefore, titanium dioxide turns into a gendered actor in our analysis in a literal and not a metaphorical sense, but more detailed theoretical arguments for this specification would be beyond the scope of this chapter.

Our reformulation of the concept of intersectionality means rejecting the conventional idea that such ostensibly independent 'social forces' as gender, class, race and ethnicity together constitute power asymmetries and identities in the social world. In our view, no real explanations of social phenomena can be accomplished with highly abstracted schemes of this kind, but the starting point for analysis must be the actual unfolding of social events through time and space. Productive interpretative concepts are still needed, of course, and we apply 'hegemonic masculine engineering culture' as one such concept in our case study, for example.

Earlier in this chapter we stated that a contextually bound version of hegemonic masculine engineering culture obviously shaped Sarah's path and development as an inventor and innovator. Gendered power asymmetry embodied by this culture was, with some probability, realized in the silencing Sarah experienced (either that or the male engineers just ignored any newcomer independently of gender), and the culture became more evident when the male engineers tried to put Sarah 'in her place' as a mother. Nevertheless, Sarah's elaborate navigation through the power-infused field can be understood only if titanium dioxide itself – and its constituent minerals already involved in the production process – is seen to carry such qualities as Sarah was able to utilize as the most supportive ally in her endeavour to build a successful career at the company.

Sarah was essentially empowered by her alliance with titanium dioxide, and so contributions from non-human actors to the intersectional construction of power relationships and identities cannot be ignored in empirical social research. This point is interestingly foregrounded in our narrative case study, because social influences attributable to ethnicity systems or class structure, for instance, seem to carry very little *difference-making* effectivity in this context. Sarah and her colleagues belonged to the same homogeneously Finnish and white ethnicity group, and it would seem quite far-fetched to argue that the few doubts expressed by Sarah's subordinates (technicians and lab assistants) toward her plans instantiated class conflict noteworthy to our analysis.

The main goal of this chapter has been to gain an interpretative understanding of certain decisive turns of a female chemistry engineer's career when she became a prominent inventor and innovator at her corporation. Narrative methodological strategy has been applied to this task, and we have also found it fruitful to revise two 'classic' concepts from gender research, that is, 'tokenism' and 'intersectionality', to utilize for our analytical purposes. Indeed, we regard it as necessary to open such concepts to the fluid and multifaceted agency of the non-human world and material reality, so that fresh insights into gendered processes of invention and innovation can be obtained beyond our case study, too. On the other hand, it may need emphasizing that what might be called the personal creative inspiration behind Sarah's inventive and innovative actions has not been – and arguably cannot be – explained away. Put differently, to presuppose that non-human actors can also make a difference in the world is not to diminish the distinctly human ability to make a difference.

## NOTES

*   The authors wish to acknowledge the funding by the Academy of Finland project 303667.

1.  Put simply, the widely shared view that abilities of doing mathematics, material sciences and technology are intrinsically male qualities with no fussing over 'feelings' or 'relationships'.
2.  Later Sarah ended up in a dispute over ownership of patents and left the company.

# REFERENCES

Acker, J. (1990), 'Hierarchies, jobs, bodies: A theory of gendered organizations', *Gender and Society*, **4** (2), 139–158.

Acker, J. (1992), 'From sex roles to gendered institutions', *Contemporary Sociology*, **21** (5), 565–569.

Acker, J. (2012), 'Gendered organizations and intersectionality: Problems and possibilities', *Equality, Diversity and Inclusion: An International Journal*, **31** (3), 214–224.

Alsos, G.A., E. Ljunggren and U. Hytti (2013), 'Gender and innovation: State of the art and a research agenda', *International Journal of Gender and Entrepreneurship*, **5** (3), 236–256.

Anthias, F. (2001), 'The material and the symbolic in theorizing social stratification: Issues of gender, ethnicity and class', *British Journal of Sociology*, **52** (3), 367–390.

Atkinson, P. and S. Delamont (2005), 'Analytic perspectives', in Norman K. Denzin and Yvonna S. Lincoln (eds), *Sage Handbook of Qualitative Research*, 3rd edn, Thousand Oaks, CA: Sage, pp. 821–840.

Beck, U. and E. Beck-Gernsheim (2002), *Individualization*, London: Sage.

Bourdieu, P. (1977), 'The economics of linguistic exchanges', *Social Science Information*, **16** (6), 645–668.

Bradley, H. (2007), *Gender*, Cambridge, UK: Polity Press.

Brewer, R. (1993), 'Theorizing race, gender and class: The new black feminist scholarship', in Stanlie M. James and Abena P.A. Busia (eds), *Theorizing Black Feminisms*, New York: Routledge, pp. 13–30.

Butler, J. (1993), *Bodies That Matter: On the Discursive Limits of 'Sex'*, New York: Routledge.

Butler, J. (2004), *Undoing Gender*, New York: Routledge.

Calás, M.B. and L. Smircich (1992), 'Re-writing gender into organizational theorizing: Directions from feminist perspectives', in Michael Reed and Michael Hughes (eds), *Re-thinking Organization: New Directions in Organizational Research*, London: Sage, pp. 227–253.

Callon, M. (1986), 'The sociology of an actor–network: The case of the electric vehicle', in Michel Callon, John Law and Arie Rip (eds), *Mapping the Dynamics of Science and Technology: Sociology of Science in the Real World*, London: Macmillan, pp. 19–34.

Caraway, T.L. (2007), *Assembling Women: The Feminization of Global Manufacturing*, Ithaca, NY: Cornell University Press.

Choo, H.Y. and M.M. Ferree (2010), 'Practicing intersectionality in sociological research: A critical analysis of inclusions, interactions, and institutions in the study of inequalities', *Sociological Theory*, **28** (2), 129–149.

Davis, K. (2008), 'Intersectionality as buzzword: A sociology of science perspective on what makes a feminist theory successful', *Feminist Theory*, **9** (1), 67–85.

Deutsch, F.M. (2007), 'Undoing gender', *Gender and Society*, **21** (1), 106–127.

Downs, L.L. (1995), *Manufacturing Inequality: Gender Division in the French and British Metalworking Industries, 1914–1939*, Ithaca, NY: Cornell University Press.

Eriksson, P. and A. Kovalainen (2008), *Qualitative Methods in Business Research*, London: Sage.

Fara, P. (2004), *Pandora's Breeches: Women, Science and Power in the Enlightenment*, London: Pimlico.

Faulkner, W. (2007), '"Nuts and bolts and people": Gender-troubled engineering identities', *Social Studies of Science*, **37** (3), 331–356.

Flick, U. (2002), *An Introduction to Qualitative Research*, London: Sage.

Fox Keller, E. (1985), *Reflections on Gender and Science*, New Haven, CT: Yale University Press.

250 *Research handbook on gender and innovation*

Frank, A.W. (2012), 'Practicing dialogical narrative analysis', in James A. Holstein and Jaber F. Gubrium (eds), *Varieties of Narrative Analysis*, Thousand Oaks, CA: Sage, pp. 33–52.

Gherardi, S. and B. Poggio (2001), 'Creating and recreating gender order in organizations', *Journal of World Business*, **36** (3), 245–259.

Grimshaw, D. (2007), 'New Labour policy and the gender pay gap', in Claire Annesley, Francesca Gains and Kirstein Rummery (eds), *Women and New Labour: Engendering Politics and Policy?*, Bristol, UK: Policy Press, pp. 133–154.

Gustafson, J.L. (2008), 'Tokenism in policing: An empirical test of Kanter's hypothesis', *Journal of Criminal Justice*, **36** (1), 1–10.

Harding, S. and M. Hintikka (eds) (1983), *Discovering Reality*, Dordrecht, Netherlands: D. Reidel.

Jardins, J.D. (2010), *The Madame Curie Complex: The Hidden History of Women in Science*, New York: Feminist Press.

Kanter, R.M. (1977), *Men and Women of the Corporation*, New York: Basic Books.

Kariv, D. (2013), *Female Entrepreneurship and the New Venture Creation: An International Overview*, New York: Routledge.

Kincheloe, J.L. and P. McLaren (2005), 'Rethinking critical theory and qualitative research', in Norman K. Denzin and Yvonna S. Lincoln (eds), *Sage Handbook of Qualitative Research*, 3rd edn, Thousand Oaks, CA: Sage, pp. 303–342.

Lash, S. and J. Urry (1994), *Economies of Sign and Space*, London: Sage.

Latour, B. (1988), 'Mixing humans and non-humans together', *Social Problems*, **35** (3), 298–310.

Law, J. (2004), *After Method: Mess in Social Science Research*, London: Routledge.

Lewis, P. and R. Simpson (2012), 'Kanter revisited: Gender, power and (in)visibility', *International Journal of Management Reviews*, **14** (2), 141–158.

Lorber, J. (1994), *Paradoxes of Gender*, New Haven, CT: Yale University Press.

Martin, Y.P. (2003), '"Said and done" versus "saying and doing": Gendering practices, practicing gender at work', *Gender and Society*, **17** (3), 342–366.

McCall, L. (2014), 'The complexity of intersectionality', *Signs*, **30** (3), 1771–1800.

Metcalfe, B.D. and C. Woodhams (2012), 'Introduction: New directions in gender, diversity and organization theorizing – re-imagining feminist post-colonialism, transnationalism and geographies of power', *International Journal of Management Reviews*, **14** (2), 123–140.

Meyer, M. (2001), 'Between theory, method, and politics: Positioning of the approaches to CDA', in Ruth Wodak and Michael Meyer (eds), *Methods of Critical Discourse Analysis*, London: Sage, pp. 14–31.

Mohanty, C.T. (1991), *Feminism without Borders: Decolonizing Theory, Practicing Solidarity*, Durham, NC: Duke University Press.

Plummer, K. (2005), 'Critical humanism and queer theory: Living with the tensions', in Norman K. Denzin and Yvonna S. Lincoln (eds), *Sage Handbook of Qualitative Research*, 3rd edn, Thousand Oaks, CA: Sage, pp. 357–376.

Poutanen, S. and A. Kovalainen (2009), 'Critical theory', in Albert J. Mills, Gabrielle Durebos and Elden Wiebe (eds), *Encyclopedia of Case Study Research*, Vol. 1, Thousand Oaks, CA: Sage, pp. 260–264.

Poutanen, S. and A. Kovalainen (2013), 'Gendering innovation process in an industrial plant – revisiting tokenism, gender and innovation', *International Journal of Gender and Entrepreneurship*, **5** (3), 257–274.

Psathas, G. (1995), '"Talk and social structure" and "studies of work"', *Human Studies*, **18** (2–3), 139–155.

Risman, B.J. (2009), 'From doing to undoing: Gender as we know it', *Gender and Society*, **23** (1), 81–84.

Romei, A. and S. Ruggieri (2014), 'A multidisciplinary survey on discrimination analysis', *Knowledge Engineering Review*, **29** (5), 582–638.

Roth, L.M. (2004), 'The social psychology of tokenism: Status and homophily processes on Wall Street', *Sociological Perspectives*, **47** (2), 189–214.

Rubery, J., M. Smith and C. Fagan (1999), *Women's Employment in Europe: Trends and Prospects*, London: Routledge.

Scott, J. (1986), 'Gender: A useful category for historical analysis', *American Historical Review*, **91** (5), 1053–1075.

Servon, L.J. and A.M. Visser (2011), 'Progress hindered: The retention and advancement of women in science, engineering and technology careers', *Human Resource Management Journal*, **21** (3), 272–284.

Shachar, O. (2000), 'Spotlighting women scientists in the press: Tokenism in science journalism', *Public Understanding of Science*, **9** (4), 347–358.

Sprague, J. (2005), *Feminist Methodologies for Critical Researchers: Bridging Differences*, Walnut Creek, CA: AltaMira Press.

Stake, R.E. (2005), 'Qualitative case studies', in Norman K. Denzin and Yvonna S. Lincoln (eds), *Sage Handbook of Qualitative Research*, 3rd edn, Thousand Oaks, CA: Sage, pp. 443–466.

Stroshine, M.S. and S.G. Brandl (2011), 'Race, gender, and tokenism in policing: An empirical elaboration', *Police Quarterly*, **14** (4), 344–365.

Sunderland, J. (2004), *Gendered Discourses*, London: Palgrave.

Turco, C.J. (2010), 'Cultural foundations of tokenism: Evidence from the leveraged buyout industry', *American Sociological Review*, **75** (6), 894–913.

Verloo, M. (2006), 'Multiple inequalities, intersectionality and the European Union', *European Journal of Women's Studies*, **13** (3), 211–228.

Wagner, I. and R. Wodak (2006), 'Performing success: Identifying strategies of self-presentation in women's biographical narratives', *Discourse and Society*, **17** (3), 385–411.

Walby, S., J. Armstrong and S. Strid (2012), 'Intersectionality: Multiple inequalities in social theory', *Sociology*, **46** (2), 224–240.

Walker, A. (2003), 'Methods, theory and the practice of feminist research: A response to Janet Chafetz', *Journal of Family Issues*, **25** (7), 990–994.

Wyer, M., M. Barbercheck, D. Cookmeyer, H. Örün Öztürk and M. Wayne (eds) (2013), *Women, Science and Technology: A Reader in Feminist Science Studies*, New York: Routledge.

Wynarczyk, P. and S. Marlow (eds) (2010), *Innovating Women: Contributions to Technological Advancement*, Bingley, UK: Emerald.

Yoder, J.D. (1991), 'Rethinking tokenism: Looking beyond numbers', *Gender and Society*, **5** (2), 178–192.

Yoder, J.D. (1994), 'Looking beyond numbers: The effects of gender status, job prestige, and occupational gender-typing on tokenism processes', *Social Psychology Quarterly*, **57** (2), 150–159.

# 13. Visualizing gender – norm-critical design and innovation

*Emma Börjesson, Anna Isaksson, Sara Ilstedt and Karin Ehrnberger*

## INTRODUCTION

The aim of this chapter is to discuss how norm-critical design with a gender perspective can reveal norms and in that way contribute to innovation. Innovation is often about questioning what is taken for granted and perceived as the natural order. Challenging this order requires a critical mind and new perspectives. We argue that norm-critical design can shift perspective, visualize neglected needs and highlight new opportunities. In order to illustrate this, the chapter is centred on a specific empirical example – the development of the norm-critical design concept the *Androchair*. The Androchair is an examination chair for men, but with a design based on women's experiences of the gynaecological examination chair.

The chapter begins with a brief description of earlier research concerning gender and innovation in order to show how our study and norm-critical design contribute to this field. This is followed by the chapter's theoretical framework, the actor–network theory (ANT). The approach regards both humans and non-humans as active social actors and is later used to analyse how the Androchair as a material object can visualize hidden norms. We then introduce the reader to norm-critical design and discuss how it can be used as a tool for debate and change. This is followed by the core of the chapter itself, which is about the development of the Androchair and how it has been received. We conclude by discussing the Androchair in light of our theoretical framework and norm-critical design in relation to innovations and innovation processes.

## GENDER PERSPECTIVES ON INNOVATION

In recent years innovation has been a recurrent topic of debate, not just in political and academic circles, but also in the public sphere. Despite innovation being a broad and multifaceted concept, issues and perspectives concerning gender have often been absent from discussions about innovation (Andersson et al., 2012). Innovation researchers have rarely focused on gender when innovation is to be interpreted, and innovation processes have been regarded as gender neutral (Fürst Hörte, 2009). On the other hand, in various ways gender studies has attempted to reveal how masculine norms characterize everything from how we think about innovations to how innovation policy is shaped and conducted. Norms have been revealed with the support of analyses of policy documents and statistics, which indicate that political priorities are beneficial to men and male-dominated industries and fields. Limiting norms have also been revealed with the help of combining action research or interactive research with what is known as the 'doing gender' perspective. Gender mainstreaming has also been used as a way to approach change and as a springboard for new innovations. In this section we provide a glimpse into some examples of all these studies. We also briefly present some design projects that reveal the well-established gender codes surrounding cars, boats, work clothing and hand tools.

**Policy and Practice**

Research has shown that innovation is often linked to (predominately male) fields such as technology, science and industry, with these dominant notions about innovation and innovators having gained stereotypically male overtones. Quite simply, men and certain constructs of masculinity have been allowed to constitute the norm of what 'real' innovations and innovators are. This has, for example, been demonstrated in studies focusing on policy documents and political priorities concerned with innovation (e.g. Balkmar and Nyberg, 2006; Berglund and Granat Thorslund, 2012; Blake and Hanson, 2005; Foss and Henry, 2010; Lindberg, 2010, 2012; Pettersson, 2007). This type of study exposes how policy documents are strongly gendered, how central government investments in innovation systems have mainly benefited developments within male-dominated sectors and how innovation and innovation systems, as noted above, have been linked to notions about technology and machinery rather than to the service sector and relationships between people. Industries are prioritized in a way that follows the gender-segregated labour market, which means that gender and innovation are created reciprocally within innovation policy.

**Processes and Products**

Researchers have emphasized that increased awareness of gender within an organization can foster conditions for innovation. However, increasing awareness is rarely sufficient. Change can only occur if there are well-thought-out methods and strategies in place. Gunnarsson (2006, 2007, 2012) proposes combining action research or interactive research with the 'doing gender' perspective in order also to convert newly acquired knowledge and insights about gender into practical actions. It will then be possible to stimulate new practices that lead to change and innovation. Action research or interactive research stresses the importance of involving both researchers and practitioners in a reflexive learning process. Together, they formulate approaches to problems, analyses and solutions (see Aagaard Nielsen and Svensson, 2006). The 'doing gender' perspective involves highlighting how gender is performed in different practices and processes (see West and Zimmerman, 1987). For example, this may involve studying how gender is performed in and through discourse, symbols, interactions and physical environments. Other studies, in line with Gunnarsson (2012), have shown that action-oriented gender research can be a productive theoretical and methodological combination in terms of creating reflection, learning and change and thus contributing to gender-aware and innovative organizations (e.g. Amundsdotter, 2009; Andersson and Amundsdotter, 2012).

There are also projects that have used women's perspectives and needs in the innovation process, resulting in new technological solutions. One example is Volvo's YCC concept car, which was designed by a team composed of nine women. The fact that this car was designed by women for a target market of European women with a lot of spending power clearly showed how many cars are designed by men for men (Lorentzi, 2009). The 'All Aboard' concept boat is a similar project in the boat industry. This involved the design of a boat with user-driven solutions that took into account the needs of women on board pleasure boats (Petersson McIntyre, 2014). The intention was not that the YCC concept car or the All Aboard concept boat would go into production; instead they were created primarily to have an impact on the market by highlighting neglected needs and target groups that had not previously been prioritized in the design of cars or boats. Another example is the Craftsman Kilt, a work-skirt that challenges gender norms in terms of what constitutes workwear for men. It began as an experiment by industrial designer Marcus Jahnke in collaboration with Blåkläder AB, but quickly entered production and was named the Swedish Textile and Clothing Industries Association's product of the year for 2007 (Lorentzi,

2009). There are also aesthetic norms governing what objects should look like, depending on who is expected to handle them and where in the home they are meant to fit in. Karin Ehrnberger exposes this in a clear and humorous way when she swaps the shape and decoration of a hand blender and a power drill (Figure 13.1). The hand blender becomes green, with rubber detailing, rev meter and battery power, while the power drill gains a soft, rounded form, simple controls and light-blue details (Ehrnberger et al., 2012).

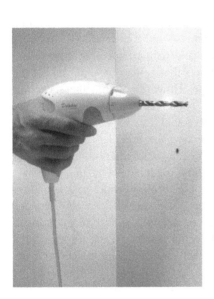 

*Source:*   Karin Ehrnberger.

*Figure 13.1    The Drill Dolphia and the Mega Hurricane Mixer*

To summarize, research and projects with an approach drawn from gender studies have made important contributions to expanding perspectives on innovation and innovation processes. In this chapter, we would like to illustrate additional ways of working to reveal norms, think outside of existing notions and thus promote innovation.

## ARTEFACTS AS ACTIVE ACTORS

We believe theories that take into account that people as well as material objects have an active and non-neutral impact on relationships and practices constitute a productive theoretical approach when it comes to thinking outside of existing notions and solutions and breaking down norms. Accordingly, the theoretical basis and concept of this chapter originate in the research approach actor–network theory.

Advocates of ANT argue that both humans and non-humans have an active role in the construction of society. Consequently, physical objects may not be interpreted as separate from the social, that is, culture, society, science, politics, economics and so on (Callon, 2001; Latour, 2003). Artefacts, for example products and technological solutions, are otherwise often regarded as neutral objects that neither have an impact on nor are affected by gender relationships. However, within the scope of ANT, artefacts are studied as active social actors, as they play an important role in the 'stabilization' of social relations (Latour, 1992). Artefacts can, from this type of perspective, be regarded as a physical manifestation of social relations. Gender, as a social relation, has a strong influence on how our society is currently organized. Oudshoorn et al. (2002) contend that cultural perceptions concerning gender and sexuality – what it means to be a man or a woman – are also built into the objects that surround us. They stress that there are no neutral technological solutions or products, but that these have an impact on us; for example, the shape of products can influence what expectation is placed on the user.

This constructivistic view of the objects that surround us means that the artefacts in our lives tell us something about values and norms of the culture in which they originated. If we regard the material world as a reflection of a society's cultural notions, then objects, like humans, can both create and recreate notions. In this regard, Latour (1986/1998) talks about the concept *translation* in order to frame how both humans and non-humans can disseminate, recreate or change ideas, expressions and objects. Translation is a constant process until it reaches what is known as a black box, that is, when something has been established as a 'truth', taken for granted and does not need to be called into question. 'A black box contains that which no longer needs to be considered, those things whose contents have become a matter of indifference' (Callon and Latour, 1981, p. 285).

In this chapter we use ANT to discuss whether design (in this case the Androchair) can work as a tool to make things 'happen' and contribute to reveal norms and unlock black boxes (see Ehrnberger et al., 2013). If material objects in network with humans can contribute towards creating and maintaining social relations, they should also be capable of being involved in changing or displacing them. Accordingly, in terms of gender and gender equality, the material objects themselves are also interesting, not only as a part in the maintenance of inequality, but also as a potential tool for change. But the objects around us are so naturalized that it is hard to catch sight of subtle issues such as gender and aesthetics, but in spite of this, or perhaps because of it, they do have a great impact on our lives and values. In this chapter we want to show how some of these hidden norms and values in physical objects can be visualized by using a norm-critical design approach.

## DESIGN AS A TOOL FOR CHANGE

Norm-critical design is in our perspective a way of creating *innovation*. As noted above, previous studies have shown how innovations have been impeded by prejudices and traditional preconceived ideas, for example regarding sex/gender, sexual orientation, class or ethnicity. Consequently, increased awareness of existing norms may be important to strengthen the innovation capacity of individuals and organizations. Tackling a field with norm-critical design methods creates new ways to approach the subject, new opportunities and new viewpoints that can lead to products and the development of services. It should be regarded as a complement to other methods within innovation and change management. As we will demonstrate in this chapter, a norm-critical design method can lead to new and unexpected results within a field.

To many people, the word 'design' suggests fashion, furniture and trends. But design now primarily denotes the *method* that is used in product development and change management, in which aesthetics is only one aspect of a larger field of knowledge. The design method is perhaps regarded today mainly as a tool for innovation and fresh approaches and is not just applicable to products for the market (Kelley, 2002). The same method can be used to meet societal challenges such as sustainable development, integration or gender equality. The concept of design has been expanded to encompass methods for working with societal challenges such as social innovation and transformative design. More speculative and investigatory approaches such as polemic design, critical design and design fiction are also included here. The latter approaches have been regarded as more artistic and investigatory phenomena, but we would like to highlight their significance to innovation.

## Critical and Norm-critical Design

Conventional design has primarily been devoted to creating new, attractive products for the market, having become a tool for companies to increase their profits. It has most frequently been used within a narrow commercial arena and with limited resources. Consequently, there has been neither the time nor the opportunity to develop alternative or critical projects. Design has thereby come to reinforce norms and values, rather than bringing them into question. Fashion and interior design, much like technology products, have reinforced existing gender norms with regard to aesthetics and function, rather than questioning them. 'Far from being a neutral, inoffensive artistic activity, design, by its very nature, has much more enduring effects than the ephemeral products of the media because it can cast ideas about who we are and how we should behave into permanent and tangible forms' (Forty, 1986, p. 6).

Critical design makes a valuable contribution with regard to the question of how artefacts and prototypes can be used to challenge notions and values relating to an object or a phenomenon and has been formulated as an alternative to design practice, which is more oriented towards problem solving (Dunne, 2006; Dunne and Raby, 2001). This approach has been developed by the design duo Anthony Dunne and Fiona Raby and is described as the opposite of affirmative design, which aims to maintain the status quo (Dunne and Raby, 2001). The aim of critical design is not to create a new and better product, but to highlight a problem, call things into question and create a discourse – asking questions rather than providing answers.

In critical design, design concepts are developed and prototypes built that look so realistic that they can be mistaken for 'actual' products. The design concept is used to embody or portray criticism, and the aim of the prototype is thus changed, from being primarily that of highlighting a function to that of revealing a problem. Critical design aims to provoke, create reflection and demonstrate alternatives and critical ways to relate to a phenomenon. In this way, design becomes a basis for a wider discussion of what is being addressed.

The discussion of gender issues in design practice and design research is in its infancy. What research there is has involved highlighting female designers and demonstrating how technology products are governed by stereotypical notions of gender (Gislén and Harvard, 2007; Kirkham,

1996; Sparke, 1995). However, there are few examples that identify the problems and suggest alternative solutions or use design methods in order to reveal these stereotypes (Ehrnberger et al., 2012; Jahnke, 2006). One example is Ehrnberger's design concept involving the power drill and the hand blender that was referred to above, with the different designs for kitchen appliances and hand tools communicating that one is to be used by men and the other by women (Ehrnberger et al., 2012). The design process is used to reveal norms, and the *design object* communicates the results of the research process. We have continued the development of a norm-critical approach in the Androchair project. From our point of view norm-critical design is a way to look at and make use of design to imagine the possibilities outside of the conventional boundaries, norms and solutions that we meet every day. It focuses on norms and power structures, primarily within gender, gender equality, ethnicity, class and intersectionality. Through the creation of design concepts and physical artefacts, issues that are subtle and elusive are given tangible form and are revealed in a way other than through text and theoretical analysis. These design concepts can be used for discussion, debate and change management within organizations and fields and can thus be a basis for innovation. The Androchair project focused on gender norms within the area of health and health technology. This project was funded by Vinnova,[1] and it was implemented through the Centre for Health Technology Halland (HCH) in 2012.

## DESIGN PROJECT: THE GYNAECOLOGICAL CHAIR

### Project Background

HCH is part of Halmstad University and works on the development of products and services, together with researchers, industry and health and social care organizations. Health technology is defined by HCH in terms of products and services that lead to improvements to or the maintenance of health and quality of life for the individual. In other words, this encompasses everything from advanced medical technologies to simple aids in everyday life. The Androchair project was formulated on the idea of producing a conceptual prototype that gives the gender perspective a tangible expression within the scope of the field of health technology. HCH already had a good deal of experience working with conceptual prototypes (so called demonstrators) that communicate a field, a technique or a need linked to health technology. Now there was an idea to do the same thing, but specifically focusing on gender issues and thus creating discourse and reflection about how the gender perspective can be a tool for innovation. A project group was assembled, consisting of colleagues from HCH and industrial designers.[2] The project began by problematizing HCH's activities, which were described as 'needs-motivated research and development', based on a gender perspective. Needs-motivated work is not entirely unproblematic; there is rarely only one need, and the needs may be many and sometimes conflicting. Products and services are often a compromise between different needs. We therefore chose to begin by specifically problematizing needs from a gender perspective.

Gynaecology was narrowed down at an early stage as a field for further development. The gynaecological examination is an unpleasant experience for many women. Cold instruments, leg stirrups, the position in the chair, uncomfortable paper covers, visible waste bowls and the lack of a mirror are some examples of physical factors that contribute to the poor perception of the gynaecological examination (Hilden et al., 2003; Millstein et al., 1984; Seymore et al., 1986). A study conducted at a women's clinic in Linköping, in the waiting room prior to an examination, found that 45 per cent of the women surveyed felt degraded in conjunction with a gynaecological examination (Wijma, 1998). Many describe feeling vulnerable and self-conscious ahead of and during the examination (Mattson, 1993). Despite women's unpleasant experiences there has been little development in the area of gynaecology when it comes to the physical environment and especially the gynaecological examination chair. The ones used today look very similar to the ones used in the 1880s (Johanisson, 2005). This captured our interest. Issues such as whose needs have been allowed to define the gynaecological examination chair guided the project further.

Gynaecology exclusively focuses on women, but there is a much less well-known counterpart, relating to men's reproductive health, called andrology. The word 'andrology' has its origin in the Ancient Greek words *andros* (man) and *logia* (the study of) and means the study of men. Andrology is not currently a field that is specifically defined by the National Board of Health and Welfare in Sweden. Nor are there any guidelines about how these patients are to be treated, which is one of the reasons why this field is not defined. Few are aware of andrology, even within the healthcare professions. In Sweden, only a few hours of medical training are currently devoted to andrology, and many nursing programmes do not cover it at all. The male reproductive system has long been a neglected area, and there is currently a lack of focus on andrology and health problems specific to men in Swedish healthcare (Pousette, 2013). In medical research, the patient has been regarded as a man, and pharmaceuticals and equipment have come to be better 'suited' to men; but andrology appears to be an exception to this rule. Neglected needs in the area of gynaecology and andrology became the core in the design process that followed in the project.

**Method**

A combination of different academic and design methods was applied to the work in the project that resulted in the Androchair. We have used the design process as a method in this research, something that Frayling (1993) calls research through design. This approach uses the design process and its creative and interpretative power to explore or reveal different problems and to find proposed solutions. The core of research through design is the design method, but the approach encompasses several other qualitative and quantitative research methods, for example often working close to the user through observations, interviews or co-design. In addition, the norm-critical approach has acted as a guide throughout the entire process. The work initially involved delimiting a problem and development area ahead of the design phase. When we decided to work on the gynaecological chair, previous research related to gynaecology and andrology was studied and compiled. Qualitative interviews were conducted with ten women, five men, midwives, gynae-cologists, andrologists and urologists. From the gynaecological field the interviews were conducted with two midwives, one registered nurse and one enrolled nurse. They were all specialized in gynaecology. Two senior physicians, both women and specialized in gynaecology and obstetrics, were also interviewed. From the andrological field, the interviews were conducted with one senior physician and two nurses, all specialized in andrology, and one senior physician specialized in urology. All except one are men. Most of the interviews were audio-recorded, while others were documented as written notes by the interviewer. Observations were made at two private gynaecological surgeries and at a public surgery at one of Stockholm's largest hospitals. In addition, we visited one private urological surgery and a public clinic. All clinics operate in Stockholm, Sweden. We also conducted a minor survey in which 20 women were asked to describe a gynaecology exam in just three words.

It was beneficial to conduct qualitative interviews and make obser-vations when the aim was to investigate individuals' perception of a phenomenon and discussion concerning a specific subject (Fejes and Thornberg, 2009). Relevant websites and current public debate in the media were studied with the help of various tools for textual analysis.

Textual analyses are important, as texts create opportunities and limitations in humans' ways of acting and thinking (Bergström and Boréus, 2000), an aspect that it is vital to highlight, not least when this involves limiting norms. The empirical material was then analysed from a norm-critical perspective. We had a so-called empirical close approach in the selection of analytical themes. This means that we developed themes based on the empirical material (Widerberg, 2002, p. 144f.). Admittedly, our critical theoretical perspectives were also present in the analysis. Widerberg means that it is positive also to be able to see the 'silence' of the material, that is, that which is not always stated but is equally important. A number of key themes were compiled and became the basis of a series of creative workshops in which the conceptual framework of the design was developed. There was then an iterative phase of sketching and concept development in which different ideas were tested against the basic concept, developed or discarded. Finally, there was a phase in which the design was defined in terms of detail, size, materials, finish and so on, and a functioning prototype was manufactured. The Androchair was then presented and displayed at HCH. The reactions analysed in this chapter consist of ten qualitative interviews with staff at HCH. It is primarily based on the reactions to the Androchair that we can say something about what it addresses, which norms are broken down and which preconceptions form the basis of these reactions. As we will discuss later, the Androchair asks more questions than it answers. It presents no solutions; instead it gives form to parts of earlier research, the testimony, experiences and reactions that emerged during the project. But first we'll present the empirical material that formed the basis for the chair's development as well as the design choices.

## EMPIRICAL MATERIAL

### 'You Have to Lie in Such a Way That You Nearly Fall Off; Then You Are in a Perfect Position'

Our interviews with women, midwives and gynaecologists painted a picture of a need that has been neglected within gynaecology. Product development in this field was described by healthcare personnel as neglected, particularly the patient-centred (and low-tech) solutions. Gynaecological examination chairs and instruments were perceived as old and out of date. Midwives and gynaecologists alike admitted that they would gladly see some improvements. They were aware that there had been some development over time, for example heating plates had been made for the tools so that they were not perceived as cold and unpleasant when used on patients. According to some of the midwives and gynaecologists, however, this type of purchase was rarely prioritized by the organizations' management, with the money being spent on high-tech equipment such as new ultrasound machines. It was clear from our interviews how gynaecological examinations are often associated with discomfort by many women, which is also confirmed by earlier research (see above and Wijma and Siwe, 2002). The physical environment in which the gynaecological examination takes place, in particular the gynaecological examination chair, symbolized much of this discomfort. Women associated it in the interviews with words such as 'exposure', 'violation', 'insecurity' and 'undignified', which made women's experiences of the gynaecological examination chair particularly interesting. We found an actual product description for a gynaecological examination chair from one manufacturer and supplier, describing how development had taken place: 'The chair is produced in consultation with healthcare personnel for maximum patient comfort, user friendliness and ergonomics' (http://www.sjobloms.com/produkter/gynekologi/gynstol.htm, accessed 10 August 2014). This raised further questions about the patient perspective in the examination context and product development.

In our survey and interviews, several women describe the chairs as high and unstable and feel that the moment they climb up into the chair is critical. Words such as 'cold' and 'hard' also kept recurring, and there was a fear of not seeing what was happening during the examination. Another perception shared by many women was that they were never lying correctly in the chair from the beginning. The doctor or midwife often needed to provide further instructions to get the patient into the right position. Healthcare personnel also described the chair as not being designed in an optimal way for getting the patient into a good position for the examination. For example, one midwife said the following during one of the interviews: 'You have to lie in such a way that you nearly fall off; then you are in a perfect position.' Despite the examination and the examination chair being associated with discomfort for the majority of women, there were few who questioned the procedure itself or the chair's design. None of the women interviewed had thought about what the chair 'actually' looks like and what improvements could be made to alleviate the uncomfortable experience. Both patients and care providers thought that the chair looked as it does because that 'was most practical' and that it quite simply 'could not look any different'. This clearly illustrates that there are invisible norms concerning the physical environment of a gynaecological examination.

There is no equivalent examination chair used in examining the lower abdomen of men, for example prostate examinations. What normally happens is that the man has to bend over a bed or lie on his side. Many men admitted that this feels uncomfortable and unsafe. In our interviews, we asked andrologists and urologists questions about whether this was the best way to examine the prostate. They said that this was perhaps not the optimal approach, but that it was smooth and simple for both the patient and the doctor.

Andrology is a neglected field, with the absence of routine check-ups for men, such as there are for women, being highlighted by both urologists and andrologists in the interviews we conducted. The fact that men do not have the same close contact with health services and are less inclined to seek care could be addressed if andrology was developed and if similar health checks were available for men as there are for women. It is not as obvious as it is for women which part of the Swedish health service men have to turn to when they have problems or concerns relating to their reproductive health. After the young people's clinic, women move on to gynaecology clinics and antenatal clinics, whereas there is no equivalent clinic for men. We found a number of discussions about this subject in online forums. For example, one person summarized their reflections on this with the words: 'Where is the fathers' health centre in this "equal society"?' (http://www.familjeliv.se/forum/thread/55750108-vart-vander-sig-en-kille-for-gyn-undersokning, accessed 10 August 2014).

Women's experiences of the gynaecological examination chair and gynaecological examinations show that there is a need that has not been taken seriously. Men lack routine check-ups and specialist care focusing on their reproductive health. These are two neglected needs largely related to societal notions concerning men and women (gender), which we found it would be interesting to work more on using a norm-critical design concept.

**The Analysis Converted into Design**

The gynaecological examination chair symbolized a large proportion of the discomfort women expressed in the interviews, while at the same time being self-evident and not called into question. If design is regarded as something that converts ideas of who we are and what we have to be or are expected to be into material objects, the gynaecological examination chair's shape and design become particularly interesting from the perspective of the notion about what it means to be a woman. Consequently, the norms associated with the gynaecological examination chair and preconceptions concerning women's reproductive health became the basis of the design process. We were also interested in asking questions concerning the norms and preconceptions associated with men's reproductive health, as andrology appeared to be neither visible nor prioritized. Accordingly, it was settled that the design concept would be to create a prototype of a gynaecological examination chair for men, based on women's experiences.

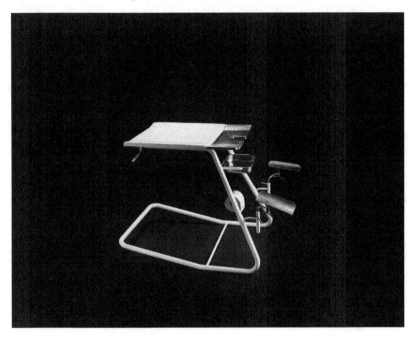

*Source:* Authors' own.

*Figure 13.2 The Androchair*

The prototype would be perceived as a realistic examination chair for men, and hence the design was initially based on how a prostate examination is performed. Doctors (andrologists and urologists) had described in our interviews how prostate examinations are performed, and one quote concerning what could be beneficial from a medical perspective was allowed to govern the design of the patient's position in the new chair: 'It is better if the legs can be pulled up as much as possible for the examination. This allows the prostate to come down' (urologist). This position involved the patient being bent away from the examiner, which was consistent with the fear described by many women of not seeing what was happening during the examination: 'It makes me anxious when I can't see what is happening' (woman, 36 years old).

From that point on in the design process it was primarily women's experiences and perceptions of the gynaecological examination chair that were allowed to define and affect the resulting design choices (see Figure 13.2). The aim of this was to ask questions about what happened when women's experiences were transferred to a product for men. In order to create the feeling of not lying correctly from the beginning, as well as to illustrate the quote 'You have to lie in such a way that you nearly fall off; then you are in a perfect position', the Androchair was equipped with a rocker function that meant the chair dropped forward slightly after the patient had adjusted himself into a comfortable position. Instability, the height and a feeling of 'climbing up' informed the shape of the chair's frame. The Androchair was also equipped with the leg stirrups typical of the gynaecological chair. The fact that many women described the gynaecological chair as cold has been primarily reinforced by the choice of materials used for the handles, leg supports and lower part of the bed. The roll of paper that sits on the Androchair symbolizes the words 'dirty' and 'undignified', words that came when women talked about their experiences, but it is also there as a counterpart to the (somewhat larger) roll of paper found on the gynaecological chair. The Androchair was also equipped, just like many gynaecological chairs, with handles (see Figure 13.3). In this case, women's hands have been used as the model for the size and shape of the handles. The objective here was for the user to feel that the chair is not really suited to them, something that was described by many women. It was important to give the Androchair an aesthetic that was largely consistent with the visual language used in healthcare today, but with a more up-to-date expression. The point is for the chair to feel realistic, that it could be a new product for the healthcare market. This makes the observer uncertain; it becomes difficult to categorize the artefact and thus open up to further interpretations. The choice of calling the prototype the Androchair (andrological examination chair, equivalent to the gynaecological examination chair) was to emphasize andrology, both to create awareness of its existence and to bring the discussion of men's health and right to specialist care to the fore.

**Reactions and Criticism**

The Androchair has been perceived as provocative, in both positive and negative senses. Criticism has been directed towards the fact that the project has only resulted in a 'subject of discussion' instead of a solution to the problems it addresses. The Androchair is not just provocative in

*Source:* Authors' own.

*Figure 13.3 Design details*

terms of the questions it addresses; it also provokes by virtue of being a norm-critical design concept: 'Can you not … create an OK chair that has things like heating, instead of wasting time on an object of revenge?' (man, 35 years old). Critical voices argue that this is not a constructive way to tackle a problem. Energy should be devoted to producing a better gynaecological examination chair instead of describing the problem in a 'new' way.

On the other hand, in a positive sense, people have expressed that the provocation itself and the physical form are key to changes being possible and to revealing problems and neglected needs:

> I think that this type of physical thing is necessary in order to be provocative and bring things to a head. You understand it then. It hits home. It becomes really clear. (Man, 41 years old)

> If you want to make a difference, this is how you have to think about a question. You have to be able to look at it from different perspectives and then I think you find what is right concerning this product because it highlights both men and women. Not black or white. (Woman, 38 years old)

In line with the quotes above, many have also underlined that it is much easier to take in a physical object than something written down in a text; the message conveyed becomes more tangible (see Isaksson et al., 2014). Furthermore, many argue that, simply because the Androchair is a physical object, it is difficult not to have an opinion about it; you have to relate to it in some way.

The Androchair poses the question of whether a situation experienced by women in the gynaecological examination chair is perceived in the same way when the patients are men: 'I wouldn't lie in that sort of chair – no chance' (man, 28 years old).

At the same time, men have expressed a recognition and understanding of the discomfort symbolized for many women by the gynaecological examination chair. However, there are some reactions that differ from these. Some men have expressed the opinion that, if a chair could make an examination easier, that is, if it was medically justified, they would have both accepted it and actually asked for it. One man, who had experienced several examinations, was also of the opinion that it might have felt better lying in an examination chair than bending over a bed.

Above all, the Androchair has resulted in many acknowledging remarks from women. Both the words and the feelings described by women in our interviews have been confirmed by other women when they have seen the Androchair. A normal reaction has been that they now look at the gynaecological examination chair in a new way, and some have raised thoughts about why the gynaecological chair is not better designed on the basis, above all, of the patient perspective. What has previously been 'a part of what it means to be a woman' is now regarded more critically. Men also admit that they look at the gynaecological chair with a more questioning gaze: 'I've thought a lot about the Androchair's real-world counterpart, the gynaecological chair, and how it can be possible that we are still working like that in 2013' (man, 57 years old).

The Androchair has also brought questions about men's health to the fore. Very few people were aware that andrology was a medical speciality and practice prior to seeing the Androchair. This has made many men reflect on the fact that they do not really know where in the Swedish health services they would turn if they had problems or concerns regarding their reproductive health. This is something they say they had not thought about before.

The collected reflections we have related above bear witness to the fact that the Androchair has revealed issues that are concerned with and in many ways have challenged preconceptions and values surrounding the gynaecological examination chair, andrology, and women's and men's health. Norms are broken and challenged by changing perspectives and transferring women's experiences to men. In the contexts in which the chair has been displayed, it has formed the basis of a wider discussion and causes those who have seen it to reflect and ask questions.

## DISCUSSION

### Challenging What Is Taken for Granted (Black Boxes)

From a theoretical perspective, the reactions to the Androchair are evidence of how the gynaecological examination chair and gynaecological examinations have been normalized and, in the terminology of

Callon and Latour (1981), have become black boxes, that is, something regarded as self-evident and unchallenged. As indicated by the review of earlier research and our empirical material, the gynaecological examination chair has – despite women's feelings of discomfort and healthcare personnel's reflections on this area being neglected – largely been accepted for some time, with an apparent absence of ideas about what the alternative could be. The Androchair, with its norm-critical design, has provided opportunities to unlock these black boxes, as, linking back to Latour (1986/1998), it has led to the gynaecological examination chair and the gynaecological examination being interpreted and called into question in various ways. The reactions we have documented contain nothing that confirms the relevance of current solutions; that is, there are no opinions or ideas stating that the gynaecological examination chair and the gynaecological examination should be accepted and be designed in the way they are today.

The Androchair has also helped to call into question and displace social relations (see Latour, 1992), as it highlights what we accept and do not accept for women and men, respectively. The powerful reactions we have elicited show that many men would never accept having to lie in the Androchair. The Androchair has also shown how deep cultural norms are ingrained in the artefacts that surround us and revealed that the gynaecological chair is an object that is far from gender neutral. It reveals something about what it means to be a woman and how this has been materialized and given physical form in a gynaecological examination chair and an examination procedure (see Oudshoorn et al., 2002) that are (have been) perceived as uncomfortable, with a counterpart for men being perceived as almost unthinkable. In a similar way, the reactions to the Androchair reveal how andrology may also be considered a black box. As we have shown above, few people know what andrology is, and the Androchair has also helped to expose the fact that few men know where to turn if they have questions about their reproductive health. In combination with what the review of earlier research and current public debate has shown, that is, how the male reproductive system has long been a neglected area and how development in the field of andrology as a speciality has been less highlighted and a low priority, we can conclude that there are strong and invisible norms concerning men's reproductive health that are only called into question on a small scale.

## CONCLUDING REFLECTIONS – NORM-CRITICAL DESIGN AND INNOVATION

The aim of the Androchair was, within the scope of the field of health technology, to problematize needs based on a gender perspective and highlight the significance of the gender perspective to innovation. As such it has been more successful than expected. The Androchair has revealed that there are several fields in which gender norms govern thought processes and stifle innovation for both men and women. But has the Androchair also been innovative from the standpoint of innovation? What would have happened if the project had created a better gynaeco-logical examination chair instead of a critical artefact? A better gynaeco-logical chair would probably have been seen as a positive contribution and in the long term would have improved the examination experience for many women if it had gone into production. However, a better gynaecological chair would not have ignited the debate and discussion the Androchair has. It would not have revealed the issue of the lack of innovation within gynaecology and the view on women in the traditional gynaecological chair. Nor would it have highlighted the issue of androl-ogy, regarding neglected needs and shortcomings, and what this says to us about the view on men and women as patients, and about those for whom innovation is performed and why. The discussion created by the Androchair forms the basis of more innovation, within both gynaecology and andrology, and of a demand for better solutions for both men and women.

Norms and preconceived ideas lock our thoughts into old paths and prevent innovation and fresh ideas. But, before we can take a step in a direction that breaks down norms, we have to catch sight of them. The problem with norms is specifically that they are invisible, naturalized, a part of our thinking and value system that we are not capable of distancing ourselves from. This is where the Androchair comes into play. Through a rhetorical and aesthetic change to the concept, it helps us to catch sight of something we would not otherwise see. It does this in a physical and direct way that we are unable to defend ourselves from. Judging by the comments and reactions, the project has aroused strong feelings, indicating that norms have been challenged and broken down.

The Androchair also contributes to research into innovation, gender and design, which is not something that normal product development can do. This demonstrates the power of creating material objects, artefacts, as tools in a change management process. We believe that norm-critical design is an unexploited tool for revealing norms and creating discussion and innovation. Norm-critical design can be a powerful tool that demonstrates needs that would perhaps otherwise be hard to see or overlooked because of various priorities. Breaking down norms provides new perspectives and creates opportunities to think outside of existing solutions. This can open doors to completely new and better innovations.

## NOTES

1. Vinnova is Sweden's innovation agency, with the aim to promote sustainable growth by improving the conditions for innovation, as well as funding needs-driven research.
2. This project was led by two of the authors of this chapter, Emma Börjesson and Karin Ehrnberger. Additional project members were Sara Ilstedt, Cristine Sundbom and Ann-Christine Hertz. Anna Isaksson became involved in the project after the Andro-chair was presented and has along with the three other authors worked on the follow-up of the reactions to the Androchair. For simplicity, we have chosen to refer to the project group as 'we'.

## REFERENCES

Aagaard Nielsen, K. and L. Svensson (eds) (2006), *Action Research and Interactive Research: Beyond Practice and Theory*, Maastricht, Netherlands: Shaker.

Amundsdotter, E. (2009), *Att framkalla och förändra ordningen – aktionsorienterad genusforskning för jämställda organisationer*, Luleå, Sweden: Luleå tekniska universitet.

Andersson, S. and E. Amundsdotter (2012), 'Developing innovative organisations – using action-orientated gender research', in S. Andersson, K. Berglund, E. Gunnarsson and E. Sundin (eds), *Promoting Innovation: Policies, Practices and Procedures*, Report 2012:08, Stockholm: Vinnova, pp. 310–327.

Andersson, S., K. Berglund, J. Granat Thorslund, E. Gunnarsson and E. Sundin (2012), 'Introduction', in S. Andersson, K. Berglund, E. Gunnarsson and E. Sundin (eds), *Promoting Innovation: Policies, Practices and Procedures*, Report 2012:08, Stockholm: Vinnova, pp. 9–20.

Balkmar, D. and A. Nyberg (2006), *Genusmedveten tillväxt och jämställd vinst – om genus och jämställdhet i ansökningar till VINNOVAs Vinnväxt-program 2006*, Stockholm: Stockholm University.

Berglund, K. and J. Granat Thorslund (2012), 'Innovative policies? Entrepreneurship and innovation policy from a gender perspective', in S. Andersson, K. Berglund, E. Gunnarsson and E. Sundin (eds), *Promoting Innovation: Policies, Practices and Procedures*, Report 2012:08, Stockholm: Vinnova, pp. 25–46.

Bergström, G. and K. Boréus (2000), *Textens mening och makt. Metodbok i samhällsvetenskaplig textanalys*, Lund, Sweden: Studentlitteratur.

Blake, M.K. and S. Hanson (2005), 'Rethinking innovation: Context and gender', *Environment and Planning A*, **37** (4), 681–701.

Callon, M. (2001), 'Actor network theory', in N.J. Smelser and P.B. Baltes (eds), *International Encyclopedia of the Social and Behavioral Sciences*, Oxford, UK: Elsevier Science.

Callon, M. and B. Latour (1981), 'Unscrewing the big Leviathan: How actors macro-structure reality and how sociologists help them to do so', in K.D. Knorr Cetina and

A.V. Cicourel (eds), *Advances in Social Theory and Methodology: Toward an Integration of Micro- and Macro-sociologies*, Boston, MA: Routledge & Kegan Paul, pp. 277–303.

Dunne, A. (2006), *Hertzian Tales: Electronic Products, Aesthetic Experience, and Critical Design*, Cambridge, MA: MIT Press.

Dunne, A. and F. Raby (2001), *Design Noir: The Secret Life of Electronic Objects*, Basel, Switzerland: Birkhäuser Press.

Ehrnberger, K., M. Räsänen and S. Ilstedt (2012), 'Visualising gender norms in design: Meet the Mega Hurricane Mixer and the drill Dolphia', *International Journal of Design*, **6** (3), 85–98.

Ehrnberger, K., L. Broms and C. Katzeff (2013), 'Becoming the energy aware clock – revisiting the design process through a feminist gaze', Nordic Design Research Conference, Copenhagen/Malmö.

Fejes, A. and R. Thornberg (eds) (2009), *Handbok i kvalitativ analys*, Stockholm: Liber.

Forty, A. (1986), *Objects of Desire: Design and Society 1750–1980*, London: Thames & Hudson.

Foss, L. and C. Henry (2010), 'Gender and innovation: Exploring the hegemonic voice', Paper presented at the Gender, Work and Organization conference, 21–23 June, Keele, UK.

Frayling, C. (1993), *Research in Art and Design*, London: Royal College of Art.

Fürst Hörte, G. (2009), *Behovet av genusperspektiv. Om innovation, hållbar tillväxt och jämställdhet*, Report VR 2009:16, Stockholm: Vinnova.

Gislén, Y. and Å. Harvard (2007), 'I skärningsfältet mellan genus och design', in S. Ilstedt Hjelm (ed.), *Under Ytan: En antologi om designforskning*, Stockholm: Raster förlag.

Gunnarsson, E. (2006), 'The snake and the apple in the common paradise – challenging the balance between surface and depth in qualifying action research and feminist research on a common arena', in K. Aagaard Nielsen and L. Svensson (eds), *Action Research and Interactive Research: Beyond Practice and Theory*, Maastricht, Netherlands: Shaker, pp. 117–142.

Gunnarsson, E. (2007), 'Other sides of the coin: A feminist perspective on robustness, science and knowledge production', *International Journal of Action Research*, **3** (3), 349–363.

Gunnarsson, E. (2012), 'Procedures for innovation', in S. Andersson, K. Berglund, E. Gunnarsson and E. Sundin (eds), *Promoting Innovation: Policies, Practices and Procedures*, Report 2012:08, Stockholm: Vinnova, pp. 271–274.

Hilden, M., K. Sidenius, J. Langhoff-Roos, B. Wijma and B. Schei (2003), 'Women's experiences of the gynecologic examination: Factors associated with discomfort', *Acta Obstetricia et Gynecologica Scandinavica*, **82** (11), 1030–1036.

Isaksson, A., E. Börjesson and K. Ehrnberger (2014), 'Att synliggöra det osynliga – design som aktör i jämställdhetsarbete', *Tidskrift för genusvetenskap*, **35** (1), 27–50.

Jahnke, M. (2006), *Formgivning/Normgivning*, Gothenburg, Sweden: Gothenburg University.

Johanisson, K. (2005), *Den mörka kontinenten*, Falun, Sweden: ScandBook.

Kelley, T. with J. Littman (2002), *The Art of Innovation: Lessons in Creativity from IDEO, America's Leading Design Firm*, New York: HarperBusiness.

Kirkham, P. (1996), *The Gendered Object*, Manchester, UK: Manchester University Press.

Latour, B. (1986/1998), 'Förbindelsens makt', in B. Latour, *Artefaktens återkomst. Ett möte mellan organisationsteori och tingens sociologi*, Stockholm: Nerenius & Santérus, pp. 41–58.

Latour, B. (1992), 'Where are the missing masses? The sociology of a few mundane artifacts', in W. Bijker and J. Law (eds), *Shaping Technology/Building Society: Studies in Sociotechnical Change*, Cambridge, MA: MIT Press, pp. 225–259.

Latour, B. (2003), *Science in Action: How to Follow Scientists and Engineers through Society*, Cambridge, MA: Harvard University Press.

Lindberg, M. (2010), *Samverkansnätverk för innovation – en interaktiv och genusvetenskaplig utmaning av innovationspolitik och innovationsforskning*, Luleå, Sweden: Luleå University of Technology.

Lindberg, M. (2012), 'A striking pattern – co-construction of innovation, men and masculinity in Sweden's innovation policy', in S. Andersson, K. Berglund, E. Gunnarsson and E. Sundin (eds), *Promoting Innovation: Policies, Practices and Procedures*, Report 2012:08, Stockholm: Vinnova, pp. 47–67.

Lorentzi, U. (2009), *Från hantverkskilt till hästföretag*, Report 2009:20, Stockholm: Vinnova.

Mattson, B. (1993), 'Gynekologisk undersökning på vårdcentral – kvinnors erfarenheter och önskemål', *Allmänmedicin*, **14**, 215–219.

Millstein, S.G., N.E. Adler and C.E. Irwin, Jr (1984), 'Sources of anxiety about pelvic examinations among adolescent females', *Journal of Adolescent Health Care*, **5** (2), 105–111.

Oudshoorn, N., A.R. Saetnan and M. Lie (2002), 'On gender and things: Reflections on an exhibition on gendered artifacts', *Women's Studies International Forum*, **25** (4), 471–483.

Petersson McIntyre, M. (2014), *Jämställdhet på köpet? Marknadsfeminism, innovation och normkritik*, Report VR 2014:02, Stockholm: Vinnova.

Pettersson, K. (2007), *Men and Male as the Norm: A Gender Perspective on Innovation Policies in Denmark, Finland and Sweden*, Nordic Research Programme 2005–2008 No. 4, Stockholm: Nordregio.

Pousette, Å. (2013), 'Kompetensen inom andrologi och tillgängligheten till andrologisk vård i Sverige 2013', Bilaga 19 i SOU 2014:6 Män och jämställdhet.

Seymore, C., R.H. DuRant, M.S. Jay, D. Freeman, L. Gomez, C. Sharp and C.W. Linder (1986), 'Influence of position during examination, and sex of examiner on patient anxiety during pelvic examination', *Journal of Pediatrics*, **108** (2), 312–317.

Sparke, P. (1995), *As Long as It's Pink: The Sexual Politics of Taste*, London: Pandora Press.

West, C. and D.H. Zimmerman (1987), 'Doing gender', *Gender and Society*, **1** (2), 125–151.

Widerberg, K. (2002), *Kvalitativ forskning i praktiken*, Lund, Sweden: Studentlitteratur.

Wijma, B. (1998), 'Gynundersökningen, ett rollspel för två', *Läkartidningen*, **95** (11), 1125–1129.

Wijma, B. and K. Siwe (2002), 'Empowerment i gynstolen. Teori, empiri och möjligheter', *Kvinnovetenskaplig Tidskrift*, **2–3**, 61–73.

# Index